# COMPLETE
# Technology AND Design

second edition

## RAYMOND CALDWELL

Hodder Murray

A MEMBER OF THE HODDER HEADLINE GROUP

Although every effort has been made to ensure that website addresses are correct at time of going to press, Hodder Murray cannot be held responsible for the content of any website mentioned in this book. It is sometimes possible to find a relocated web page by typing in the address of the home page for a website in the URL window of your browser.

Orders: please contact Bookpoint Ltd, 130 Milton Park, Abingdon, Oxon OX14 4SB. Telephone: (44) 01235 827720. Fax: (44) 01235 400454. Lines are open 9.00–6.00, Monday to Saturday, with a 24-hour message answering service. Visit our website at www.hoddereducation.co.uk

© Raymond Caldwell 2001, 2005

First edition published in 2001
by Hodder Murray, an imprint of Hodder Education,
a member of the Hodder Headline Group
338 Euston Road
London NW1 3BH

Second edition published in 2005

Impression number  10 9 8 7 6 5 4 3 2 1
Year                    2010 2009 2008 2007 2006 2005

Cover photo Gusto/Science Photo Library
Typeset by Fakenham Photosetting Limited
Printed and bound in Italy

A catalogue record for this title is available from the British Library
ISBN-10: 0340 907 789
ISBN-13: 978 0340 907 788

# CONTENTS

# Acknowledgements

The Publishers would like to thank the following for permission to reproduce copyright material:

**Photo credits**
Every effort has been made to trace all copyright holders, but if any have been inadvertently overlooked the Publishers will be pleased to make the necessary arrangements at the first opportunity.

pp. 2, 9, 99, 211 © Emma Lee; p. 226 Mecmesin Systems; p. 232 © Royalty-Free/Corbis; pp. 15, 47$b$, 69$t$, 68$t$ John Townson/Creation

All other photographs supplied by the author.

**Acknowledgements**
The author is grateful to the following individuals, organisations and schools for their support in the writing of this book:

**Raymond Moffatt, Principal Moderator for CCEA Technology and Design, without whose support, guidance and editing this book would have not been possible.**

Ronnie Lee for his technical editing. Denis Currie, Sidney Conn, Willy McKeown and Nigel Gamble for providing technical help, support and resources. Glenn Currie for extracts from his GCSE portfolio. Dalrida Voluntary Grammar, Our Lady and St Patricks College Knock, Glengormley High School, St Mary's Grammar (Magherafelt), St Colmans High School, Potora Royal School, Ballycastle High School, Newbridge Integrated College, City of Armagh High School and St Fanchea's College for exemplar coursework. SMC Pneumatics for illustrations and Technical support. NTCADCAM's Claire Shields and Paul Pearson for Solidworks exemplar material. Jim Neal and New Wave Concepts for software used to develop the electronic systems used in this book.

# CHAPTER ONE

# Focused tasks associated with designing

Your role as a designer within technology and design is to select a situation or problem for which there is no meaningful solution and, using creativity and imagination, to come up with a possible design for a product. However, the task does not stop there. You are then required to make and evaluate your product and design.

The first two chapters of the book will help you do this by setting out a number of **focused tasks** designed to develop specific skills and knowledge. Examples of students' work will be used where possible. The focused tasks fall into two main groups:

- Designing
- Communicating

There are two main areas of designing. The following focused tasks are designed to help you with these. They are:

- Product analysis
- Product evaluation

If you are studying for the CCEA GCSE in Technology and Design you will be required to complete one focused task associated with designing and one focused task associated with communicating as part of your coursework. Each focused task will carry a maximum mark of 5%.

When identifying a product for your focused tasks, you must choose a technological product. A technological product is one that incorporates a system. Products such as a mobile phone, Game Boy, electric kettle, paper stapler or a lever-operated corkscrew are all technological products and suitable for your focused tasks.

## Product analysis

Product analysis can be a useful exercise. It can help you find a starting point for your own design through redesigning or improving an existing product.

If you are studying for the CCEA GCSE in Technology and Design and electing to produce a focused task on product analysis you will be required to:

1. Write a clear description of the purpose of the technological product selected.
2. Write a detailed specification of the selected product.
3. Name the materials used and give reasons why they were selected for the product.
4. Describe the method of manufacture.
5. State how convenient the product is to use and service.

The *Dyson* vacuum cleaner is a good example of a product that resulted from product analysis. As the user of a domestic vacuum cleaner, Mr Dyson was unhappy with its performance and started to analyse it. From this simple process was born one of the most successful vacuum cleaners on the market, the *Dyson*.

**Figure 1.1** *Dyson vacuum cleaner*

While no one is expecting you to design a new cleaner, this technique can be used on more modest products and can form the starting point for your design.

The focused task of product analysis can be broken down into five sections. They are:

1. Give a clear description of the purpose of the technological product. Try to speculate on, and justify your understanding of what the designer had in mind when he/she conceived the product.
2. Write a detailed specification of the product. This can be obtained from your description of the purpose of the product and from the manufacturer's literature. The specification is simply a list of what you think the product was meant to do.
3. Name the materials used in the product. One way of doing this is to make a table identifying the materials used and give your reasons why you think they were chosen for use in the product.
4. Describe the method of manufacture. You will be required to list and discuss some of the main techniques used in the manufacturing of the product.
5. Show how convenient the product is to use and service. This should be a written explanation of how convenient you found the product is to use and service (changing the battery or dust bag, etc).

When undertaking a product analysis you should select a technological product you are familiar with. Keep your selection simple; unless you are a qualified automotive engineer do not try to analyse the internal combustion engine! Start with a product similar to one listed in Table 1.1.

**Table 1.1** *Examples of technological products suitable for focused tasks*

| | |
|---|---|
| Mobile phone | Electric smoothing iron |
| Camera | Electric kettle |
| Calculator | Paper stapler |
| Game Boy | DIY tools |
| Nintendo controller | Electric kettle |
| Joystick for a computer | Lever-operated corkscrew |
| CD Walkman | Electric screwdriver |
| Computer mouse | Desk lamp |
| Electric toothbrush | Battery-operated torch |
| Hairdryer | MP3 player |

To help you with the task of product analysis a number of case studies are included in this chapter. Most of these are from students who have recently completed their focused task in product analysis.

| Case study 1 | **Product analysis of a hairdryer** |
|---|---|

If you wish to practise the skill of product analysis you might like to complete this case study.

### 1 Give a clear description of the product

This can be obtained from a number of sources, such as the user manual that comes with the product, catalogue or in-store promotional leaflets.

The product selected for this case study was a 1800 watt hairdryer. It has a deep bowl diffuser which allows larger sections of the hair to be dried at the roots for a fuller, more natural look.

**Speculation on what the designer had in mind**
You are required to speculate on, and justify your understanding of what the designer had in mind when he/she conceived the product.

- In my opinion the main function of the hairdryer was to dry hair quickly and effectively. It had to be lightweight as well as being attractive to look at.

### 2 Specification

The following are just a few possible specification points the designer appears to have had in mind while designing the hairdryer. You may have more that you wish to add to the list.

- Dry hair more quickly, hence the 1800 watts of output power.
- Include a deep bowl attachment to the air output nozzle. This feature is designed to add the appearance of volume to the hair.

- As the product has to be held for long periods during drying it must be made from lightweight but attractive materials.
- As the dryer is giving out 1800 watts in the form of heat the product must be made from heat resistant materials.
- Consider the product's life expectancy.
- Consider how the product will be manufactured.

### 3 Analysis of the manufacture and materials

### Analysis of materials

When choosing the materials for a product a number of factors are important and you should comment on these during the product analysis. Analysis of materials used in the hairdryer might consider:

- heat resistance
- manufacturing process
- durability
- finish
- cost
- colour
- ergonomics
- weight
- insulation properties
- availability
- environmental considerations.

If you consider the point of heat resistance then the main body of the dryer would need to be made from a material that lends itself to large-scale production yet can withstand the heat from both the hot air and the heating element. A plastic such as melamine could be used. This material can be moulded, has a high quality finish and will not change shape with temperature.

**Table 1.2** *Choice of materials and reasons for their choice*

| Material used | Reasons for choice |
|---|---|
| Plastic body (melamine) | • Heat resistant. Suitable for the injection moulding process.<br>• Durable in that it is not easily chipped or cracked when dropped.<br>• Low cost of manufacture.<br>• Can be coloured to give a range of different colours from which you can choose.<br>• Readily available material.<br>• Good electrical insulation properties that are important when drying wet hair with a product that uses mains voltage.<br>• High quality finish to the material that is difficult to scratch. |
| Rubber coated handle | • Soft to the touch.<br>• Easy to hold with wet hands.<br>• Good electrical insulation properties. |

A way of presenting your work could be to use a table in which you identify the materials and the reasons for their choice. An example of this is shown in Table 1.2.

**Analysis of manufacture**

It is important to understand how the product was manufactured. To do this you will need to refer to the appropriate sections of this or other books.

Once again it is useful to make a drawing of your selected product, which you can then refer to during this section.

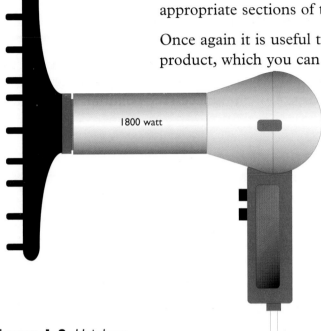

**Figure 1.2** *Hairdryer*

Manufacturing processes you might wish to consider are:

- making by wasting
- making by fabrication
- moulding
- final assembly techniques
- scale of production
- cost
- availability of components
- hazards associated with its manufacture.

### 4 Ease of use and service

Comment on the serviceability of the product. You may also wish to comment on:

- safety during use and servicing
- ergonomic factors
- anthropometric factors
- complexity of instructions
- ease of fitting batteries
- cleaning
- weight
- portability.

If you consider the hairdryer shown in Figure 1.3, you may wish to comment on some of these points.

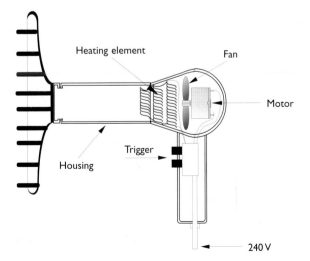

**Figure 1.3** *Sectional drawing of the hairdryer*

- The bowl diffuser can be removed for cleaning. This is important due to the need for regular cleaning in hot soapy water.
- The dryer itself is a sealed unit, which is not designed for servicing.
- As the dryer is a sealed unit, this will mean the product will have to be thrown away if it is faulty.
- This type of throw-away product can and often does have a serious impact on our natural resources. Many of the components used in the product, such as melamine, decompose very slowly and will have a long-term impact on the environment through unnecessary pollution of landfill sites.

## Case study 2 — Product analysis of a lever-operated corkscrew

### Product Purpose

The product I have selected for this "Product Analysis" is a lever corkscrew. This product can be obtained from a number of sources e.g. supermarket, off-licence. With the use of rack and pinion it makes bottle opening much easier.

**What is it?**
It is a lever corkscrew, which is basically a normal corkscrew that uses a rack and pinion to make this job much easier.

**Where is it used?**
It is a household utensil used for removing corks from bottles.

**What does it do?**
It is held over the neck of a bottle and used to remove the cork in much less time and with much less effort than a normal corkscrew.

**Who is the user?**
Cooks/chefs, waiters and householders.

**How does it function?**
The lever corkscrew consists of a cylinder-shaped body. Inside the body is a normal corkscrew which extends up through a long metal tube at the top of the main body to a handle. Between the screw itself and the handle, the piece of metal that actually moves through the tube has teeth and, on either side of the tube, is a lever with a cog on the end that fits with the teeth, and as the handle is turned and the screw is twisted deeper and deeper into the cork, the cogs turn and the levers lift into the air. Then, when pressure is put on top of the levers, they are pushed down, causing the screw to rise up, lifting the cork out of the bottle.

**Figure 1.4** *A clear description of the purpose of the technological product*

### Design brief

Size; It must be small and light to add to the ease of use.

Shape; It has to be a particular shape so it will fit over the neck of a bottle.

Storage; It will be small so it can be stored with all the other kitchen utensils.

Cost; It will be relatively cheap so you might not go looking for it but if you saw it you'd think it was useful and just buy one.

Function; It will be used to remove corks from bottles more easily.

Manufacture; It will have to be easily and cheaply mass produced.

Materials; It will have to be made of strong material (e.g. metal) so it will not break when pressure is applied to the levers or screw.

### Ergonomics (ease of use)

You get an idea of how to use this because you can see it has a handle and a corkscrew so you know what it is right away. When someone picks it up and sees that, when the screw moves down and up and the levers move as well, they figure out that the levers are designed to lift the screw out of a bottle.

The corkscrew is a good size, so it can fit over a bottle neck and it is the right shape so it fits on a bottle and can be held over it with one hand, leaving the other hand free to twist the handle.

It is quite obvious how this works. All someone has to do is lift it up, fiddle with the handle and they can soon figure out what it is used for and how.

This corkscrew is very easy to use. All you have to do is place the cylinder over the bottle neck, turn the handle and when the levers lift up just push them down and the cork lifts out.

### Servicing

You would service this piece of equipment by making sure you don't let the cogs get stiff and oil it regularly using a mild lubricant. As with all kitchen utensils it should be washed after use and stored in a clean dry place.

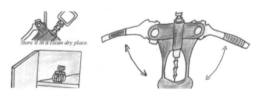

**Figure 1.5** *Specification and servicing*

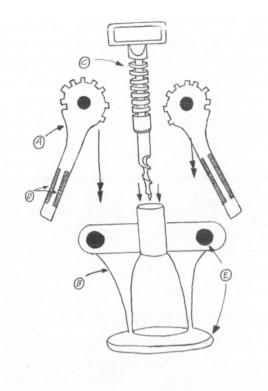

**General arrangement**

| Components | Materials | Manufacture |
|---|---|---|
| A Handle/levers | Stainless Steel | Drop Forging |
| B Frame | Stainless Steel | Die Casting |
| C Screw | Stainless Steel | Die Casting |
| D Grips | Rubber | Injection Moulded |
| E Hinges/mouth | Plastic | Injection Moulded |

**Product Performance**

This product uses a rack and pinion to convert rotary motion into linear motion. By twisting the screw deeper into the cork the mechanism causes the arms to lift and when they are pushed down the mechanism again causes the screw to lift, removing the cork.

**How Could It Be Improved?**

If the rack and pinion remain the same size, but they had less teeth on them and the screw was made longer, it would make the arms lift quicker and make them easier to push down. This would mean that this job would be quicker and you would use less energy to push down the handles.

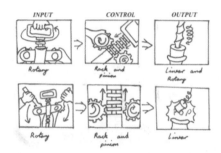

**Figure 1.6** *Method of manufacture*

**Figure 1.7** *Materials used, method of manufacture and use*

Author's comments on the focused task shown in Figures 1.4 to 1.7.

*Activity 1: Give a clear description of the purpose of the technological product selected.*

*The purpose of the product has been clearly defined and the student has clearly demonstrated the rationale for such a product. A good clear illustration of the product is included. It is important to include a clear graphic or image of the selected product and display this on either the front cover sheet or on the first page, showing the nature of the product under review.*

*Activity 2: Write a detailed specification of the selected product.*

*The specification for the product was not clearly defined; it appears under several other headings such as 'Design brief'. The main relevant points of the specification are present including the technical data, however closer attention to the criteria would have facilitated the marking process.*

*Activity 3: Name the materials used and give reasons why they were selected for the product.*

*This student has clearly listed and named each part of the device and stated the material used in each case and the manufacturing processes involved. This is good practice and good use of a table.*

*Activity 4: Describe the method of manufacture.*

*As well as describing the method of manufacture the student has also shown the method of assembly through the use of an exploded diagram.*

*Activity 5: State how convenient the product is to use and service. The clear exploded diagram of the product provides a good understanding of the corkscrew's assembly and the excellent sequence of sketches show very clearly how it is used. Also, the important note on ergonomics makes reference to how easy the product is to use.*

# Product evaluation

Product evaluation is an important part of any design-and-make activity. It is that part of the process that enables you to reflect on the final outcome. This reflection should be based on the product specification, for this was the initial requirement for the design. The product's success or otherwise should be judged against the original specification.

This focused task is an opportunity for you to practise and develop this skill before starting your major design-and-make project. Product evaluation can be divided into four main sections that should help you through this activity. These are:

1. Select an appropriate product, which will lend itself to critical appraisal, and justify the selection.
2. Write a detailed specification of the selected product.
3. Evaluate the product against the detailed specification.
4. Make realistic proposals for modification.

## 1 Select a technological product for evaluation

Selection: Select a technological product that you use on a regular basis and keep it manageable. Do not try to evaluate the jet engine even though you go on holiday ten times a year! Evaluate something like your watch, an electric kettle, an adjustable reading lamp, a Game Boy, a mobile phone or a DIY tool.

Description: Start by giving a description of the technological product you plan to evaluate and what it does.

Reason for your choice: Say why you have chosen this product to evaluate over all others. It may be because it is used for your hobby, or you use it every day at home.

## 2 Write a detailed specification of the selected product

You may have access to the original specification, which can often be found in the user's manual that comes with most products. If not, you will have to try and put yourself in the position of the designer and make a list of what you think the product was designed to do.

## 3 Evaluate the product against the detailed specification

One way to do a critical appraisal is to take each of your specification points and comment on how well the product did or did not meet that point. To make a realistic critical appraisal you will now test the product and record your findings. This can be done in the form of a table or short notes.

## 4 Make realistic proposals for modification

In this section you must suggest and make modifications to the product you are evaluating. These modifications should be based on what you said in section 3. The best way to do this is to make a drawing of the product showing the changes you would make to improve the design. You should annotate your drawing to explain how the changes would make the design or parts of the design better.

| Case study 3 | Evaluation of an electric kettle |
|---|---|

### 1 Justification for selecting the product

I have decided to evaluate an electric kettle for two main reasons:

- The Swan free-standing cordless jug kettle is a product that I use every day to boil the water when making coffee or tea.
- It is a technological product and as such is suitable for my focused task of product evaluation.

### 2 Detailed specification of the selected product

The kettle is shown in Figure 1.8.

It is my opinion that this electrical kettle was designed with the following points in mind:

1. hold 1.7 litres of water
2. indicate the level of water in the jug
3. free-standing
4. stop when the water is boiled
5. easily filled
6. stable
7. pour water effectively
8. portable
9. sell for under £20.00
10. safe to use
11. boil 1.7 litres of water in under 3 minutes
12. colour matches the rest of this kitchen equipment range.

**Figure 1.8** *Electric jug kettle*

### 3 Evaluation of the jug kettle against the detailed specification

The following comment is an extract from the student's evaluation of an electrical jug kettle specification:

**Point 6: Stability**

Comment: The kettle has a wide base for stability and four rubber feet to stop it sliding on a wet worktop. The wide base was fine when the kettle was quarter full but when it was filled to the top the centre of gravity was very high. When filled like this it could be toppled over with relative ease. We tend to only fill the kettle half way to avoid this problem.

When the kettle was plugged into the wall the flex became a problem in that it became an obstacle on the cluttered work surface. Several times there have been near accidents as the kettle was pulled over by the flex getting caught as other equipment was being moved.

### 4 Modifications to the jug kettle

- I would make the kettle wider at the base for increased stability.
- I would have an opening lid that opened inside the handle so that my hand was always above and behind the lid. This should help stop the kettle falling over as you try to pull the lid up.
- I would lower the centre of gravity by making the kettle barrel shaped. This would mean that more water was at the base than at the top.
- I would have the on-off switch at the back and top of the handle so that the action is more of a downward push rather than a horizontal push. This would help prevent accidentally pushing the kettle over.
- I would make it from the same materials and keep the colour to match the range.

A drawing of the modified kettle is shown in Figure 1.9.

### Author's comments on case study 3

*This is not a complete case study but it is included because it addresses all the criteria for GCSE Technology and Design in that:*

- *The product selected was a technological product and this is a requirement.*
- *The reasons for the selection were based on a product the student was familiar with. This is important if the evaluation is to be meaningful and you are to learn from the exercise.*
- *The specification was realistic and meaningful.*
- *As only part of the evaluation is given in the example it is difficult to comment fully on it. However if point 6 is typical of the rest of the evaluation then this is an excellent standard.*
- *The suggested modifications are excellent, realistic and practical, and directly based on the evaluation and this is important. The*

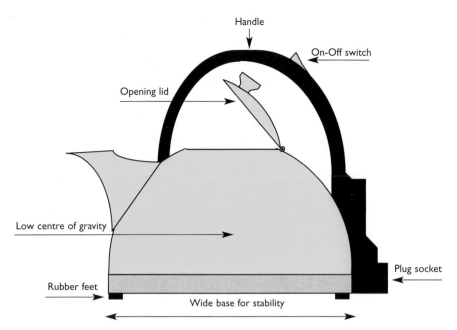

**Figure 1.9** *Drawing of the modified kettle*

*use of CAD to show the modifications to the kettle was excellent. However a sketch would have been adequate and may have taken less time. However if CAD is a technique that you are familiar with, are good at and you find it quick and easy to use, then use it.*

| Case study 4 | Evaluation of a Bosch jigsaw |
|---|---|

The following example of product evaluation was by a year 11 student studying for CCEA's Technology and Design examination.

### Justification for selecting the product

I have chosen to evaluate a Bosch jigsaw because I find it has a problem with cutting. The jigsaw has a regular speed that can't be controlled and can be a problem when I'm trying to cut around corners and cutting different materials of different thickness. It is a problem because the blade often twists and breaks. It would be better if there was a speed control as this would help to cut different materials of different thickness. For example, for cutting metal it would be more suitable to operate the jigsaw at a lower speed but when cutting wood a higher speed would be better.

### Specification of the product

In my opinion when the jigsaw was being designed it was to fulfil the following points:

**Figure 1.10** *Picture of a Bosch jigsaw*

- The jigsaw should have a locking button so you can cut without holding the trigger in the on position.
- The jigsaw should have a vacuum adapter to vacuum up the harmful dust made during cutting.
- The jigsaw should have an on/off switch so you can operate it.

11

- The jigsaw should have a safety guard to protect the operator from the blade when the blade is in motion.
- The jigsaw should be able to cut wood up to a thickness of 53 mm.
- The jigsaw should be able to cut aluminium up to a thickness of 12 mm.
- The jigsaw should be able to cut mild steel up to a thickness of 3 mm.
- The jigsaw should have an adjustable base-plate to allow for cutting at angles up to 45 degrees.
- The jigsaw should have a stroke rate of 2700 revs/min.
- The jigsaw should have ventilation slots so that the motor can operate for a long time without overheating.
- The jigsaw, its accessories and packaging should be manufactured to be environmentally friendly and recyclable.

### Evaluation of the product against the specification

- The jigsaw did have a locking button so you can cut without holding the trigger in the on position, which made it easier to hold when cutting.
- The jigsaw did have a vacuum adapter to vacuum up the harmful dust made during cutting but this was not very effective when the dust was very fine.
- The jigsaw did have an on/off switch so you can operate it and this was easy to use.
- The jigsaw did have a safety guard to protect the operator from the blade when the blade is in motion and this was good but when cutting wood it became dusty making it hard to see the blade.
- The jigsaw did cut wood up to a thickness of 53 mm but it was difficult to operate at this thickness.
- The jigsaw did cut aluminium up to a thickness of 12 mm with ease.
- The jigsaw did cut mild steel up to a thickness of 3 mm but it was difficult to operate at the fixed speed because it vibrated, making it difficult to hold.
- The jigsaw did have an adjustable base-plate to allow for cutting at angles up to 45 degrees.
- I think the jigsaw did have a stroke rate of 2700 revs/min but this was too difficult to measure accurately.
- The jigsaw did have ventilation slots but these were not very effective as the motor overheated and stopped when I used it for a long time.
- I think the jigsaw would be environmentally friendly and recyclable except for the body of the saw that had to be plastic for safety reasons and plastic is hard to recycle.

## MODIFICATIONS

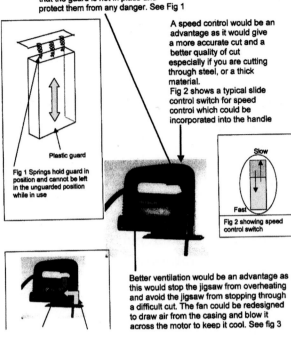

The safety guard, instead of being manually operated could be spring operated this would alert the operator that the guard is not in place and protect them from any danger. See Fig 1

A speed control would be an advantage as it would give a more accurate cut and a better quality of cut especially if you are cutting through steel, or a thick material.
Fig 2 shows a typical slide control switch for speed control which could be incorporated into the handle

Plastic guard

Fig 1 Springs hold guard in position and cannot be left in the unguarded position while in use

Slow

Fast

Fig 2 showing speed control switch

Better ventilation would be an advantage as this would stop the jigsaw from overheating and avoid the jigsaw from stopping through a difficult cut. The fan could be redesigned to draw air from the casing and blow it across the motor to keep it cool. See fig 3

**Figure 1.11** *Modifications to the Bosch jigsaw*

*Author's comments on case study 4*

*Case study 4 is a good product evaluation focused task that was submitted for CCEA's GCSE Technology and Design. It is realistic and achievable for most students. It is good in that it satisfies all the criteria to some degree.*

- *It clearly identified a technological product suitable for evaluation. The student gives clear reasons for the choice of product. The use of an image of the Bosch jigsaw taken from the Internet is all that is required; it is not necessary or advisable for a student to spend time drawing the product as this rarely shows a true image.*
- *The specification was detailed, relevant and clearly set out.*
- *The evaluation was directly linked to the original specification and the comments, if lacking in detail at times, were clearly derived from the student's knowledge of the jigsaw in use.*
- *The suggested modifications are good. They are clearly presented through the use of sketches and notes along with images of the original jigsaw.*

| Case study 5 | Product evaluation of a Palm 111e Desktop Handheld Organiser |
|---|---|

The following example of product evaluation of a Palm 111e Desktop Handheld Organiser was by a year 11 student studying for CCEA's Technology and Design examination.

### Product justification

For my GCSE Product Evaluation I have decided to research the Palm 111e Desktop Handheld Organiser. The Palm 111e Desktop Handheld Organiser is the third generation in the family of products manufactured on the Palm platform. It has several capabilities as well as improvements on earlier Palm handhelds.

I have decided to start by asking myself challenging evaluation questions in a number of specific categories covering a range of the product qualities. I then plan to answer these questions in detail to learn more about my product. The specific questions are:

### *Specification*

Aesthetics, ergonomics, anthropometrics, cost, durability, environment, function, maintenance, materials, performance, reliability, safety, size, storage, usefulness, weight, where the product can be purchased, user friendliness and modifications. (The following is a sample of the student's questions. These were in a booklet that preceded the drawing shown in Figure 1.12.)

## Aesthetics

- Is the product pleasing to look at?
- Does the product have a colour scheme?
- Is the product curvaceous?
- Does the product look more pleasing than similar products?
- Does the product stand out?
- Was the product designed with looks in mind?
- Does the product have eye-catching logos?

## Ergonomics

- Is the product easy to hold?
- Is the product smooth to the touch?
- Does the product have rounded corners?
- Does it have any special grip?
- Does the user feel the product was designed just for him/her?
- Is it more ergonomically pleasing than similar products?

## Anthropometrics

- Is it the right size for the intended user?
- Is the product easy to hold?
- Is it easy to work?
- Is the product more anthropometrically pleasing than other similar products?

## Cost

- How much does the product cost?
- How does the price compare with other similar products?
- Is the product expensive to manufacture?
- Is the product expensive to run?
- Is the product expensive to maintain?
- Does it have a recommended retail price?

## Durability

- How long will the product last?
- How long before the batteries need changing?
- Is it shock absorbent?
- Is it waterproof?
- Can it withstand being stood on?
- How does the durability compare with similar products?

I personally think that the Palm III Desktop is aesthetically pleasing to look at because it is translucent. All the product's electronics are clearly seen through the cover. It looks very technological, however I can understand that some people might find it dull to look at. If this is the case, it is available in many other different colours. The product is for an executive adult so the colours are not that important. The product is curvaceous with rounded corners and folds out to be able to operate it. The product might not have been designed with looks in mind although it does have all the other good qualities about it. I don't think that it would stand out in a room other than just another piece of technical equipment such as a calculator or electronic diary. However, it is much more than that. The buttons and large screen are set out neatly to give it a good presentation of the whole product.

The product is designed to suit your hand, therefore easy to hold. It comes with a hard tipped pen called a stylus to touch the screen with. Its edges do not cut into your hand or begin to feel uncomfortable after a long period of time. The product is rough on the outside cover giving it a good firm grip in your hand but when opened it has a smooth surface with comfortable and responsive buttons. I feel the product must have been designed for an adult and would probably be essential for a business working man/woman, as it is incredibly useful for storing dates and other pieces of information. Although the new updated version of the Palm III can hold more information and is more ergonomically pleasing. The stylus is very ergonomically pleasing because it fits in your hand just like a pencil.

The cost of the product is between £130–£150. Other similar products are roughly the same price. The product is not that expensive to make. Like most electrical equipment, when you make the original, copies are easy to manufacture by the thousands. The product runs on batteries so once bought all you have to worry about is the cost of the batteries. There are no running costs to the Palm III handheld. The recommended retail price of the manufacturer is as stated above and you can get the Palm III handheld in any electrical store.

I tend to look at this product as a mini laptop, just not as advanced. It is a perfect size to carry around like a mobile phone and the user can operate it at any time. It is the ideal size for the intended purpose and it is very easy to hold and operate. With the product in one hand and the stylus in the other, which fits into a slot at the back, it is just like writing on paper. The company has clearly researched previous models and have taken the time in modifying a whole new design. I have not seen other similar products more anthropometrically pleasing than this product and would be surprised to see a newer model beat its standards in anthropometrics

**Figure 1.12** *Evaluation of a Palm IIIe Desktop Handheld Organiser*

### Environment
- Is it environmentally friendly?
- Will it be easily recycled?

### *Modification to the Palm IIIe Desktop Handheld Organiser*

I cannot suggest any meaningful modifications to the product design. However, I would include metric and currency conversions and a more scientific calculator because they could prove useful. Other than that I am very pleased with the modifications the company have made since the previous models. It does not have any flaws that I have encountered yet. There is an updated model available called the 'Blue-Tooth' that has increased memory and more features. Also it has satellite remote/Internet access.

*Author's comments on case study 5*

*This example of a student's product evaluation is a quality piece of coursework. It satisfies the five elements mentioned earlier. The use of probing questions based on the specification was an excellent technique to help start the process of evaluation. The standard of work in my opinion is more than would be required of a student at the GCSE level.*

## Questions on product analysis

1 With reference to either case study 1 or 2:
- Write down the product chosen by the student for product analysis.
- Why did the student choose this product?
- Write down four specification points listed by the student.

2 Within the context of a focused task on product analysis, write a *short* sentence to explain what each point means:
- A clear description of the purpose of the technological product selected.
- Write a detailed specification of the selected product.
- Name the materials used and give reasons why they were selected for the product.
- Describe the method of manufacture.
- State how convenient the product is to use and service.

3 With reference to the list of technological products set out in Table 1.1 (page 3), select one of these products or a technological product of your own choosing and answer the following questions. Your answers should be on a maximum of four sides of A4 paper.
- Write a clear description of the purpose of the technological product (try to speculate on, and justify your understanding of, what the designer had in mind when he/she conceived the product).
- Write a specification for the product. This can be obtained from the manufacturer's literature or you can list what you think it should be. Include some technical and non-technical points in your specification.
- Name the materials used in the product. You can do this by making a table or writing short paragraphs identifying the materials used and giving your reasons why you think the material was chosen for use in the product.
- Discuss the method of manufacture by explaining some of the main techniques used in the manufacturing of the product.
- Explain how easy or otherwise it is to use and service the product.

## Questions on product evaluation

1 Within the context of a focused task in product evaluation, write a *short* sentence to explain what each of the following points means:
- Select an appropriate product to evaluate, which will lend itself to critical appraisal, and justify the selection.
- Write a detailed specification of the product.
- Evaluate the product against the detailed specification.
- Make realistic proposals for modification.

2 Within the context of a focused task in product evaluation and with reference to the list of technological products set out in Table 1.1 (page 3), select one of these products or a technological product of your own choosing and answer the following questions. Your answers should be on a maximum of four sides of A4 paper.

- For your selected product, and under the heading 'Justification for selecting the product', explain why you have chosen this product. Include a picture of your chosen product.
- For your selected product, and under the heading 'Specification', write a detailed specification for the product. This can be obtained from the manufacturer's literature or you can make a list of what you think the product should do. Include some technical and non-technical points in your list.
- For your selected product, and under the heading 'Evaluation', evaluate the product against the detailed specification explaining how well or otherwise your product satisfied the points in the specification.
- For your selected product, and under the heading 'Modifications', explain the changes you would make to the product if you had to make it again. You should use sketches and notes to explain your modifications and improvements.

# CHAPTER TWO

# Focused tasks associated with communicating

There are two main areas associated with communicating that the following focused tasks are designed to help you with. These are:

1. Computer Aided Design Presentation
2. Freehand Presentation Drawing

## CAD (Computer Aided Design) presentation

Computer generated drawings are very useful when you are designing. Possibly the main advantage they have is that they allow you to save a drawing and either use it again later or make slight modifications to show the design as it develops. You can also make a library of your drawings or parts of drawings to be used at any time in the future.

If you are studying for the CCEA GCSE in Technology and Design you will be required to submit one focused task in either Computer Aided Design Presentation or Freehand Presentation Drawing as part of your coursework. It will carry a maximum mark of 5%.

If you chose the Computer Aided Design Presentation as your GCSE focused task, you will be required to demonstrate knowledge, understanding and skills associated with Computer Aided Design.

CAD is a very wide topic and there are numerous software packages you can buy. All of these packages have their own purpose and style that makes them different.

1. 2D CAD using Micrografx Windows Draw
2. 2D/3D CAD/solid modelling using Pro/DESKTOP V8
3. 2D/3D CAD/solid modelling using Solidworks

**Micrografx Windows Draw** is an old software package and is coming to the end of its useful life. However it is still to be found in many schools and for this reason it will be included in this chapter.

**Pro/DESKTOP** was launched in schools in 1998 and is an excellent CAD/CAM package and is available through DATA. Once the basic principles have been mastered it is a very powerful and impressive solid modelling design tool. Designs produced in Pro/DESKTOP can then be downloaded to a CNC machine enabling you to model your design in 3D before committing time and effort to the manufacturing process. Pro/DESKTOP requires your teacher to have an operating licence. However once the licence is in place you can borrow a copy of the software to use on your computer at home.

**Solidworks** is a drawing and solid modelling package produced primarily for industry. However an educational package is available to schools. Details of the educational package are available through NTCAD/CAM at www.ntcadcam.com. Alternatively if your school has C2K on the school network you can access it through this platform.

This focused task is an opportunity for you to practise and develop skills and draw a technological product from first principles. There are a number of skills and techniques associated with a focused task in Computer Aided Design Presentation, which you will have to demonstrate your ability in. These are:

1. Convey the intended information accurately.
2. Accurately use the graphic tools and facilities offered by the computer software in a suitably challenging context.
3. Use carefully considered annotation.
4. Generate the drawing from first principles.
5. Show at least two drawing views to help clarify details, i.e. pictorial, front views, and side views, sectional or exploded views, etc.

Your presentation should be on a maximum of one side of A3 or two sides of A4 paper.

It is important that you attempt to draw a technological product that you are familiar with. The chosen product should also have a level of complexity compatible with the specification for GCSE. Often students attempt to draw products such as sports cars, jet fighters, or the internal combustion engine, all of which are much more than is required for GCSE. Common technological products such as digital radio alarms, Walkmans, etc are much more suitable to draw.

Table 1.1 (page 3) gives a list of technological products which are suitable for this focused task. These are only suggested products; there is nothing stopping you from choosing one of your own. A case study for each of the three different software packages is shown in detail based on one of these technological products.

## Computer Aided Design (CAD) presentation of a mobile phone using Micrografx Draw

**Figure 2.1** *Ericsson mobile phone*

### Assignment

Your assignment is to complete the following exercise using Micrografx Draw. To undertake this assignment you will need access to a suitable PC and Micrografx Draw software.

### Getting started

The technological product chosen for this assignment is the Ericsson GA628 mobile phone drawn from first principles. The completed drawing is shown in Figure 2.1.

This assignment will show you how to use Micrografx Draw and by the end of this exercise you should be able to:

- draw and arrange shapes
- create a library of shapes to use in your drawing
- draw types of lines
- add colour to your drawing
- add shading
- group components
- draw a surface development
- add text and convert text to graphics.

### Getting to know Micrografx Windows Draw

In Micrografx you are able to draw different types of lines and shapes by selecting them from the top menu bar. You can draw free-hand lines, arcs, pie/pie wedges, polylines, curves, circles, rounded triangles, rectangles/squares and straight lines. To draw any of these lines click on the draw button (pencil) in the left-hand menu. The top menu will now change to show all the line tools. Figure 2.2 shows you where to find these.

### Reshape tool

The reshape tool is useful if the shape you have drawn is not quite correct. To use this tool, click on the drawing you wish to edit. Click on the fourth button along on the pointer menu. This will bring up a series of editing handles. You can pick up one of the editing handles (small black square boxes) at a time and move it around. As you do this you will notice the shape changing.

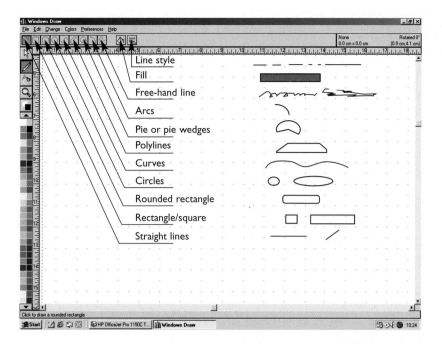

**Figure 2.2** *Selecting the Micrografx Draw tools*

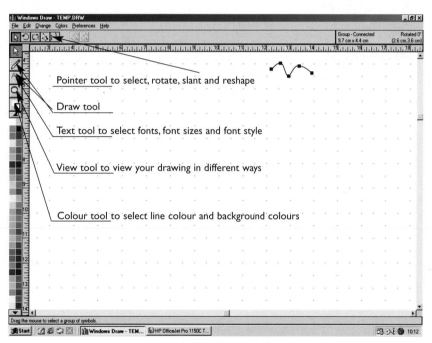

**Figure 2.3** *Micrografx vertical menu bar*

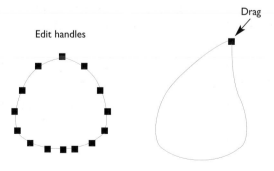

**Figure 2.4** *Pointer tool*

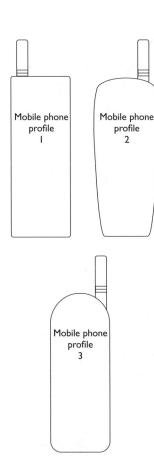

**Figure 2.5** *Mobile phone profiles*

### Drawing profiles using Micrografx

When drawing an object that is the same shape on both sides of the centre line, it is good practice to draw one half before copying and pasting it on the other side. This way you are sure of both halves being the same. Figure 2.6 shows how each profile was drawn.

### Selecting the phone profile

There are a few basic front profiles that mobile phone makers seem to use. Three of these are shown in Figure 2.5.

All three profiles were drawn inside a rectangular box. A line was drawn down the middle so that lines and shapes could be positioned on either side of it. This line was removed at the end. The same aerial was used for each profile. The aerial and the cross bands were drawn using the same rounded rectangle tool.

### Profile 1

This is the simplest shape and was drawn using the rounded rectangle tool from the top menu bar.

### Profile 2

This was the most difficult to draw. One side was drawn using the arc and curve tools. This was then copied, pasted and flipped horizontally to form the other side. The lines were then captured and connected.

### Profile 3

One half was drawn using the arc and straight-line tools. This was then copied, pasted and flipped horizontally to form the other side. The lines were then captured and connected.

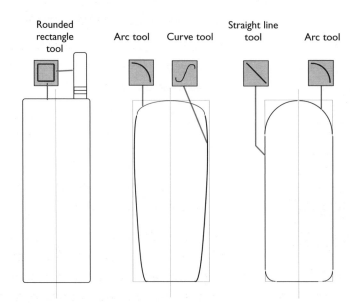

**Figure 2.6** *Using the draw tool to draw a profile*

**Figure 2.7** *Shading the profile*

### Drawing the Ericsson GA628 Mobile Phone

The Ericsson GA628 uses profile 1 shown in Figure 2.5. The drawing of this phone is set out showing the different stages.

### Stage 1 Drawing the profile

Draw the profile. This should be selected and coloured black. If you wish you can select the gradient from the fill menu and shade the phone black to grey by clicking on the colour palette down the left-hand side.

### Stage 2 Drawing the sound recess

Working from the top of the drawing down, draw the sound recess as follows.

Use the arc tool to draw two arcs (Figure 2.8). Copy and paste these before flipping over and joining them to the first two. Next capture all four and go to the drop-down menu. Change and select, arrange – connect to join the four arcs. The drawing can now be filled. Finally draw three ovals and drop these on to form the sound holes.

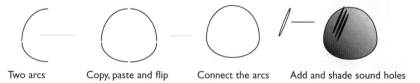

**Figure 2.8** *Drawing the sound recess*

Two arcs     Copy, paste and flip     Connect the arcs     Add and shade sound holes

### Stage 3 Drawing the display

Draw a rectangle and use the fill/gradient tool to shade it grey-white. Draw the background outline using a polyline and two arcs. Connect these together before filling black. Select the display rectangle and drag it over the background.

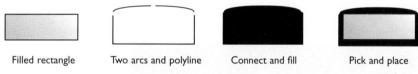

**Figure 2.9** *Drawing the display*

Filled rectangle     Two arcs and polyline     Connect and fill     Pick and place

Charging light

**Figure 2.10** *Placing the drawing on the profile*

### Stage 4 Adding the sound recess and display

It is advisable to group your drawing of the sound recess before picking and placing it close to the top of the phone profile.

Do the same with the display drawing before picking and placing it on the profile. Make sure it is centred on the centre line.

Draw a small oval and fill it green. This will be the charging light. Place it on the profile before sending it to the back.

### Stage 5 Drawing the buttons

The yes/no buttons are the same shape as the sound recess so copy this and reduce it in size to act as a button. The number buttons are all one unfilled oval outside and one solid oval

**Figure 2.12** *Button panel*

inside. You will need 15, so simply draw one and copy it 15 times for all the numbers and functions.

**Figure 2.11** *Drawing the buttons*

### Stage 6 Adding text to the buttons

Select the text menu from the left-hand menu bar. Next select a font. Micrografx always defaults to *Swiss* but this is not a true font so you will have to select one from the drop-down menu.

Place the number on your button and change the colour to white before grouping.

Draw a rectangular button panel and locate the buttons on it. Group the finished button panel before picking and placing on the phone profile.

### Stage 7 Adding text to the drawing

To add the white texts, simply select text from the menu, type the name and highlight it. Now select white from the colour palette and click on it. The text will change to that colour. Pick and place this on your phone profile. Your drawing should look like the drawing in Figure 2.13.

**Figure 2.13** *Final drawing of Ericsson GA628 mobile phone*

| Case study 2 | Computer Aided Design (CAD) presentation of a digital alarm clock using Pro/DESKTOP V8 |
|---|---|

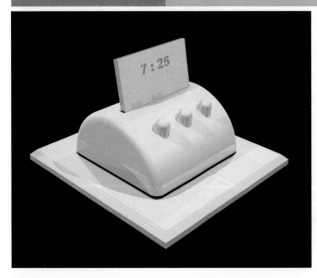

**Figure 2.14** *CAD digital alarm clock drawn in Pro/DESKTOP V8*

### Assignment

Your assignment is to complete the following exercise using Pro/DESKTOP version 8. To undertake this assignment you will need access to a suitable PC and Pro/DESKTOP software.

The technological product chosen for this assignment is a digital alarm clock drawn from first principles. The digital alarm clock you will be drawing is shown in Figure 2.14.

This assignment will introduce you to Pro/DESKTOP version 8. It assumes you have some knowledge of the introductory exercises found in the help files provided on the CD.

By the end of this exercise you should be able to:

- select and/or reposition a workplane
- create a new sketch
- use the ellipse tool
- view in isometric
- use autoscale
- extrude a sketch
- select and use the edge tool to create a radius
- view onto a workplane and create a centre line
- create a slot, extrude and subtract material
- create a workplane on an angle
- create a sketch and project it into your main sketch
- modify a solid, and deform a face
- create a shell image of your drawing
- create a final assembly
- render a drawing.

**Figure 2.15** *Digital Alarm Clock drawn in Pro/DESKTOP V8*

### Solid modelling of a digital alarm clock design drawn in Pro/DESKTOP V8

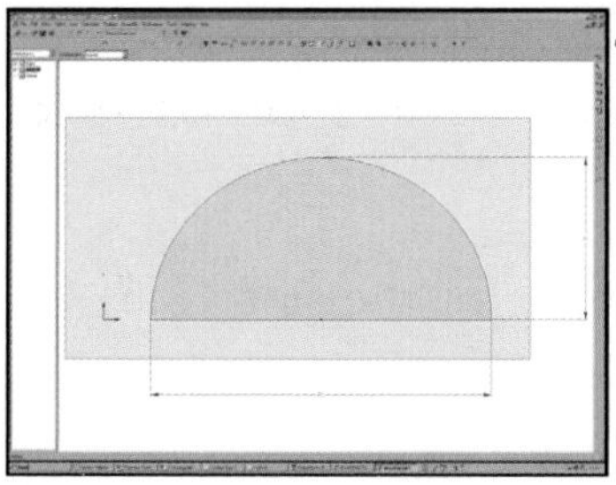

1. Right click on the frontal Workplane icon in the browser – new sketch, OK, and view onto workplane – select lines in the Design toolbar.

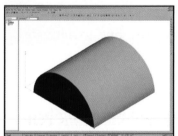

**Figure 2.16** *Ellipse drawn on frontal workplane*

2. Select the Ellipse tool and draw an ellipse major axis 65 mm and minor axis 30 mm. View in Isometric and (Shift + A) to Autoscale (Figure 2.16).

3. Extrude to a depth of 65 mm and OK (Figure 2.17).

**Figure 2.17** *Extruding*

4. Select the Edge tool  , click on the round edges to select, right click and radius to 5 mm as shown in Figure 2.18.

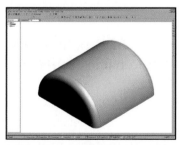

**Figure 2.18** *Rounding the edges*

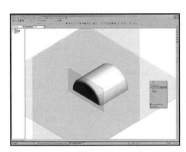

**Figure 2.19** *Creating a new workplane*

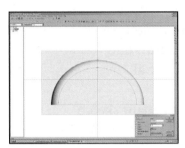

**Figure 2.20** *Adding a new workplane*

**Figure 2.21** *Adding centre line to the workplane*

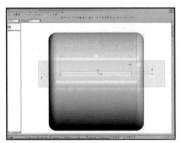

**Figure 2.22** *Drawing the rectangle for the slot*

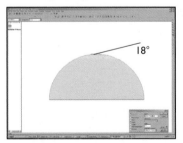

**Figure 2.23** *Setting the workplane to 18 degrees*

5. Select the workplane icon from the Design toolbar, click on the base workplane, right click and select new workplane (Figure 2.19).

6. Off-set or slide the workplane to the top of the arc, OK, then right click and add a new sketch (Figure 2.20).

7. View onto workplane, select the line tool and add a centre line dimension 32.5 mm from the end of the drawing (Figure 2.21).

8. View in Isometric and with the centre line **highlighted** select workplane from the top menu bar – new workplane or Ctrl + L.

9. Position the workplane to an angle of 10°, OK, and add a new sketch.

10. View onto and draw the rectangle for the slot 48.5 × 3 mm (Figure 2.22).

11. Extrude and subtract material to a depth of 10 mm.

12. Select Lines icon, double click centre line to activate the sketch.

13. Select workplane from the top pull-down menu bar, new workplane or Ctrl + L. Set the workplane to an angle of −18° and OK (Figure 2.23).

14. With the workplane selected (Figure 2.24) right click, new sketch and OK. You may wish to name each new sketch.

15. View onto and draw three circles diameter 7 mm as shown in Figure 2.25. Start by adding a centre line.

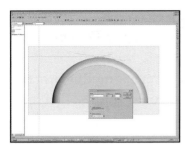

**Figure 2.24** *Selecting the workplane*

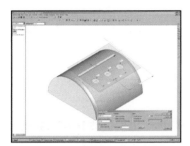

**Figure 2.25** *Drawing the circles onto the workplane*

**Figure 2.26** *Selecting the project icon*

**Figure 2.27** *Modifying a solid*

**Figure 2.28** *Deforming all three faces*

16. Select the Project icon from the features toolbar (Figure 2.26); ensure the dialogue box is ticked as shown below.

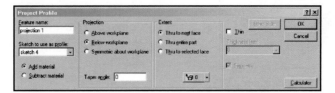

17. Select the Face tool from the Design toolbar, select one of the circle's faces, go to Features from the pull-down menu, Modify Solids, Deform Face and set the height to 3 mm in the dialogue box and OK (Figure 2.27).

18. Continue and deform all three faces for the buttons (Figure 2.28).

19. Select the Edge tool from the Design toolbar and radius the ends of the buttons (Figure 2.29).

20. Select the Face tool from the Design toolbar and use the cursor keys to tumble the casing and select the bottom face. Right click and shell  0.5 mm (Figure 2.30).

21. Zoom in or (Shift + Z) to the casing edge (Figure 2.31). Use the Face tool to select the face, right click and add a new sketch. View onto (Shift + W).

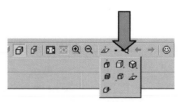

22. Select the Line tool and draw a Vertical Centre line (Ctrl + G) to change the line to a construction line (Figure 2.32).

23. Draw concentric circles close to the top left-hand corner, diameter 4 mm and 2 mm (Figure 2.33).

**Figure 2.29** *Adding a radius to the edges of the buttons*

**Figure 2.30** *Shelling the sketch*

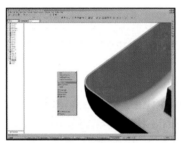

**Figure 2.31** *Selecting the bottom edge*

**Figure 2.32** *Adding a vertical centre line*

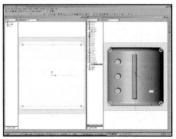

**Figure 2.33** *Drawing the concentric circles*

24. To Mirror the circles, first select the circles ◎, now in red, select Line from the top menu bar, Mirror, select axis in the dialogue box and OK.
    By drawing a horizontal line and repeating this process the concentric circles can be mirrored to the other side of the casing design (Figure 2.34).

25. Hold down the Shift key and multi-select all circles, select the Project tool, click below workplane through to next face and OK.

26. Select Assembly from the top menu and New Design in Context. A new window will appear with a wire image of the casing design (Figure 2.35).

27. Select the bottom face using the Face tool (Figure 2.36), right click and add a new sketch.

28. Select the Edge tool and multi-select the outer lines by holding down the Shift key.

29. Right click and Project (Figure 2.37).

30. Extrude to a depth of 2 mm (Figure 2.38) and save this sketch as Base. Close the sketch.
    You will notice in your original sketch of your casing design that this base is now attached.
    It is **important** to select the Parts tool and Delete this before saving your drawing.
    Shown opposite is the assembled view of the digital display and the casing assembled.

**Figure 2.34** *Adding circles to all four corners*

**Figure 2.35** *New design in context*

**Figure 2.36** *Selecting the bottom face*

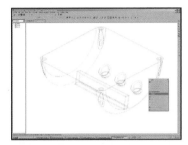

**Figure 2.37** *Projecting the base edges*

**Figure 2.38** *Extruding the base*

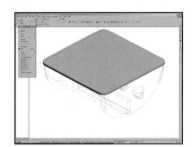

**Figure 2.39** *Completing the attached base*

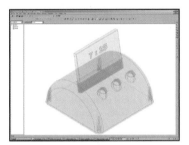

**Figure 2.40** *Adding the display to the drawing*

**Figure 2.41** *Creating an assembly*

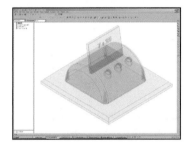

**Figure 2.42** *Adding a tabletop to the drawing*

**Figure 2.43** *Rendering the drawing*

31. Having drawn the body of the clock, you should be able to go on to complete the drawing of the digital alarm clock by adding the base and display panel (Figures 2.40 to 2.42).

### Questions

1 From the knowledge and skills you have gained from this exercise, draw the digital display.
Activate the sketch of the casing design to find the dimensions for the slot or go to Assembly, New Design in Context.

2 Use New Sketch, Assemble from the pull-down menu and add a component to connect (mate) the three parts of the electronic clock.

3 Draw a table-top of your own design and mate the base of the clock to the top of this table.

4 Open the Album feature and make a presentation drawing by rendering each part in different materials. Render in the

29

presentation mode before exporting as a jpeg and annotate to make a final presentation of the product.

### Focused tasks for Computer Aided Design presentations drawn in Pro/DESKTOP

The examples of students' work shown in Figures 2.44 to 2.47 are all suitable for the GCSE focused task 'Computer Aided Design Presentation'. All the examples were drawn using Pro/DESKTOP. They were chosen for four main reasons:

1. The level of complexity of the chosen product was appropriate.
2. They show a standard of presentation achievable by students.
3. Good use of annotation to explain specific details or views within the drawing.
4. The chosen product was a technological product (i.e. it contained a system).

| Examples | Focused tasks using Pro/DESKTOP |
| --- | --- |

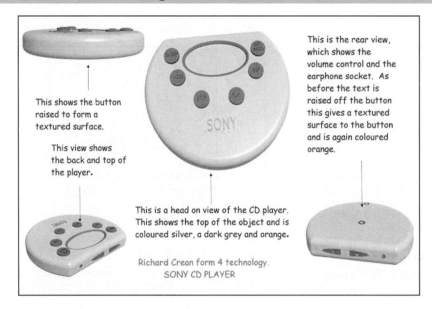

**Figure 2.44**

*Pro/DESKTOP presentation focused task of a Sony CD player*

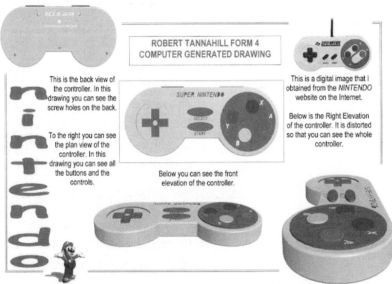

**Figure 2.45**

*Pro/DESKTOP presentation focused task of a Sony CD player*

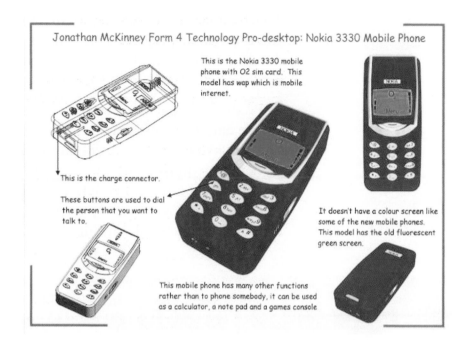

**Figure 2.46**

*Pro/DESKTOP presentation focused task of a Nokia 3330 mobile phone*

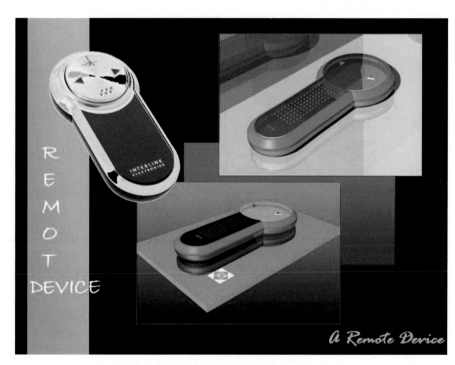

**Figure 2.47**

*Pro/DESKTOP presentation focused task of a remote device*

*Author's comments*

*The products shown in Figures 2.44 to 2.47 are all suitable for a GCSE focused task in Computer Aided Design Presentation. The standard of work is excellent. In the CAD presentation shown in Figure 2.47, while this is a suitable product the presentation would need to be annotated for GCSE.*

## Computer Aided Design presentation using Solidworks

To undertake this assignment you will need access to a suitable PC, Solidworks software and a Solidworks dongle.

This focused task is an opportunity for you to practise first- and third-angle projection techniques and communicate your design information. The task can be broken down into five sections. These are:

1. Produce a range of views of your design, showing front, top, side and isometric views.
2. Demonstrate hidden detail on the drawing and show section views if required.
3. Show a good understanding of scale.
4. Use annotations where appropriate to convey information.
5. Produce a pictorial drawing in the form of a solid model of your design.

| Case study 3 | Computer Aided Design (CAD) presentation of a CD storage rack using Solidworks |
| --- | --- |

### Assignment

Your assignment is to complete the following exercise using Solidworks.

**Figure 2.48** *CD storage rack drawn in Solidworks*

The product chosen for this assignment was a CD rotating/security storage system. The design brief was based on a class theme of CD storage. The CD storage rack was to be individually drawn in Solidworks as a class project before being cut out of acrylic by a laser cutter at the area board centre. The drawing and its rotating/security base were to be drawn from first principles. An example of a CD storage rack is shown in Figure 2.48.

Before attempting this focused task it is recommended that you complete lessons 1, 2 and 3 from the online tutorial in the Solidworks Help menu.

### Getting started

To do this task you will need a dimensioned drawing of a CD rack. The one used in this example is shown in Figure 2.57 on page 37.

This assignment will show you how to:

- Create a two-dimensional sketch in Solidworks.
- Turn the sketch into a three-dimensional solid part file.
- Add material to the solid part.
- Group components together in an assembly.
- Create front, side and plan elevations in a working drawing.

### Getting to know Solidworks

In Solidworks you can create parts, assembly and drawings. A part is created by first sketching a 2D shape using the sketch tools provided (lines, arcs, circles, rectangles, splines, etc.) and then turning that sketch (2D) into a solid (3D) by extruding it. Once you have a solid extrusion you can add more material or take it away by cutting.

To create a sketch, simply start a new part and click the sketch toolbar at the top, select the tool you want to use and sketch by clicking once where you want to start and a second time where you want to finish. The interactive help will assist you in what you want to do.

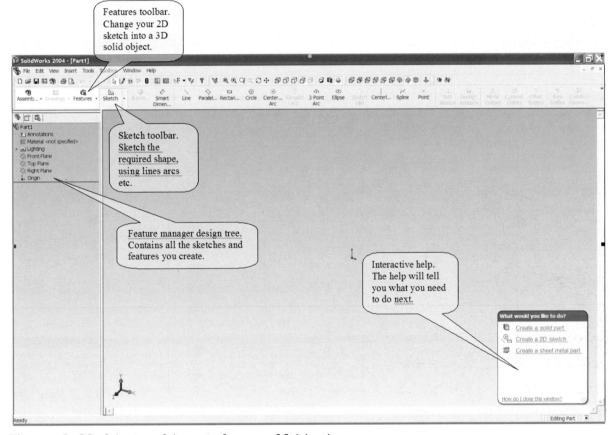

**Figure 2.49** *Selection of the main features of Solidworks*

### Creating the CD rack

This CD rack is made from three individual parts:

- two side plates
- eleven tops/shelves
- one locking bar.

You will need to create a sketch for each part and extrude it into a solid. The first sketch you need to create is the side plate. You can draw half the image and mirror this to create the full image. This process is referred to as creating half of the geometry and then mirroring it using a centre line. This is shown in Figure 2.50.

### Adding dimensions

You can add dimensions to the individual drawings that make up the side plate by using the Smart Dimension tool.

### Creating the 3D image from the 2D drawing

Once you have created the 2D drawing, simply click the Features toolbar at the top and select Extruded boss/base. Enter a depth for the extrusion or drag the arrow on the screen, then click the green tick. This will create the 3D image (Figure 2.51).

Once you have created a 3D solid image you can select a material to make it from. The tool to enable you to do this can be found in the feature manager menu shown on the left of the screen. In here you will find the Materials folder. Right click and edit material.

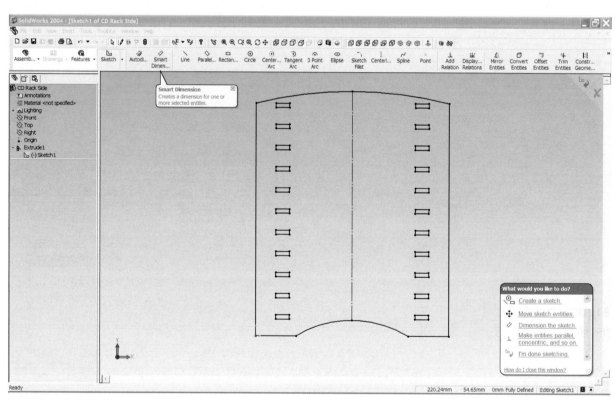

**Figure 2.50** *Creating a mirror image of the side plate by using a centre line*

### Creating the shelf and locking bar for the CD rack

You will need to create a drawing of the shelf and locking bar using the same techniques used in the drawing of the side plate. The drawings are shown in Figures 2.50 and 2.51, while the main dimensions can be found in Figure 2.57 on page 37. The side lugs on the shelf must fit into the rectangular holes in the side plate shown in Figure 2.50. Whatever length and distance apart you have drawn the rectangular holes will determine the size and position of the side lugs.

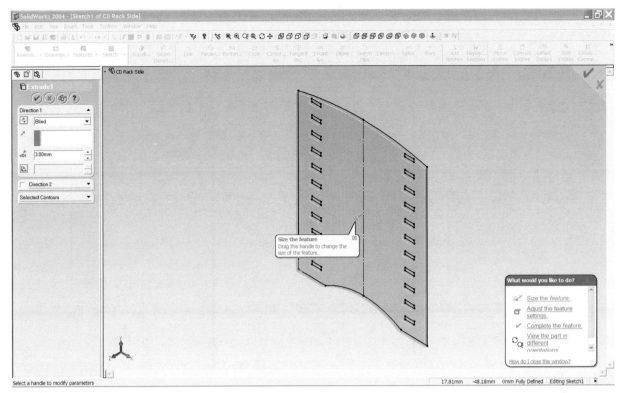

**Figure 2.51** *Creating a 3D image from a 2D drawing*

**Figure 2.52** *Drawing of the shelf*

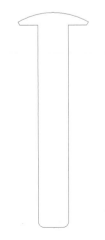

**Figure 2.53** *Drawing of the locking bar*

The same will also apply to the locking bar (Figure 2.53). Whatever width you have drawn the slot at the top of the shelf will determine the width of the locking bar as the bar has to slide into the slot. The length of the bar can be found in Figure 2.57.

**Creating an assembly drawing of the CD rack**

Once you have you completed your drawings of the three different parts of the CD storage rack you can bring them together in an assembly. The three individual parts that make up the assembly are shown in Figure 2.54.

Start a new assembly and insert the first component using the browse button on the left-hand side. Use the interactive help to insert more components and mate the components together (Figure 2.55).

Figure 2.56 shows what the assembled CD rack should look like. Front, plan and side elevations with an exploded isometric are shown.

Creating parts and assemblies are central to the design process. Using 3D CAD like Solidworks allows you to do real design checks without having to create time-intensive prototypes. The final stage of the process is to create an orthographic 2D drawing. This is a quality drawing showing both pictorial and isometric views.

35

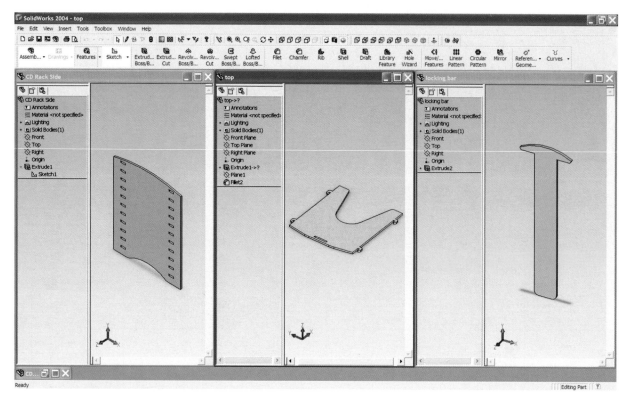

**Figure 2.54** *View of all the parts of the CD rack*

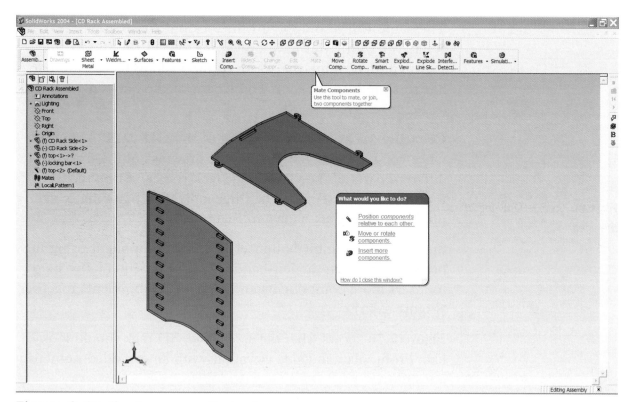

**Figure 2.55** *Creating an assembly drawing*

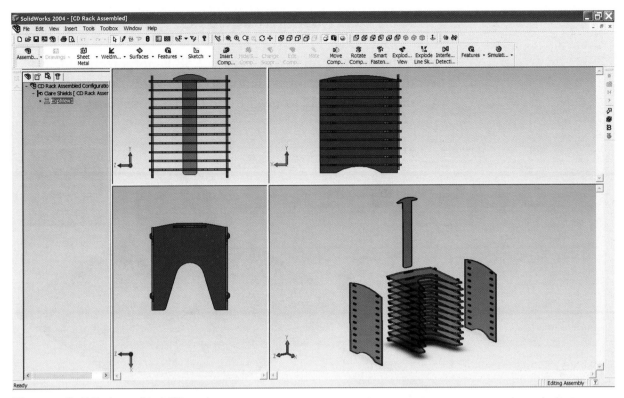

**Figure 2.56** *Assembled CD rack*

A completed drawing of the CD rack showing all the dimensions and a number of different views is shown in Figure 2.57.

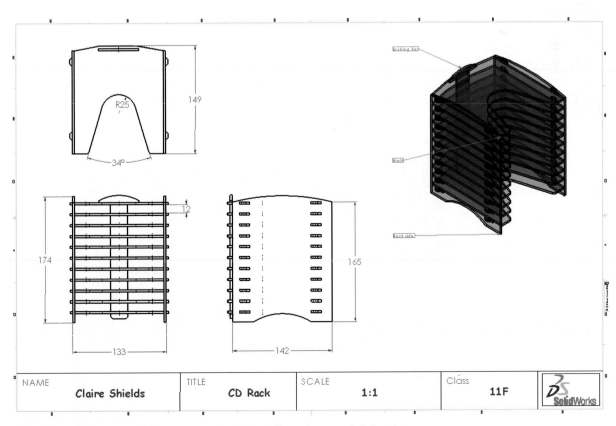

**Figure 2.57** *Final CAD presentation of the CD rack using Solidworks*

While the drawing shown in Figure 2.58 is not a technological product, it is a good introduction to Solidworks. It covers a range of skills you are likely to need to undertake your focused task.

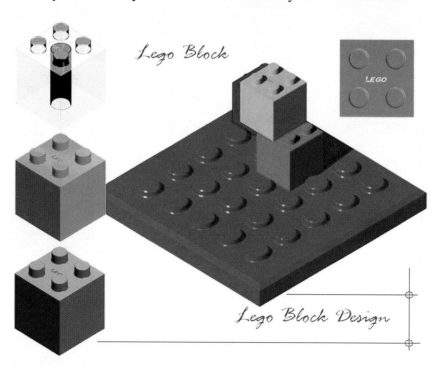

**Figure 2.58**

*Introductory exercise in Solidworks CAD presentation: Lego blocks*

It is important that you attempt to draw a technological product that you are familiar with. The chosen product should also have a level of complexity suitable for GCSE. Often students will attempt to draw products such as sports cars, jet fighters, or the internal combustion engine, all of which are much more than is required at this level. Common technological products such as radio alarms and Walkmans are much more suitable products to attempt. Examples of suitable tasks are shown in Figures 2.59 to 2.63.

**Figure 2.59** *Solidworks CAD presentation focused task of a cam-operated toy frog*

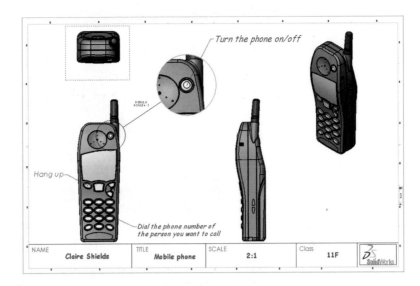

**Figure 2.60** *Solidworks CAD presentation focused task of a mobile phone*

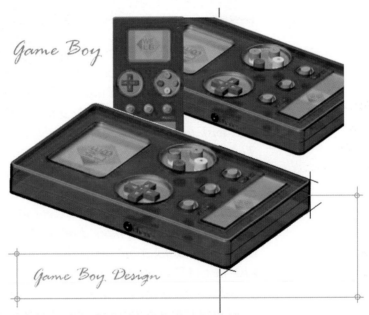

**Figure 2.61** *Solidworks CAD presentation focused task of a Game Boy, design 1*

**Figure 2.62** *Solidworks CAD presentation of a Game Boy, design 2*

39

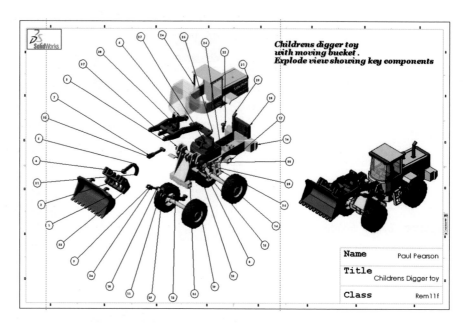

**Figure 2.63** *Solidworks CAD presentation of a toy digger*

*Author's comments*

*The choice of technological product you attempt is important. The complexity of the focused task should be such that you can complete it successfully. Ideally it should be a product that is familiar to you. You may wish to refer to the list of suitable products in Table 1.1 on page 3. The drawings of the cam-operated frog, mobile phone and Game Boy 1–2 shown in Figures 2.59 to 2.62 are all excellent standards of work. However if these drawings were to be entered for GCSE they would have to be annotated. Except for the minimal annotation added to the mobile phone drawing in Figure 2.60 all the others have little or no annotation, which is required for a CCEA GCSE focused task in CAD presentation.*

*The drawing of the toy digger in Figure 2.63 is an excellent example of how Solidworks can be used to produce quality Computer Aided Drawing presentations. However, the complexity of these drawings is more than one would expect from a CCEA GCSE candidate.*

# Freehand presentation drawing

Sketching and drawing are central to designing. They are the means by which you explain and record your thinking as you struggle to find a solution to your problem. A presentation drawing is the final stage of this process. It is a quality drawing that allows you to show what your final idea will look like.

A presentation drawing must be in the form of a pictorial drawing. A pictorial drawing is defined as an illustration of a technological product which contains expression and suggests a mental image. This focused task is an opportunity for you to practise and develop this skill should you wish to do so.

It is possible to break the focused task down into five sections that should help guide you through the activity. These are:

1. Select a technological product and produce a freehand pictorial representation, which accurately depicts the product.
2. Employ drawing techniques which are appropriate for your selected product, to have the desired impact on the intended audience.
3. Demonstrate rendering skills on the drawing using appropriate media (e.g. line, pattern, texture, tone and colour in coloured pencils, watercolour or markers).
4. Demonstrate a good understanding of scale and proportion in your drawing.
5. Use carefully considered annotation on your drawing.

You should be able to produce a good presentation drawing on one A3 page or two A4 pages. All the information should be on these pages. This includes notes (annotation) and extra details such as sections, etc.

When undertaking a presentation drawing, select a product which reflects the type of product you are likely to be drawing in your major project. Remember that you are developing a skill, so select a product of a similar complexity. Don't attempt to draw a Formula 1 racing car when all you are likely to design is a security system, an aid for the disabled or a lifting mechanism.

The following technological products are suitable for the focused task 'Freehand Illustration Presentation'. These are only suggested products; there is nothing stopping you from choosing one of your own:

- mobile phone
- digital camera
- calculator
- Game Boy
- Nintendo controller
- joystick for a computer
- CD Walkman
- electric toothbrush
- electric screwdriver
- electric smoothing iron
- computer mouse
- electric kettle
- paper stapler
- DIY tools.

### Two-dimensional (2D) drawing

By drawing one or more flat two-dimensional (2D) views of a technological product and using coloured pencils, pastel chalks, dry markers or a mixture of all three, it is possible to shade and texture your drawing to make it appear three-dimensional (3D).

When attempting pictorial drawing for the first time it is a good idea to start with one or two 2D views of the product as shown in Figure 2.64. These then can be rendered to give the drawing the desired impact. By doing this you will become more familiar with the product. This knowledge can then be used to generate a 3D drawing of the product if you so desire.

| Case study 4 | 2D presentation drawing of a moisture probe |

A pencil drawing was made of the electronic moisture probe before using coloured pencils to add shade and texture to enhance the drawing. The next stage was to attempt the drawing in 3D.

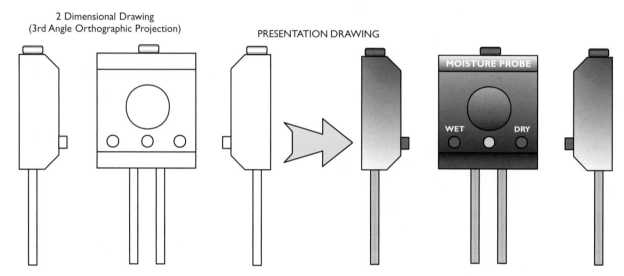

**Figure 2.64** *2D Drawings of a moisture probe*

### Drawing the moisture probe in 3D

The technique used in Figure 2.65 was isometric projection. In this method, the sloping lines are drawn at 30 degrees to the horizontal as shown. The isometric circles were drawn using an isometric ellipse drawing template.

#### *Adding colour to the isometric drawing of the moisture probe*

By using coloured pencils you can add colour and shading to a 3D view. The technique involves holding the pencil on its side to lay down more colour with a single pass. By making repeated passes over the same area you can add depth to the colour. This will give the effect of shading. A black pencil can be used to form a shadow under the drawing. Finally a white pencil can be used to highlight the edges. The coloured pencils used were Derwent Artists Pencils. These or similar artist's pencils give a good coverage and depth of colour.

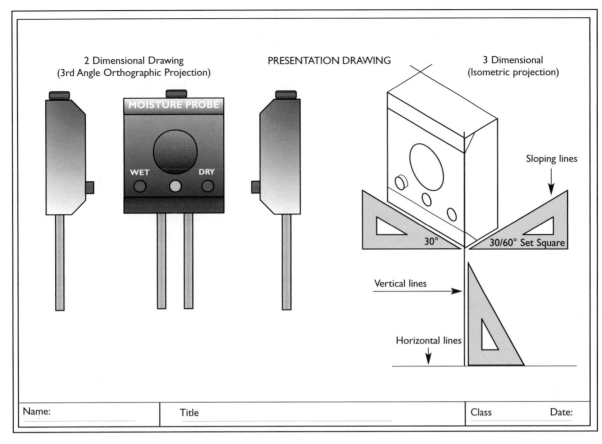

**Figure 2.65** *Generating a 3D drawing from a 2D drawing*

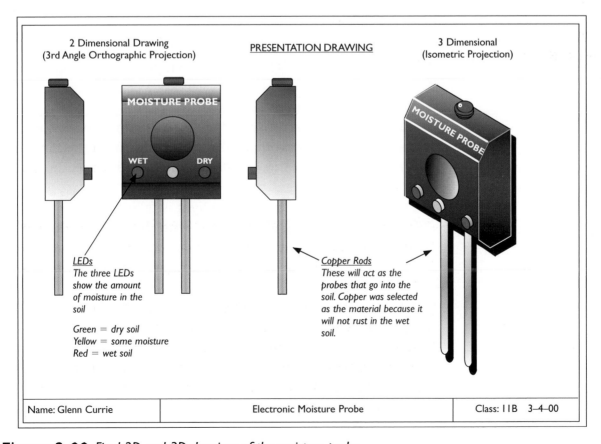

**Figure 2.66** *Final 2D and 3D drawings of the moisture probe*

## Adding annotations to your drawings

To annotate a drawing means to add short explanatory notes to it. The purpose of annotation is to provide more information about your design. The presentation drawing in Figure 2.66 has some annotations added to explain the purpose of the LEDs and the material used for the probes.

## Dry markers

The dry marker is a fast drying spirit-based marker. While it takes a little bit of getting used to, the final results are more striking than coloured pencils. The two markers that students seem to get the most success with are the Edding 2000/2200 grafix permanent art markers and the Pantone. For everyday school use, the Edding are a good all-round choice. They are fast drying, refillable and give off a low odour.

### The technique of using markers

The technique involves using a chisel point marker to lay down a strip of coloured ink, leaving this to dry then laying down another layer on top. The more passes over the same line the deeper the colour will become. This process will add shade and texture to your presentation drawing.

The steps necessary to complete a dry marker rendering of your drawing are:

1. Make a light 2D pencil drawing of the technological product.
2. Make a photocopy. This way you can practise the technique.
3. Select the light colours first. If necessary it is then possible to go over this with a dark colour.
4. Using a chisel point marker lay down the foundation colour. Use a 'T' square and make these lines all run in the same direction. Don't worry about running past the outside edges of the drawing.
5. Decide on which direction the light is falling on your product. By making another pass with the same marker you can start to darken the areas in shadow. The more passes you make the deeper the colour will appear. This is shown in Figure 2.67.
6. Use a white coloured pencil to add highlights. The Berol Karisma white 938 is a good pencil for this job.
7. Use a black pen to outline your drawing.
8. When completely dry, place the drawing on a cutting mat. Using a sharp craft knife and safety rule cut around the outside of the drawing. Finally, paste the drawing on to your presentation page.

Figure 2.68 shows the final presentation drawing for the cordless drill. Additional information has been added in the form of annotation and a 3D drawing of the chuck.

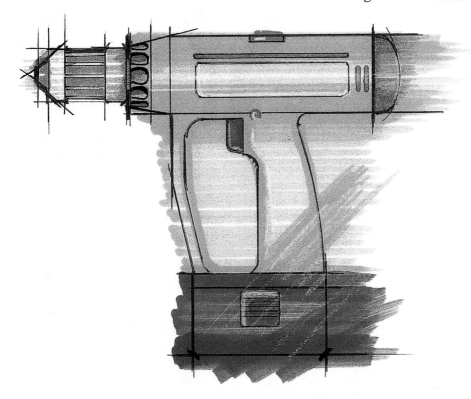

**Figure 2.67** *Dry marker drawing of a cordless drill*

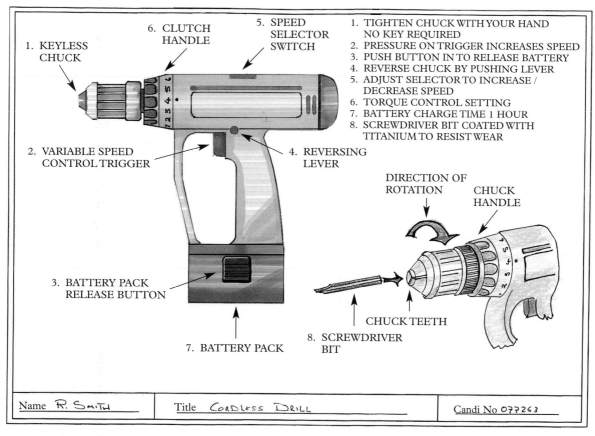

6. CLUTCH HANDLE

5. SPEED SELECTOR SWITCH

1. KEYLESS CHUCK

1. TIGHTEN CHUCK WITH YOUR HAND NO KEY REQUIRED
2. PRESSURE ON TRIGGER INCREASES SPEED
3. PUSH BUTTON IN TO RELEASE BATTERY
4. REVERSE CHUCK BY PUSHING LEVER
5. ADJUST SELECTOR TO INCREASE / DECREASE SPEED
6. TORQUE CONTROL SETTING
7. BATTERY CHARGE TIME 1 HOUR
8. SCREWDRIVER BIT COATED WITH TITANIUM TO RESIST WEAR

2. VARIABLE SPEED CONTROL TRIGGER

4. REVERSING LEVER

3. BATTERY PACK RELEASE BUTTON

DIRECTION OF ROTATION

CHUCK HANDLE

CHUCK TEETH

7. BATTERY PACK

8. SCREWDRIVER BIT

Name R. SMITH          Title CORDLESS DRILL          Candi No 077263

**Figure 2.68** *Completed dry marker drawing of a cordless drill*

## Students' use of dry markers when designing

The examples shown in Figures 2.69 and 2.70 are from a student's design portfolio for an activity game that would help a child learn about the clock. Figure 2.71 is from a student's design portfolio for an educational toy that would teach a young child about the planets. In both portfolios the student has enhanced her/his illustrations using a mix of markers directly onto the page and some cutting and pasting. Markers have also been used on simple pencil drawings as a background to make them stand out on the page, helping to illustrate a specific part of the design.

The drawing shown in Figure 2.72 is a focused task presentation drawing that uses markers to enhance the illustration.

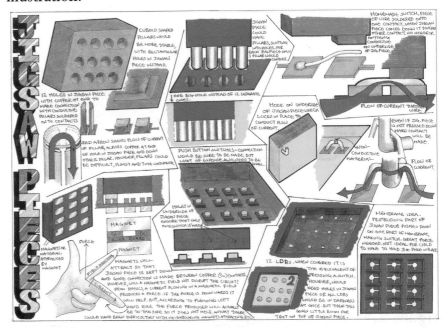

**Figure 2.69** *Markers used on concept sketches for a child's activity toy*

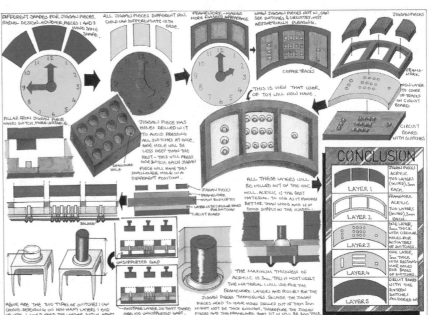

**Figure 2.70** *Markers used on development sketches for a child's activity toy*

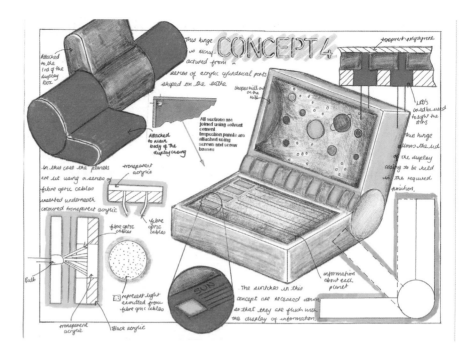

**Figure 2.71** *Markers used with cut and paste technique on concept sketches*

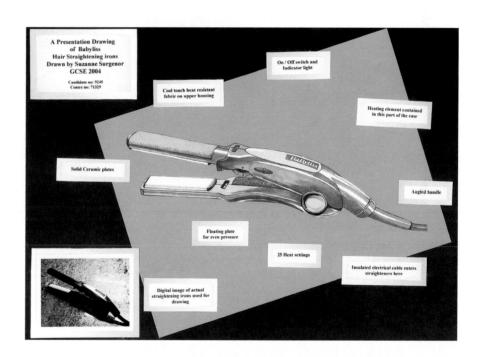

**Figure 2.72** *Markers used in a presentation drawing of a pair of hair straightening irons*

---

| Examples | **Students' presentation drawings using colouring pencils** |

The drawings shown in Figures 2.73 and 2.74 are rendered using quality colouring pencils with a black ink pen used to give definition to the outline and details. All drawings were first drawn in 2D and as the student became familiar with the product he/she was drawing they attempted the 3D drawing of all or part of the product. This is a good technique to use as it enables you to attempt the more difficult 3D drawing with some knowledge and experience of what you are drawing.

47

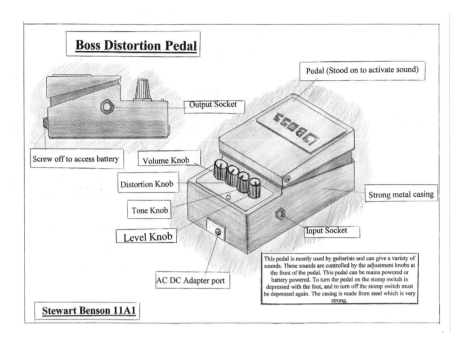

**Figure 2.73**

*Presentation drawing of a Boss distortion pedal*

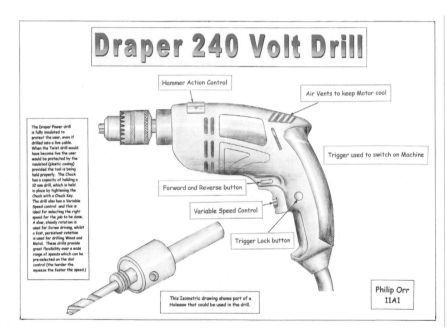

**Figure 2.74**

*Presentation drawing of a Draper 240 volt drill*

## Dimensioned working drawing

A dimensioned working drawing is an important part of any design. It enables you to add precise dimensions to the product you have just designed. This should speed up the manufacturing process as well as ensuring all the different parts fit at the assembly stage.

Every part of a working drawing must conform to a common standard called the **ISO standard**. This will ensure that anyone looking at your drawing will know precisely what it shows. The type of drawing you will be doing in this focused task is called **orthographic projection**.

This focused task is an opportunity for you to practise and develop these skills before starting your major design-and-make project activity.

## Orthographic projection

Orthographic projection is a standard method of drawing where you draw a number of flat views of your project looking from the front, top and side. The drawing is normally drawn to scale. The number of views and the order in which you show them is also important. For example, Figure 2.75(a) shows the top view of a wood joint. The top view alone has insufficient information for anyone to know precisely which joint it is. If on the other hand you add a second view looking in from the front, as shown in Figure 2.75(b), the joint starts to become clear.

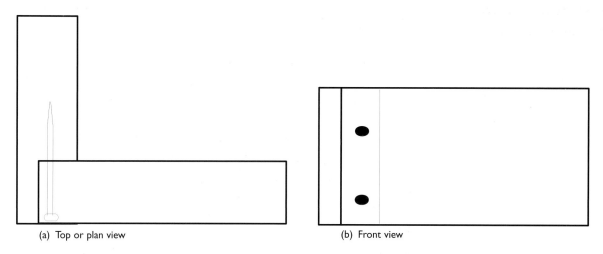

(a) Top or plan view

(b) Front view

**Figure 2.75** *Wood joint*

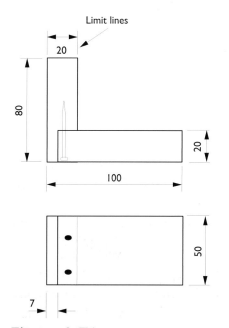

**Figure 2.76**

*Dimensioning a drawing*

## Adding dimensions

The wood joint shown in Figure 2.75 may be recognisable as a joint called an end lap but you would still be unable to make it from just these drawings. You would need to know the dimensions of each piece. Figure 2.76 shows the same wood joint with dimensions added. It would now be possible to mark out and make the joint.

Dimensions should conform to the following:

- Dimension lines should be drawn slightly lighter in weight than the drawing.
- Dimensions should be above or at right angles to the line but not resting on it.
- Dimension limit lines must indicate the full length of the dimension line and extend out from but not touch the drawing.

- Arrowheads must be closed. They must also touch the dimension limit lines.

### Third-angle orthographic projection

Third-angle orthographic projection has to a large extent replaced first-angle throughout Europe. Therefore presentation drawings should now conform to this standard.

If you consider the pictorial drawing of a joint shown in Figure 2.77 you will notice four of the faces have the letters A, B, C and P on them. This drawing will be used to explain third-angle projection.

Third-angle orthographic projection has the side view appearing next to the front view on the drawing.

You should start by looking at the joint from the front, view A, and take this as your first view. This is called the **front elevation**.

Now go above the joint and look down on the top, P. What you see is called the **plan** and this view must be drawn above the front elevation (Figure 2.78).

If you then look to the right-hand side, B, what you see must be drawn beside the front elevation on the right. This is called the **side elevation**. The left-hand side, C, would then be drawn to the left as shown.

The correct way to present a third-angle orthographic drawing is to draw the views using a 2H pencil or pen and ink. You must not use colour or shading on your drawing.

**Drawing lines:** These are the lines used for the actual drawing. They must be drawn heavier than dimension lines.

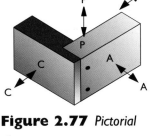

**Figure 2.77** *Pictorial view*

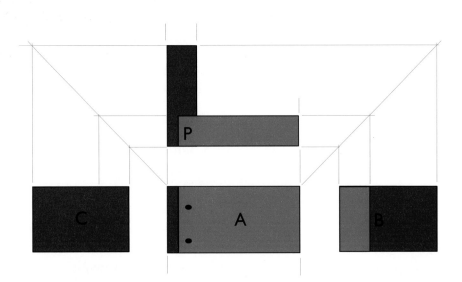

**Figure 2.78** *Third-angle orthographic projection*

**Projection and construction lines:** These are light lines used during the construction of the drawing. They should be removed from the final drawing.

**Hidden detail lines:** These are light dotted lines that show parts of the object that are hidden behind others.

**Third-angle symbol:** This is shown at the top of Figure 2.79.

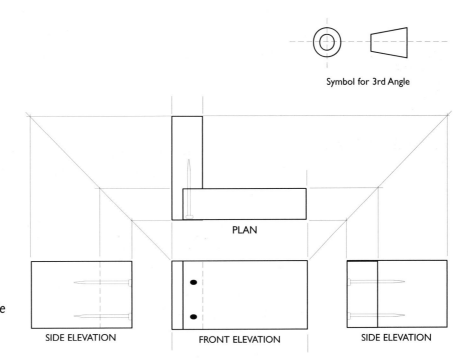

Symbol for 3rd Angle

PLAN

SIDE ELEVATION | FRONT ELEVATION | SIDE ELEVATION

**Figure 2.79** *Third-angle orthographic projection of an end lap joint*

| Example | **A third-angle orthographic projection working drawing** |

Figure 2.80 shows a working drawing of a toy frog. You can use either conventional pencil and paper or a CAD package to produce your drawing. If you are planning to practise drawing a product in third-angle orthographic projection it is a good idea to draw a technological project you are familiar with. The example shown was produced by a year 9 student.

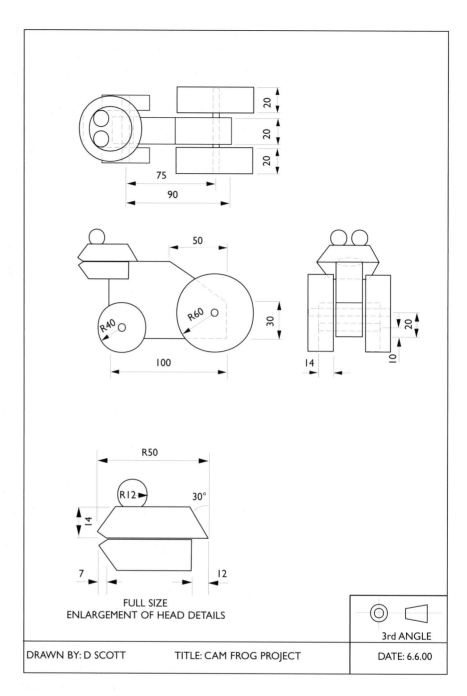

**Figure 2.80** *Working drawing of a cam-operated frog*

---

### Questions on 2D CAD using Micrografx Windows Draw

1  What do the letters CAD stand for?
2  Complete the following sentence: When choosing a product for a CAD focused task it must be a t_____ product.
3  A technological product is one that involves energy and c_____.
4  Name three technological products suitable for a CAD focused task.
5  Figure 2.2 lists a number of Micrografx Draw tools. Name three of these tools.
6  Micrografx Draw software was used to draw the phone in Figure 2.1. Name the type of phone used in the example.
7  Figure 2.3 refers to a vertical menu bar. What is a vertical menu bar?
8  Micrografx Draw has a Reshape tool. What is this used for?

9 The mobile phone shown in Figure 2.1 has a display panel. List the four processes used in drawing this display.

10 Using Micrografx Draw 3 software copy the Ericsson GA628 mobile phone shown in this chapter.

11 There are five skills and techniques associated with CAD presentation. Choose one of these and write a short paragraph to explain what it means. The five skills are:

● Convey the intended information accurately.

● Accurately use the graphic tools and facilities offered by the computer software in a suitably challenging context.

● Use carefully considered annotation.

● Generate the drawing from first principles.

● Show at least two drawing views to help clarify details, i.e. pictorial, front views, end views, sectional or exploded views, etc.

12 Decide on a technological product you wish to draw and, using Micrografx Draw, produce a 'Computer Aided Drawing Presentation'. Your presentation should be on a maximum of one side of A3 or two sides of A4 paper. A list of technological products that are suitable for the focused task is given in Table 1.1. These are only suggested products; you may choose one of your own if you wish.

## Questions on 2D/3D CAD/solid modelling using Pro/DESKTOP and Solidworks

1 The worked example of a digital alarm clock design refers to a number of Pro/DESKTOP drawing tools. Name three of these tools.

2 Using Pro/DESKTOP software, copy the drawing of the digital alarm clock shown in Figure 2.15.

3 Decide on a technological product you wish to draw and using Pro/DESKTOP produce a 'Computer Aided Drawing Presentation'. Your presentation should be on a maximum of one side of A3 or two sides of A4 paper. A list of technological products suitable for the focused task is given in Table 1.1. These are suggested products; you may choose one of your own if you wish. Repeat this task using Solidworks.

4 Figure 2.49 lists a number of Solidworks sketch tools. Name three of these tools.

5 Using Solidworks complete lessons 1, 2 and 3 from the online tutorial in the Solidworks 'Help' file.

6 Solidworks was used to draw the product shown in Figure 2.58. What is this product? Is it a suitable technological product for a CAD Presentation focused task? Explain your answer.

7 With reference to the section entitled 'Getting to know Solidworks', complete the following questions:

● Which would you draw first, a 2D or a 3D sketch?

● How is a 2D sketch turned into a solid 3D sketch?

● Name three Solidworks sketch tools.

- Complete the following sentence: To create a sketch you simply start a new part by clicking on_____.

8  In Solidworks there are two ways to extrude a sketch. What are these?

9  The CD rack drawn in Solidworks has three different component parts. Name all three.

10  What is the Solidworks term used when bringing two or more parts together to make a complete drawing?

11  Using Solidworks software, copy the drawing of the side plate shown in Figure 2.50.

12  Explain how you would add dimensions to your drawing of a side plate.

13  What is meant by 'show at least two drawing views to help clarify details'?

## Questions on working drawings

1  Figure 2.79 shows a third-angle projection of an end lap joint. Name the four views shown on this drawing.

2  In the context of third-angle projection, what is meant by the term 'hidden detail'?

3  What type of line would you use to show hidden detail on a third-angle projection drawing?

4  The following are three different types of projection lines used to produce the drawing shown in Figure 2.79:
- vertical
- horizontal
- 45 degree.

Using each type of line only once, complete the following sentence: When projecting lines across from the plan view _____ lines are used until they meet the _____, at this point they drop down _____ to be used in drawing the side elevation.

5  Should drawing lines be drawn darker or lighter than construction lines?

6  Third-angle orthographic projection is the recognised drawing standard for a working drawing. Using this standard, reproduce the drawing of the lap joint shown in Figure 2.79. Your drawing should satisfy the following criteria:
- Be drawn full size and show all four views.
- Have all four views correctly labelled: side elevations, front elevation and plan.
- Show all construction lines. These lines must be drawn lighter than the main drawing.
- Dimensions correctly added to the drawing as shown in Figure 2.76.
- Show hidden detail.
- In the bottom right-hand corner of your drawing, show the symbol for third-angle orthographic projection.

7  Using third-angle orthographic projection, reproduce the drawing of the cam-operated frog shown in Figure 2.80. The main drawing should be drawn half full size; that is, each line is drawn half its true length while all dimensions are listed as the actual sizes. So a part that has a

length of 100 mm would be drawn as 50 mm. The head should be drawn full size.

---

### Questions on freehand illustration presentation

1  Name three technological products suitable for the task 'Freehand Illustration Presentation'.

2  There are five skills and techniques associated with the focused task 'Freehand Illustration Presentation'. Choose one of the these and write a short paragraph to explain what it means. The five skills are:
   - Select a technological product and produce a freehand pictorial representation which accurately depicts the product.
   - Employ drawing techniques which are appropriate to your selected product, to have the desired impact on the intended audience.
   - On the drawing demonstrate rendering skills using appropriate media (e.g. line, pattern, texture, tone and colour in coloured pencils, watercolours or markers).
   - Demonstrate a good understanding of scale and proportion in your drawing.
   - Use carefully considered annotation on your drawing.

3  Figure 2.65 shows how to turn a 2D drawing of a moisture probe into a 3D drawing. On one A3 page or two A4 pages complete the following assignment:
   - Using an HB pencil, copy the 2D drawing.
   - Render your 2D drawing using coloured pencils or dry markers to create the sense of light coming from the top.
   - In pencil and using a 60/30-degree set square, draw the moisture probe in 3D (isometric projection).
   - Add colour to your drawing using coloured pencils or dry markers.
   - Add short notes (annotations) to your drawing to explain the different parts and what they do.

4  Decide on a technological product you wish to draw for the focused task 'Freehand Illustration Presentation' and using a technique described in the chapter, produce a presentation drawing. Your presentation should be on a maximum of one side of A3 or two sides of A4 paper. The following is a of list technological products that are suitable for this focused task. These are only suggested products, there is nothing stopping you from choosing one of your own.

   - mobile phone
   - camera
   - calculator
   - Game Boy
   - Nintendo controller
   - joystick for a computer
   - CD Walkman
   - electric toothbrush
   - electric screwdriver
   - electric smoothing iron
   - computer mouse
   - electric kettle
   - paper stapler
   - DIY tools.

# CHAPTER THREE    The design project

As a technology and design student you will be required to design and manufacture a product that involves energy and control. The choice of project will be made by you in consultation with your teacher and should reflect the content of the syllabus. You have to submit a product you have manufactured, accompanied by its portfolio.

It is this part of your GCSE that will attract the most marks. If you are studying for CCEA GCSE Technology and Design the project and its portfolio can be awarded up to 50% of the total marks for the course, so it is well worth your while putting time and effort into it. The common areas associated with designing, regardless of tier, are:

- designing
- communicating
- manufacture
- using energy and control.

# Elements of designing

While there is no single design process that will guide you through every design problem to the ultimate solution, there are a number of common elements that appear in most technology and design projects. The order in which you consider and address each of these elements will change from project to project.

What is common to all technology and design projects is the constant going back to earlier elements of your work to monitor and evaluate what you are doing. Some refer to this as the circular nature of design: the constant going round and round until you arrive at the best possible solution.

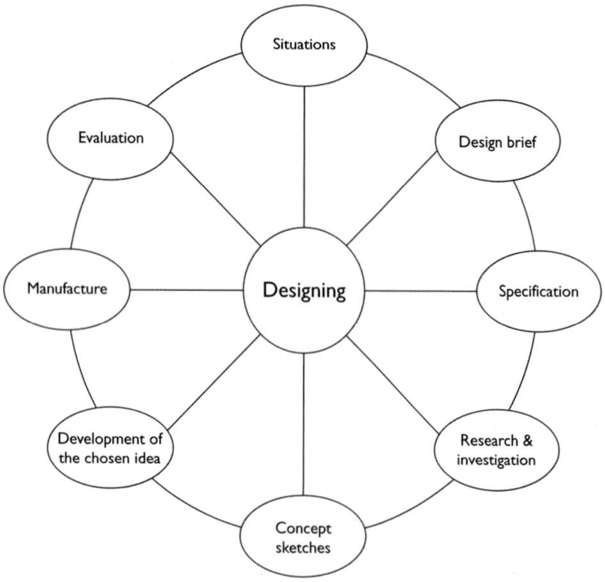

You can think of the design process as a giant wheel. At its centre is the activity of designing. Around the outer edges are all the activities associated with it. You are constantly going out to these activities in order to undertake specific tasks which you bring back into your central activity of designing. This is shown in Figure 3.1.

It is possible to break down the design portfolio into eight elements or topics. Each element should help guide you through the design and manufacture of a product. The elements are:

**Figure 3.1** Design elements

1. Identify a situation/s or problem/s.
2. Write a design brief.
3. Write a detailed specification for your product.
4. Research and investigate the problem.
5. Draw a series of concept sketches.
6. Choose one of your ideas and show its development.
7. Manufacture your product.
8. Evaluate your product and suggest modifications.

To help you with your design portfolio, the eight design elements or stages are explained in detail in the remainder of this chapter. This will happen in three ways:

- Each of the eight elements will be explained in detail.
- Extracts from three different case studies will be used to explain a specific element and put it in the context of a GCSE Technology and Design portfolio.
- The layout for a 15-page portfolio (as suggested by CCEA as a maximum size for a portfolio) is set out as one possible way of presenting your design work.

## 1: Identify a situation/s or problem/s

You should start your design portfolio by identifying a small number of different situation/s (usually one or two) that have the potential of leading you to the design and manufacture of a technological product. A technological product is one that involves energy and control, e.g. a CD rack that rotates as shown in Figure 3.40 would be a technological product, however a simple CD holder that didn't involve a system would not.

The ideal situation is one for which there is currently no satisfactory solution.

There are a number of ways of finding different situations or problems. You could consider:

- your hobby or sport
- problems around the house
- redesigning an existing product
- aids for the disabled
- educational aids or toys for young children
- safety within the home
- personal safety
- environmental control systems
- aids for your pet.

Select only one situation. Carry out some research into the chosen situation and comment on what you find out. Photographs showing the problem can really help explain the situation in detail. If possible interview people who are familiar with the problem and record their comments.

## 2: Design brief

Write a design brief for your chosen situation.

A brief should be a short paragraph describing what you intend to design and make. It is important to write an open-ended design brief that identifies a need or opportunity but keeps your design options open.

## 3: Specification

The specification is a list of short statements listing what the client or end user wants your final product to do or have. The specification is important; it will be central to all your early thinking. It is also one of the means by which your final project will be judged. At this stage of design it is not possible to be precise about what you want from the product; this will come later when you have arrived at a possible solution. Only then can you put precise boundaries on the performance you expect from your final product in the form of a final specification.

In industry the initial specification usually comes from the client and may be a few lines to one page long. The final specification comes from the manufacturing team after some research and development and will be drawn up in consultation with the client and end user. Final industrial specifications could be up to fifty pages long and cover every component and all the materials used in the product. You are not required to produce an industrial specification but it's good practice to write a specification that identifies:

- what the person/s using your design would want the product to do
- the technical limits you want to put on the final product.

## 4: Research and investigation

This section of your portfolio should be based on the specification. It will provide you with the opportunity to find out more details about the problem. This should help you at the next stage of the process, producing possible solutions in the form of concept sketches.

One way of starting your research and investigation is to take some points from your specification and find out and record as much information as possible about each point.

## 5: Concept sketches

These are at the very core of designing. They should show what you are thinking as you struggle for the best solution. They should be quick freehand sketches that occasionally have colour added to highlight a good idea.

Figures 3.2 to 3.6 show concept sketches from students' portfolios.

### Concept sketches of a study lamp

Figure 3.2 shows concept sketches for a study lamp. The sketches are based around a simple mechanical pivot on which a balancing lever would sit. The lamp would be on one end of the lever with a counter-balancing weight on the other. The sketches show simple pencil drawings with some colour added to enhance the concept.

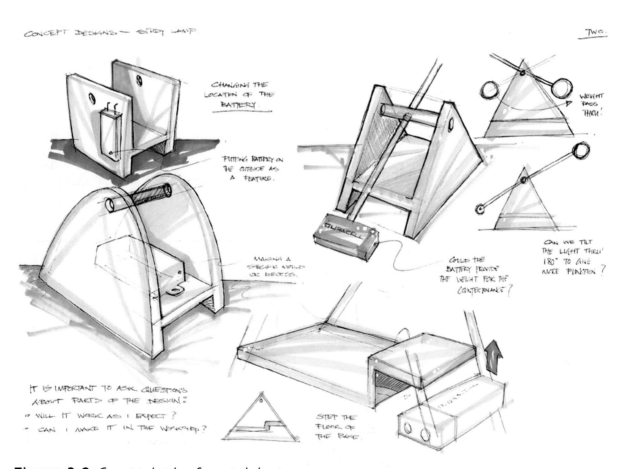

**Figure 3.2** *Concept sketches for a study lamp*

### Concept sketches of an educational toy

The brief was to design and manufacture an educational toy that would teach a child how to identify the planets. Figure 3.3 shows concept sketches from the student's design portfolio. The student has enhanced the presentation of the concept sketches by using a mix of dry marker work direct onto the page and a cut-and-paste technique.

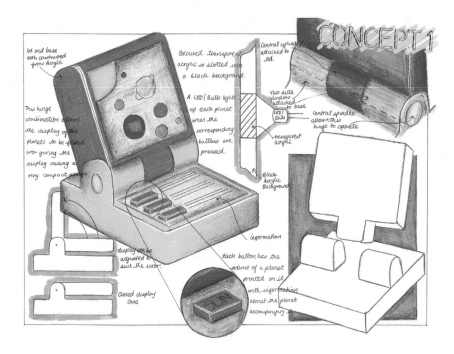

**Figure 3.3** *Educational toy concept sketch*

### Concept sketches of a child's toy

The design brief was for a child's pull-along toy. Figure 3.4 shows the use of CAD in the production of concept sketches. If you are familiar with a CAD solid modelling package there is nothing to stop you from using it to produce your concept sketches. The example shown was produced using Pro/DESKTOP.

**Figure 3.4** *CAD concept drawing of a toy steam engine (Pro/DESKTOP)*

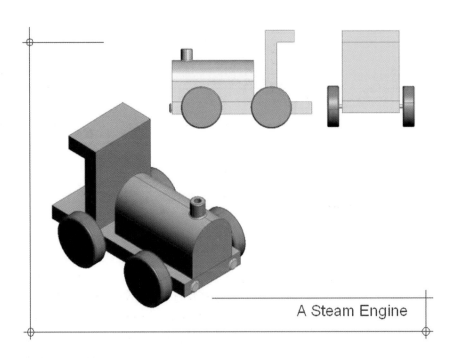

A Steam Engine

### Ideas for concept sketches

If you are having difficulty finding different ideas for your concept sketches you could apply the technique of using different technologies to find different solutions. For example, a student is working on the problem of an aid for her arthritic grandparents. The aid is to assist them with the opening of jars. The student considers pneumatic, electronic and microprocessor solutions as alternatives. The pneumatic solution is shown in Figure 3.5. You may think this is an impractical solution but is not as impractical as it may at first seem. It is possible to buy a quiet pneumatic compressor smaller than a bag of sugar. This could then be used in the final design.

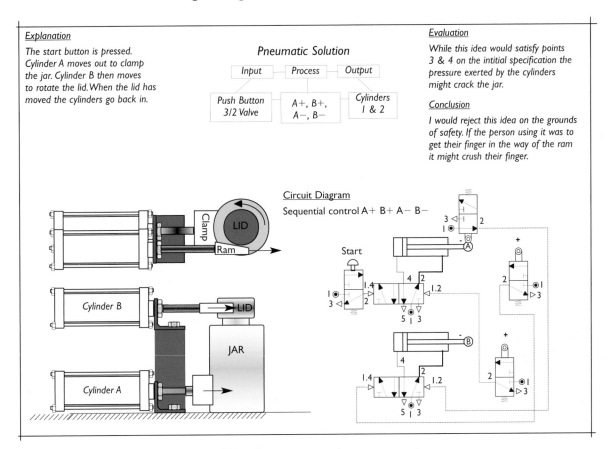

**Figure 3.5** *Concept drawing using CAD of a pneumatic device to open jars*

### Author's comments

*The way one concept sketch leads to the next and the way details flow out of the idea is what you should be striving to achieve and show in this section of your portfolio.*

*The work shown in Figure 3.2 was a page of concept sketches from a student's portfolio and shows the student's thinking and development of an idea. It is an excellent standard. It is evident that the student had a good understanding of mechanisms and was able to draw upon this knowledge for inspiration at the concept stage. Figure 3.3 shows concept sketches that are also of an excellent standard. However they are of a standard greater than one would expect to see at GCSE.*

*In Figures 3.4 and 3.5 the student has used CAD to show a concept. If you are really experienced in the use of a specific piece of software this is a good technique to use; if not, CAD may be best left to the modelling and/or presentation stage of your portfolio.*

### 6: Choose one of your concepts and develop possible solutions

From your range of concept sketches you will have to select one idea and based on this you will start to refine your idea. This refinement will be in the form of sketches of possible solutions and will take account of your specification. At this stage you start to explain how the idea will work.

## Development of the chosen idea

You should now be in a position to develop your chosen idea through to a final project.

The development is likely to include a section on each of the following:

- development of the system
- development of the product housing or unit
- a presentation drawing of the final product
- a working drawing or sketch of the final product with dimensions
- a cutting list/bill of materials for the casing and/or system
- a plan for manufacture listing the main or critical stages in the manufacture.

### Development of the system

You will have to incorporate energy and control into your product. If your chosen idea incorporates electronics or a microprocessor (PIC) it is good practice to develop this system first before starting the casing design. In this way you will be sure that the circuit works and you can keep the details of the system in mind as you develop the product.

It is a good practice to start with a simple system and keep developing it until you have a working system that satisfies the specification. At this stage CAD software can help model the system before you make it. Software such as PCB Wizard, Livewire, Bright Spark, Control Studio, Crocodile Clips, or Logicator really comes into its own when developing your system as you can model the circuit, PCB (printed circuit board), program or mechanism on the computer before committing time and effort to making it.

## Development of the product

If your product is a mechanical system then the system itself will be the product, e.g. a clamp to hold a bicycle lamp. However, if the system incorporates electronics then you will need a casing in which to house the electronic circuit. In either case you will show the final design in detail. This should include information about:

- constructional details
- dimensions
- servicing details
- choice of materials
- type of finish.

## Working drawing

The working drawing or sketch should contain enough information to enable you or others to manufacture your design. The drawing can be either a dimensioned sketch or an orthographic drawing.

If you choose to do your working drawing in orthographic projection then this should be in third-angle projection. Third-angle projection is explained in detail in Chapter 2. It may be worth reading this section before attempting this part of your portfolio.

## Cutting list/bill of materials

This is a list of all the materials you will need to manufacture your product. You should set out your cutting list in a precise way so that others will understand it. An example of a template for a cutting list is shown in Table 3.1.

**Table 3.1** *Template for a cutting list*

| Name: | | | | Class: | Date: |
|---|---|---|---|---|---|
| Date required for (one week's notice required) | | | | Teacher's Int: | |
| Cutting list | | | | | |
| Name of part | Number required | Length | Width | Thickness | Material |
| | | | | | |

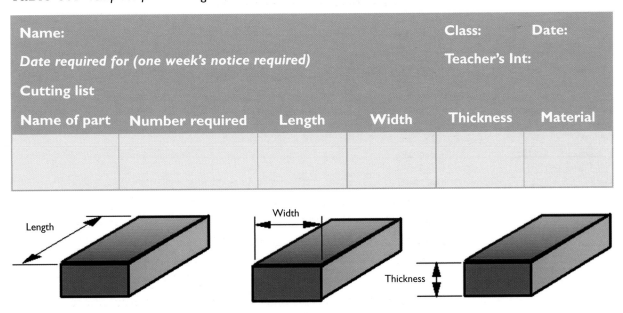

**Figure 3.6** *Understanding the difference between length, width and thickness*

Figure 3.6 will remind you of the meaning of some of the terms used in the cutting list.

A bill of materials is similar to a cutting list in that it is a list of all the bits and pieces you will need for the circuit, etc. In a bill of materials you must specify the value and/or type of component you wish to purchase.

**Table 3.2** *Template for a bill of materials*

| Name: | | | Class: | Date: |
|---|---|---|---|---|
| *Date required for (one week's notice required)* | | | Teacher's Int: | |
| Bill of materials | | | | |
| Name of part and value | Number required | Code number | Supplier | Cost |
| | | | | |

## Manufacturing plan

This is a plan showing the sequence in which you plan to manufacture your product.

Set this out as a list that identifies the main stages in the manufacture of your product and the sequence in which you will undertake these. An example of a student's manufacturing/production plan for a basketball counter project is shown in Figure 3.7.

**Production Plan**

**Project:** BASKETBALL COUNTER.

| | | | Week Number | | | | | | | | | | | |
|---|---|---|---|---|---|---|---|---|---|---|---|---|---|---|
| **No** | **Process** | **Material/Tools** | **1** | **2** | **3** | **4** | **5** | **6** | **7** | **8** | **9** | **10** | **11** | **12** |
| 1 | Design Circuit | PCB WIZARD (COMPUTER) | ✓ | | | | | | | | | | | |
| 2 | Produce PCB | etching tank + drill | | ✓ | | | | | | | | | | |
| 3 | Solder components | Soldering Station | | | ✓ | | | | | | | | | |
| 4 | Make MDF mould for casing | MDF, SAW, SANDER PVA GLUE | | | | ✓ | | | | | | | | |
| 5 | Vacuum Form mould | VACUUM FORMER, ACRYLIC | | | | ✓ | | | | | | | | |
| 6 | Make back for casing | SAW, SANDER (coping), ACRYLIC | | | | | ✓ | | | | | | | |
| 7 | Cut + shaped steel for trigger | HACKSAW, VICE GRINDER, MILDSTEEL | | | | | ✓ | | | | | | | |
| 8 | Weld steel | ARC WELDER | | | | | | ✓ | | | | | | |
| 9 | Fitted components into case | DRILL, COPING SAW, HOT GLUE GUN | | | | | | | ✓ | | | | | |
| 10 | Added switch + springs to trigger | BOLTS + NUTS, SPRINGS, DRILL | | | | | | | ✓ | | | | | |
| 11 | Painted trigger | PAINT BRUSH + PAINT | | | | | | | | ✓ | | | | |
| 12 | TESTING PRODUCT | | | | | | | | | | ✓ | | | |
| 13 | | | | | | | | | | | | | | |

**Figure 3.7** *Example of a manufacturing/production plan*

# Evaluation of the product

Evaluation of the product will be an ongoing process throughout the design and manufacture, and comments should be made as this work progresses. You will also need to evaluate the final outcome after you have made and tested it. This entails returning to your detailed specification and design brief and commenting on how well you feel your final product satisfies these.

You should start your evaluation by testing your product against as many points in the detailed specification as you can. You can do this in written form or in table form where you set down the points in one column and your findings in another. Try to be critical in your remarks on how well your product satisfied each point. Product evaluation is explained in detail in Chapter 1. You may wish to refer to this before starting on this section.

### Modifications

Every product, no matter how well it is made, can be improved upon. In this section of your portfolio you have the opportunity to say what you would change to improve your design. Where appropriate you should include sketches of any modification you would make.

# Design portfolio

The portfolio will contain your design work. It should contain evidence of your ability to investigate, generate, evaluate, communicate and use energy and control.

The portfolio should contain quality work not quantity. It should be summative in nature, that is, as you think something through you should record your thinking in the form of sketches and notes. You should include important research and investigation material. You should show evidence of constant evaluation and modification of your evolving designs. If you are studying for a GCSE in Technology and Design then you must use energy and control in your design.

One possible layout for a GCSE in Technology and Design portfolio is shown in Figure 3.8. This layout uses 15 A3 pages, which should be more than sufficient to show all relevant information. An example of a portfolio based on the 15 layouts is shown in Figures 3.9 to 3.16.

| GCSE Technology and Design portfolio cover page | 1. Problem identification<br>Design brief<br>Specification | 2. Research and investigation<br><br>3. Research and investigation |

**Cover page content**

- Project title
- Your name
- Exam no
- Level of GCSE
- Images

**Guidance for page 1**

- Identify a problem
- Write a brief
- Specification

**Guidance for pages 2–3**

- Research the problem and make it relevant to your study
- Make judgements about the research and explain how the research has been of use to you
- Explain how you plan to use this information

| 4. Concept sketches<br><br>5. Concept sketches | 6. Proposed idea/s<br><br>7. Proposed idea/s<br><br>8. Proposed idea/s | 9. Proposed idea developed<br><br>10. Proposed idea developed |

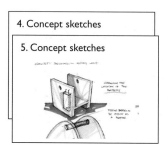
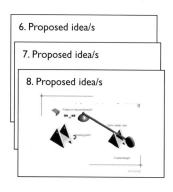
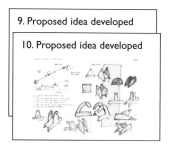

**Guidance for pages 4–5**

- Generate a range of concept sketches
- Show different ideas and be creative
- You should show different ideas not just variations of the same idea
- Select one of these for further development as your proposed idea

**Guidance for pages 6–8**

- Draw proposed ideas
- These should come from one of your concept sketches and be a development of it

**Guidance for pages 9–10**

- Develop your best idea
- Show as much detail as possible

| 11. Energy and control system | | 14. Working drawing | | 15. Evaluation, modifications and improvements |
| 12. Energy and control system | | | | |
| 13. Energy and control system | | Plan | | |

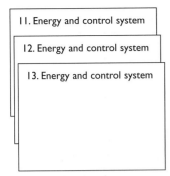

14. Working drawing

Plan

Elevation          Elevation side

15. Evaluation, modifications and improvements

## Guidance for pages 11–13
- Develop your system
- Explain how it works
- If an electronic system, show PCB layout, etc
- Sometimes the design of the system may come earlier in your portfolio

## Guidance for page 14
- Produce a detailed working drawing or sketch showing the main dimensions necessary to manufacture your idea

## Guidance for page 15
- Show evidence of evaluating your product against the specification
- Suggest possible modifications to your product if you were to make it again

**Figure 3.8** *Possible layout for a 15-page portfolio*

**Example**          **Design portfolio based on the 15-page layout**

**Figure 3.9** *Identification of the problem and the specification*

## Research and investigation
- The research and investigation was clearly related to the study.
- The research was relevant and referred to later in the portfolio.

## Problem identification and brief
- The problem was clearly identified.
- The design brief was short and precise.

## Specification
- The student has produced an initial specification based on the needs of the user. Some students like to make a comprehensive specification at this point. Others like to list only what the end user will want, waiting until the design is finalised before adding in the technical points.
- The latter possibly leads to a more realistic specification.

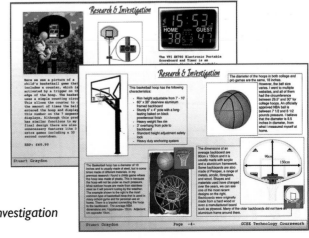

**Figure 3.10** *Research and investigation*

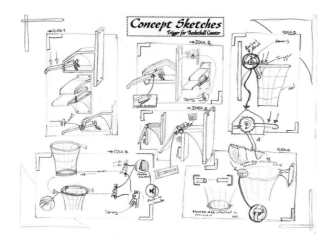

**Figure 3.11** *Concept sketches*

### Range of concept sketches

- The concept sketches clearly show the student's thinking.
- The sketches are freehand, free flowing and show different ideas that may or may not be developed later.
- The work is clearly creative and spontaneous.

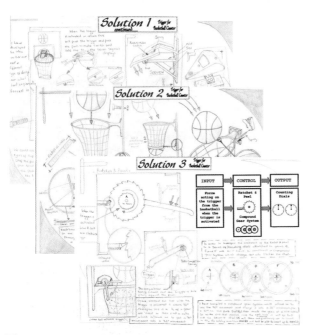

**Figure 3.12** *Possible/proposed ideas*

### Possible/proposed ideas

- The range of possible solutions is clearly based on one of the concept sketches.
- The student has clearly started to develop an electronic solution. However in solution 3 consideration was given to the possibility of a mechanical system.
- The work is free flowing.
- Detail is being added as the work progresses.
- From studying the work it is possible to get a feel for how the student has worked through the problem, leading to the development and refining of an idea.

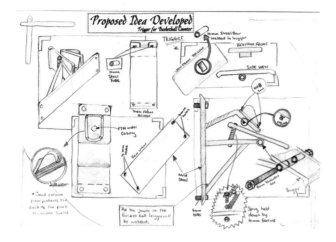

**Figure 3.13** *Development of the proposed ideas*

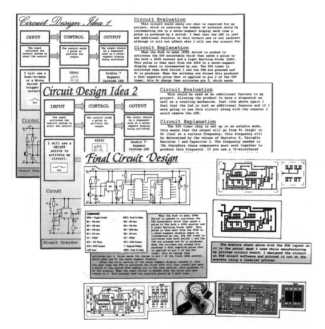

**Figure 3.14** *Development of the control system*

## Development of the proposed idea

- Having decided on an electronic solution that will count as the ball passes through the net, the student is now in a position to fine-tune the idea.
- This fine-tuning is where you show the precise detail of your design.
- The only thing missing so far is the development of the electronic system.
- Some students like to design the system first and have this ready to be included in the final design.
- Other students like to leave the system until they have the design finalised before making the system fit the design. There is no right or wrong way to do this, it will just depend on how your idea develops.

## Development of the control system

- The standard of work shown in circuit design is excellent.
- However the student has started to design a very complex system and while there is nothing to stop you doing this it may be better to start with a simple solution and develop your system from this, e.g. a simple 555 timer circuit used to pulse an LCD counter display may have been a possible solution.
- The student's notes are clear. The notes explain, evaluate and suggest modifications to the circuit design.
- Dividing the system into manageable blocks of input, control and output is good practice and has been used to good advantage to explain the circuit design.
- The final page shows all the necessary detail to enable the circuit to be manufactured.

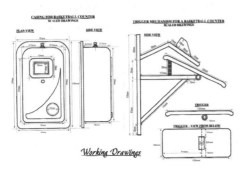

*Working Drawings*

**Figure 3.15** *Working drawing*

### Working drawing/s

● This shows almost enough detail for the student to make the product. However colour should not be used on a working drawing.

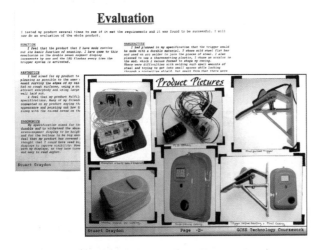

**Figure 3.16** *Evaluation of the final product*

### Evaluation/modifications

● This is a good realistic evaluation based on the specification.
● It is good practice to suggest possible improvements or modifications that you could make to your product if you were to make it again as a conclusion to your evaluation.
● Good use of digital image to show the final product.

# Starting points for Technology and Design GCSE coursework

There are a number of different ways you can get started on your Technology and Design GCSE coursework. The two most common approaches are:

● Individual situations: On your own identify a situation or problem for which you wish to design and make a technological product. Possible situations are discussed throughout this chapter.
● Based on a theme: Working on a common theme set by the teacher, a group of students derive a situation or problem for which they wish to design and make a technological product.

Not all GCSE coursework has to start with you working on your own situation/problem. It is possible for you to get together with other students to work on a common theme. The teacher will usually set a theme but it is also possible for a group of students to decide on one.

A theme is a common design problem, which the entire group come together in the beginning to research and investigate. This is followed up by you working on your own to produce a solution.

Advantages of coursework themes are:

- You can get started right away on a common problem.
- Much of the early research will be provided for you by the teacher, or by the group.
- The group can discuss the problem collectively.
- You are not on your own.
- You can overcome the problem of what to design and make.
- Common resources can be purchased for the group.
- The organisation and management of your project is more manageable.

The main disadvantages of coursework themes are:

- You may not like the theme given.
- You may have a problem you want to solve.
- You may prefer to work on your own.
- It may be difficult to mark your contribution to the project.
- Not all members of the group will share.

Most of these problems can be overcome if the theme is well thought out and leaves enough room for you to produce your own work to the highest standard. Some commonly used themes are:

- night-lights
- robotic toys
- rotating displays
- board games
- security
- toys for young children.

The following are examples of the first four themes.

## Theme: Night-lights

The class were given a common situation/problem. This was to design a night-light for a room of your choice in your home. The teacher provided reference materials in the form of photos and extracts from design magazines. Some of these resources illustrate existing lighting: free-standing desk lights for a study, cantilevered lighting and free-standing lights based on a nature theme. Figures 3.17 to 3.20 show the reference materials on the left and a student's solution on the right.

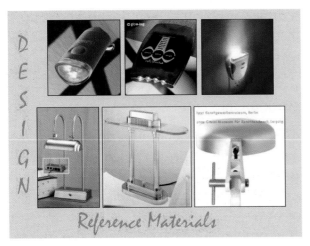

**Figure 3.17** *Reference material for the desk lighting*

**Figure 3.18** *Student's design for the desk lighting*

**Figure 3.19** *Reference material for a cantilever light*

**Figure 3.20** *Student's design for a cantilever light*

### Theme: Robotic toys

The theme was microprocessor-controlled robotic toys. The class were given a common situation/problem. This was to design a robotic toy that would be either controlled by the computer through an interface or freestanding using a PIC.

In preparation for the theme the students worked through a series of exercises using Logicator software involving the control of small motors. A number of the students' outcomes are shown in Figures 3.21 to 3.24.

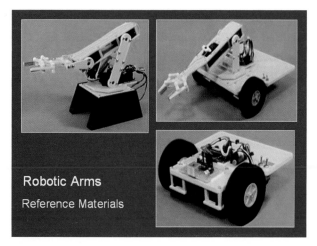

**Figure 3.21** *Reference material for robotic arms*

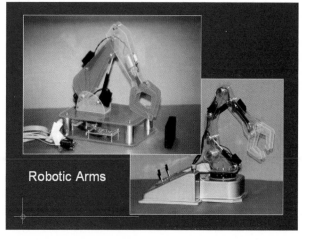

**Figure 3.22** *Students' designs for robotic arms*

**Figure 3.23** *Reference material for robotic vehicle*

**Figure 3.24** *Student's design for a robotic vehicle*

## Theme: Rotating displays

The class were given a common situation/problem. This was to use the gearbox motor provided to design and make a display. In preparation for the theme the teacher had each student assemble a small gearbox motor that turned at 10 revolutions/minute. The gearbox motor had a 4 mm diameter centre shaft onto which the display could be fixed. The student had to design a unit to hold the gearbox motor as well as designing the display to go on the top. Figure 3.25 shows the reference material given to the students. It sets out the type of gearbox motor and asks the student to design a suitable base unit for the gearbox motor. Figures 3.26 to 3.28 show examples of students' work based on this theme.

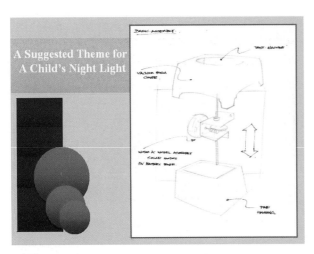

**Figure 3.25** *Reference material for rotating display*

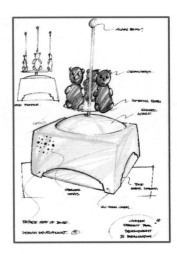

**Figure 3.26** *Student's design for a rotating display*

**Figure 3.27** *Student's rotating CD display*

**Figure 3.28** *Student's rotating trophy display*

## Theme: Board games

The theme was to design a product that incorporated a board game. The students were asked to work in groups of no more than six, to work on the common situation/problem. Two outcomes are shown in Figures 3.29 to 3.32. The counter game incorporates a storage

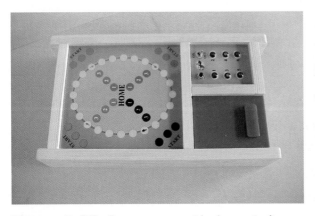

**Figure 3.29** *Counter game with electronic dice*

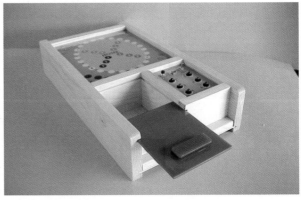

**Figure 3.30** *Storage for the counters*

compartment for the counters and an electronic dice to determine the number of moves each player has to make. The chess game incorporates a move timer as well as storage for the chess pieces.

**Figure 3.31** *Chess board with built-in storage*

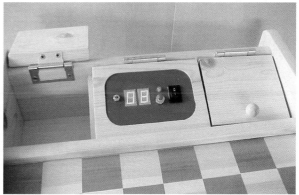

**Figure 3.32** *Electronic chess move timer*

# Case studies

To help you better understand what is expected in your GCSE Technology and Design portfolio three case studies are set out for your consideration. Each case study deals with a number of the eight design elements shown in Figure 3.1. The three case studies are:

**Case study 1:** This shows a section from the portfolio of a student who looked at a number of situations before selecting one. The selected situation was 'Aid to comfort a crying baby'. This case study will cover the topics:

- design situation/s
- select one situation for further investigation
- research and investigate the chosen situation
- write an open-ended design brief.

**Case study 2:** This shows a section from a portfolio on an 'Aid for the disabled'. It covers the topics:

- open-ended design brief
- specification
- research and investigation
- concept sketches
- find ideas for concept sketches
- select your best idea from your concept sketches.

**Case study 3:** This shows a section from a portfolio for a 'CD storage system'. It covers the topics:

- development of the system
- development of the product housing or unit
- a working drawing

- a cutting list
- a bill of materials
- evaluation of the product
- modification of the product.

| Case study 1 | Aid to comfort a crying baby |

### Design situation/s

The following extracts are from a student's portfolio. It sets out four design situations that are then explained in brief. One is then selected and an investigation/research is carried out. Finally an open-ended brief is written.

Four design situations were identified. These were:

1. Watering plants in the greenhouse
2. Aids for elderly relatives
3. Getting wet while opening and closing the garage door
4. Aid to comfort a crying baby

One design situation was selected. This was number 4 'Aid to comfort a crying baby'.

### Chosen situation

My nine-month-old nephew wakes up very early in the mornings. His mother is frequently in the kitchen making breakfast and fails to hear him crying. The crying wakes his older brother, aged 2, who is sleeping in the next room.

### Research and investigate the chosen situation

As part of my investigation I have chosen to interview my aunt and uncle who are the mother and father of the baby and record the findings. I also plan to take photographs of the situation and make further observations of the problem.

**Figure 3.33** *Picture of the baby's cot*

**Student's interview with the baby's mother**

The following are the notes the student made during the interview with the baby's mother.

Student   At what time in the morning does the child wake up?
Mother    Around 6 am.

Student   How does this bother you?
Mother    It does not bother me as much as his brother in the next room. It wakens him out of his sleep.

Student   What does the child do when he wakens?
Mother    Cries until he is lifted.

Student   Is there anything you can do to comfort him?
Mother    Yes. He responds well to nursing and he also responded well in the past to the music of a moving toy.

**Student's conclusion from the interview**

It appears that there is a real problem that I might be able to help with. It also appears that the child can be comforted by nursing, music or movement. I think that I have enough information about this situation to proceed.

### Design brief for a baby-calming device

Design and manufacture a device that could be located close to or be attached to the baby's cot. This device should have a calming effect on the child and if possible be educational.

| Case study 2 | Aid for the disabled |
|---|---|

### Design brief

The brief is a short written statement of what you plan to design and make. It should be open-ended, i.e. it leaves the design options open to a number of possible solutions. An example of an open-ended design brief is this one, which was for an aid for the disabled:

Design and manufacture a device to assist my elderly arthritic grandparents remove a lid from commonly used screw-topped jars.

### Specification for an aid to open jars

**Part 1. What the grandparents wanted the final design to be able to do**

- Remove the lid from a range of jars
- Usable by both grandparents
- Cost no more than £15.00

- Freestanding on the kitchen worktop
- Must be a device that is able help the grandparents overcome their disability
- Easily cleaned in case of spillage
- Hold one jar at a time.

## Part 2. What limits do you want to put on your final product?

- Operated by a large push switch
- Have an automatic clamping and releasing system
- A mix of mechanisms and electronics
- Easily serviced
- No larger than 300 mm square
- Hold a range of jars that vary in size from 60 mm to 80 mm in diameter.

### Jar-opening unit concept 1

The first idea, shown in Figure 3.34, is based on an inclined plane or wedge to release the lid from the jar.

### How it works

As the crank handle is turned the wedge moves along the bar that is threaded along its length. The inside of the wedge has two bolts glued in place, one at each end. The rollers at the back of the lid prevent it from moving away from the wedge. The rollers have bearings for ease of rotation. The bearings have a bolt passing through the centre for fixing to the base plate. The only problem with this concept is the fact that to remove the lid the wedge would have to be brought back and this would retighten the lid.

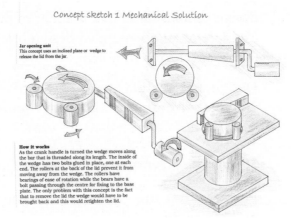

**Figure 3.34** *Concept sketch using mechanical wedge to release the jar lid*

### Jar-opening unit concept 2

The second idea uses a mechanical clamp to hold the jar. This is shown in Figure 3.35.

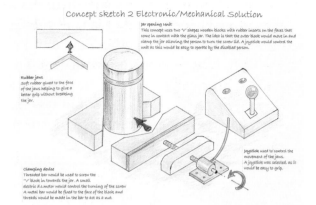

*Concept sketch 2 Electronic/Mechanical Solution*

**Jar opening unit**
This concept uses two 'V' shapes wooden blocks with rubber inserts on the faces that come in contact with the glass jar. The idea is that the outer block would move in and clamp the jar allowing the person to turn the screw lid. A joystick would control the unit as this would be easy to operate by the disabled person.

**Rubber jaws**
Soft rubber glued to the face of the jaws helping to give a better grip without breaking the jar.

**Clamping device**
Threaded bar would be used to screw the "V' block in towards the jar. A small electric d.c.motor would control the turning of the screw A metal bar would be fixed to the face of the block and threads would be made in the bar to act as a nut.

**Joystick** used to control the movement of the jaws. A joystick was selected as it would be easy to grip.

**Figure 3.35**
*Electromechanical clamp used to hold the jar*

## How it works

The jar is placed in the unit. A motor comes on and moves the vee block in to grip the jar. With the jar held firmly both hands can be used to turn the lid.

| Case study 3 | Storage system for CDs |
| --- | --- |

These examples were taken from a GCSE student's portfolio. He wanted to design and make a compact storage system for CDs. The full specification is listed below. However, we will be looking in detail at Part 2 of the specification.

### Part 1. What the user (in this case the student) wanted the final design to be able to do

- Hold a minimum of 40 CDs
- Be compact so that it would sit on a desk
- Good visibility of the CD title labels
- Cost no more than £35
- Protect the CDs from dust and dirt.

### Part 2. What limits the student put on the final design

- Should be battery operated
- Should move slowly and quietly
- Must turn through 90° and stop
- Compact rotating design
- Easy removal of the CDs from the unit
- Made from plastic as this is easily cleaned
- Have an electric motor to rotate the unit
- No larger than 350 mm cube
- Electronic logic circuit to turn the unit
- Gearbox with a speed of no greater than 25 revs/min.

Extracts from the student's GCSE Technology and Design portfolio for the rotating CD storage unit are shown in Figures 3.36 to 3.40.

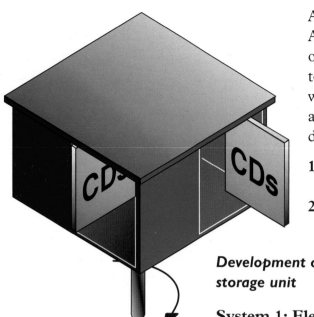

As specified, the unit had to hold 40 CDs. As some of the CDs would be behind others the unit had to rotate through 90° to give access. The design work progressed with the concept sketches drawn first. After a selection was made the system was designed in two parts:

1. Electronic system to turn on a DC motor for a set time
2. Mechanical system to turn the unit at the correct speed.

### Development of a system to control a rotating CD storage unit

### System 1: Electronics

The electronic system started out as a simple circuit incorporating a motor, battery and push-to-make switch and concluded with a RS flip-flop outputting to a relay and a secondary circuit.

**Figure 3.36** *Rotating CD storage unit*

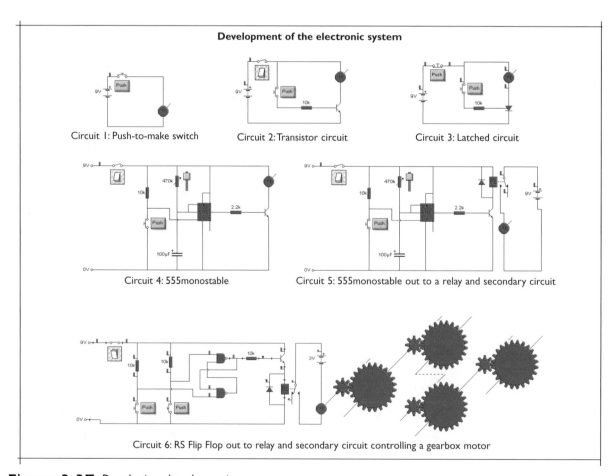

Figure 3.37 Developing the electronic system

## System 2: Mechanics

A relay was used to turn the final drive system, which incorporated a gearbox motor, pulleys and belt. This system was developed around a simple gearbox motor unit which had a series of plastic gears that could be assembled to give different gear ratios.

The student was given the speed of the motor in revs/min and a number of different gear wheels. From this, the student was able to calculate a suitable output speed for the final drive shaft of 22.4 revs/min.

This was finally reduced by a ratio of 4:1 by using a belt and pulley system. The final output speed of the rotating storage unit was approximately 6 revs/min when the pulley system was added.

Some of the student's development work for the gearbox is shown in Figure 3.38.

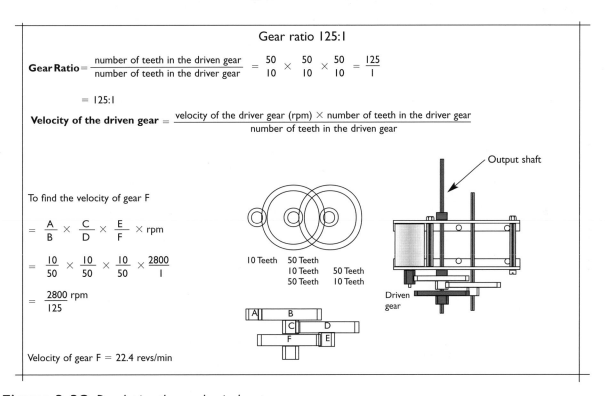

**Figure 3.38** *Developing the mechanical system*

### Developing the product housing for the system

Having developed the electronics/PIC system the student then had to incorporate this into the product. This is something you must keep in mind as your design develops.

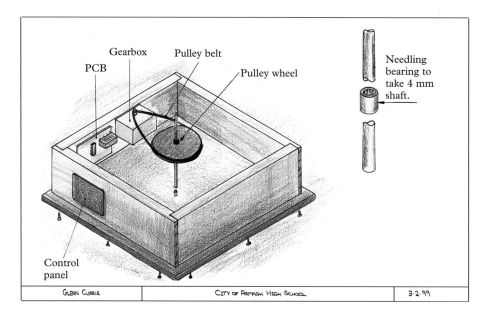

Gearbox — Pulley belt
PCB
Pulley wheel

Needling bearing to take 4 mm shaft.

Control panel

GLENN CURRIE          CITY OF ARMAGH HIGH SCHOOL          3·2·99

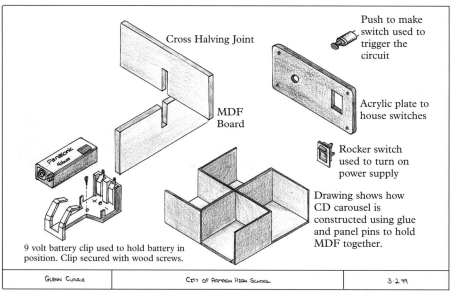

Cross Halving Joint

MDF Board

Push to make switch used to trigger the circuit

Acrylic plate to house switches

Rocker switch used to turn on power supply

Drawing shows how CD carousel is constructed using glue and panel pins to hold MDF together.

9 volt battery clip used to hold battery in position. Clip secured with wood screws.

GLENN CURRIE          CITY OF ARMAGH HIGH SCHOOL          3·2·99

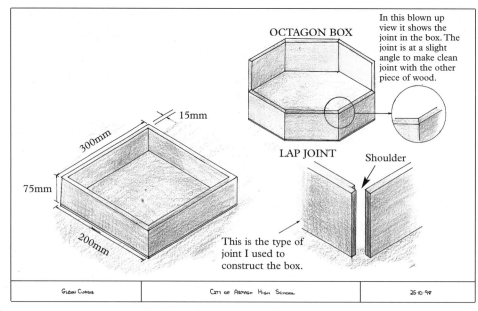

OCTAGON BOX

In this blown up view it shows the joint in the box. The joint is at a slight angle to make clean joint with the other piece of wood.

15mm

300mm

LAP JOINT

Shoulder

75mm

200mm

This is the type of joint I used to construct the box.

GLENN CURRIE          CITY OF ARMAGH HIGH SCHOOL          25·10·98

**82**     **Figure 3.39** *Developing the product housing*

Figure 3.40 shows the working drawing in third-angle projection for the rotating CD storage unit.

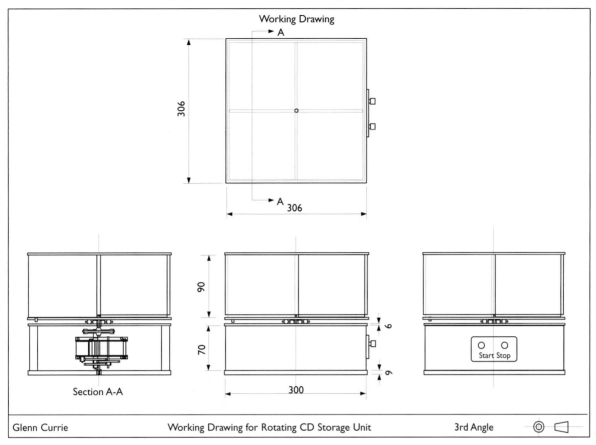

**Figure 3.40** *Working drawing for the rotating CD storage unit*

## Cutting list

**Table 3.3** *Cutting list for the rotating CD storage unit*

| Name: Glenn Currie | | Class: 12A | | Date: 4th Sept | |
|---|---|---|---|---|---|
| *Date required for (one week's notice required)* | | | | Teacher's Int: | |
| **Cutting list** | | | | | |
| Name of part | Number required | Length | Width | Thickness | Material |
| **Base unit** | | | | | |
| L.side | 2 | 300 | 70 | 20 | Pine |
| R.side | 2 | 288 | 70 | 20 | Pine |
| Motor plate | 1 | 260 | 70 | 14 | Pine |
| Base | 1 | 306 | 306 | 9 | MDF |
| Top | 1 | 306 | 306 | 5 | Acrylic |
| **Storage unit** | | | | | |
| Sides | 4 | 153 | 90 | 6 | MDF |
| Top | 1 | 306 | 306 | 6 | MDF |
| Bottom | 1 | 306 | 306 | 6 | MDF |
| Middle | 2 | 288 | 90 | 6 | MDF |

### Bill of materials for the system

A bill of materials is similar to a cutting list in that it is a list of all the bits and pieces you will need for the circuit, etc. In a bill of materials you must specify the value and/or type of component you wish to purchase.

**Table 3.4** *Bill of materials for the system*

| Name: Glenn Currie | | | Class: 12A | Date: 17th Sept |
|---|---|---|---|---|
| *Date required for (one week's notice required)* | | | | Teacher's Int: |
| **Bill of materials** | | | | |
| **Name of part and values** | **Number required** | **Code number** | **Supplier** | **Cost** |
| PP3 battery clip | 2 | 18-0157 | Rapid Electronics | £0.10 |
| PP3 battery | 2 | 18-3275 | Rapid Electronics | £3.40 |
| Battery holders | 2 | 12-2965 | Rapid Electronics | £0.80 |
| Transistor BC108 | 1 | T018 | Rapid Electronics | £0.11 |
| Transistor holders | 1 | 22-0000 | Rapid Electronics | £0.05 |
| Gearbox/motor | 1 | Stock | | £5.15 |
| 4011B chip | 1 | Stock | | £0.40 |
| DIL socket | 1 | 22-0150 | Rapid Electronics | £0.05 |
| Variable resistor | 1 | 67-0245 | Rapid Electronics | £0.07 |
| Relay DPDY 12V DC | 1 | 60-1115 | Rapid Electronics | £1.30 |
| Rocker switch SPST | 1 | 75-0275 | Commotion | £0.40 |
| Push-to-make switch | 1 | 78-0100 | Rapid Electronics | £0.10 |
| Micro-switch SPST | 1 | 78-2404 | Rapid Electronics | £0.90 |
| Resistors: | 3 | | | |
| 10k | 2 | 62-0358 | Rapid Electronics | £0.02 |
| 2.2k | 1 | 62-0358 | Rapid Electronics | £0.02 |
| Cable and solder | | Stock | | |
| Diode | 1 | IN4001-1000 | Rapid Electronics | £0.02 |
| Pulley belt and pulleys kit | 1 | 37-0370 | Commotion | £1.25 |

### Evaluation of the product

Evaluation of the product will be an ongoing process throughout the design and manufacture, and comments should be made as this work progresses. You will also need to evaluate the final outcome after you have made and tested it. This entails you returning to your detailed specification and design brief and commenting on how well you feel your final product satisfies these.

Extracts from a student's product evaluation of a rotating CD storage unit are shown on the following pages.

### Specification point 1: The unit should be battery operated

**Test results:** A 9-volt PP3 battery housed inside the base box powered the circuit. While this circuit worked well, I had to unscrew the baseboard to gain access to the battery each time it needed changing.

**Critical appraisal:** The problem with unscrewing the base was that all the CDs had to be removed so that the unit could be turned upside-down to enable the screws to be removed. By modifying the front panel of the base box I was able to change the battery without turning the unit upside-down.

### Specification point 2: The unit should move slowly and quietly

**Test results:** The unit's gearbox was geared down to a 625:1 ratio, which enabled it to turn slowly, but the gearbox was still very noisy.

**Critical appraisal:** The speed of rotation was fine but the noise was a constant source of annoyance. I was never able to solve this problem although when I oiled the gears it improved. If I were to make the unit again I would used a better quality gearbox. I discovered that you can buy a silent running gearbox for about twice the cost of the one I used.

### Specification point 3: The unit must turn through 90° and stop

**Test results:** At first the circuit worked fine but after a few weeks, as the batteries ran down, the unit would stop before turning through 90°.

**Critical appraisal:** This became a constant source of annoyance, as I could not always see the titles on the CDs. Even though I had modified the unit to ease the changing of the batteries, batteries would only last a few weeks. The problem was solved when I fitted a jack plug socket and connected an old unused 9-volt DC power supply in parallel with the batteries. The batteries are now used as a back-up power supply.

### Modifications to the product

An example of part of the product modification for the rotating CD storage unit is shown in Figure 3.41.

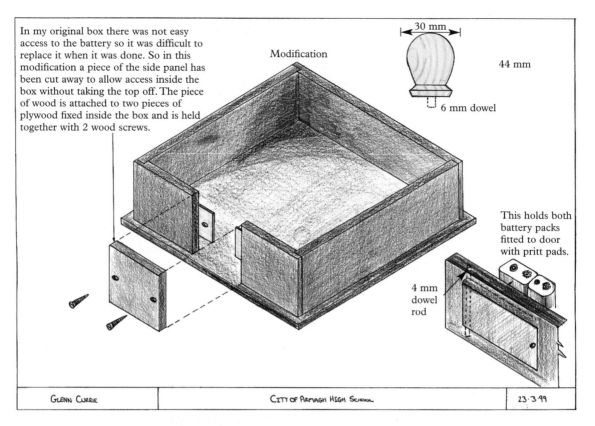

In my original box there was not easy access to the battery so it was difficult to replace it when it was done. So in this modification a piece of the side panel has been cut away to allow access inside the box without taking the top off. The piece of wood is attached to two pieces of plywood fixed inside the box and is held together with 2 wood screws.

Modification

30 mm

44 mm

6 mm dowel

This holds both battery packs fitted to door with pritt pads.

4 mm dowel rod

GLENN CURRIE          CITY OF ARMAGH HIGH SCHOOL          23·3·99

**Figure 3.41**

*Modifications to the final product*

## Questions

1  What is the maximum mark you can be awarded for a CCEA GCSE Technology and Design project and its portfolio?

2  There are eight elements or stages associated with these design projects. What are the eight elements?

3  Figure 3.8 shows an example of a possible 15-page portfolio layout. With reference to this example:

   a. List all the page titles

   b. Explain what you would expect to see on each page.

4  As a starting point for your design portfolio you have to identify situations or problems that are suitable for your Technology and Design coursework.

   Make a list of two possible situations or problems that would satisfy this part of your coursework.

5  What is a design brief?

6  What is a specification?

7  A product specification can often come in two parts. What are these?

8  What are concept sketches?

9  When designing an electronic product your design usually develops in two separate parts. One is the system, what is the other?

10 Copy and complete the following sentence:

   A working drawing should contain enough
   _____ your design.

11 When you have designed and manufactured a product, why is it important to evaluate it?

12 Using either a computer or a pencil and ruler make a template for:
   a. a cutting list
   b. a bill of materials.

On no more than 15 A3 drawing sheets (example shown in Figure 3.8) produce a coursework design portfolio for your chosen situation/ problem. If you are entered for the foundation tier you should attempt portfolio 1 below. If you are entered for the higher tier you should attempt portfolio 2 which satisfies either the foundation tier or higher tier assignments.

---

## Portfolio 1: Generate a foundation tier design portfolio for your GCSE coursework

Working on your own or on a class theme set by your teacher, complete a design portfolio that includes a section on each of the following:

### ● Situation

In the form of a short paragraph, explain the problem you have to solve.

### ● Design brief

As part of a team or on your own, write a design brief for your product. You may wish to start your sentence with: I plan to design and make a . . .

### ● Write a specification for your product

As part of a team or on your own, write a list of what the final product you will be making must do or have to make it a success. You may wish to start your specification with:

1  Material. The materials must be . . .
2  Finish. The finish must be able to . . .
3  Cost. The product must cost no more than . . .

Remember you will have to use the specification to evaluate your design as it progresses and at the end.

## ● *Research and investigation*

As part of a team or on your own, research and investigate things that are relevant to the product you are designing, e.g. are there similar products and how do these work?

## ● *Generate a range of concept sketches*

On your own, you should sketch different ideas that would solve the problem. Include short notes on your sketches to explain your idea (annotation). These sketches should show different solutions to the problem, not different variations of the same solution.

## ● *Proposed ideas*

Having generated a number of concept sketches and on your own, you should select one of these and develop it further, explaining your thoughts and evaluating your ideas by making reference to your specification.

## ● *Develop proposed idea*

Having completed your work on your proposed idea, you should make a fresh drawing of it, showing as much detail as possible, e.g. working drawing, cutting list.

## ● *Develop the energy and control system*

Working as part of a team or on your own, develop a system for your product. You should:

1 Develop a simple system that would solve or partly solve your problem.
2 If possible use Software like PCB Wizard, Bright Spark, Livewire, Control Studio, Logicator, PIC Logicator to show some development of your system.

## ● *Working drawing/s*

On your own, produce a detailed drawing or sketch showing the main dimensions and sufficient detail to enable you to make your product. This should also include a materials/cutting list.

## ● *Evaluation and modifications*

Finally, reflect on how well or otherwise your final product satisfied your specification. Do this by referring back to your specification. You should also comment on and even sketch changes you might make to your final product if you had to design it again.

### Portfolio 2: Generate a higher tier design portfolio for your GCSE coursework

● **Situation**

In the form of a short paragraph, identify a situation or situations for which there is no satisfactory solution and one for which you would like to design a suitable technological product. Research and investigate your chosen situation to find out as much information as you can about the problem and add this to your portfolio (this can be in the form of notes, pictures, photos, or even a taped interview with a person who is going to use your product).

● **Design brief**

Write a design brief for your product based on your research and investigation. This should be in the form of a short statement of what you intend to design and make and what the product must do.

● **Write a specification for your product**

This will usually include a list of what the client/end user wants and the technical limits you will put on the final product. This specification will be used to evaluate your design as it progresses and at the end.

● **Research and investigation**

Research and investigate things that are relevant to the product you are designing. You should explain why each reference is important to you and how you intend to use it.

● **Generate a range of concept sketches**

These sketches should show divergence and creative thinking. The sketches should show different solutions to the problem, not different variations of the same solution. A useful tip to get you started is to think of different technologies you could use to solve the problem, e.g. a mechanism or electronics. You should also include short notes on your sketches to explain the idea (annotation).

● **Proposed ideas**

Having generated a number of concept sketches, you should select one of these and develop it further, explaining your thoughts and evaluating your ideas by making reference to the specification.

● **Develop proposed idea**

At this point in your portfolio you should show as much detail as possible, e.g. how things will fit together, constructional details, how parts are secured, how you might service the product (e.g. change the battery), materials you intend to use, explain and evaluate your ideas making reference to the specification.

● *Develop the energy and control system*

At this point, or earlier in some cases, you should develop your system along with a PCB, etc (if relevant). You may find it helpful to develop your system from a simple one that would solve or partly solve your problem before trying to come up with a complicated system. It is at this point that CAD modelling comes into its own. Software like PCB Wizard, Bright Spark, Livewire, Control Studio, Logicator, PIC Logicator, etc can be very useful in developing and modelling your system.

● *Working drawing/s*

Produce a detailed drawing showing the main dimensions and sufficient detail to enable you to make the product. This should include an additional page showing your materials/cutting list and manufacturing plan.

● *Evaluation and modifications*

Finally, you should reflect on how well or otherwise your final product satisfies your initial specification. Do this by referring back to your specification. You should also comment on and even sketch changes you might make to your final product if you had to design it again.

# CHAPTER FOUR  **Materials**

## Timber

For thousands of years, trees have been used to make wooden products. Timber is one of our managed natural resources and is used all around the home. In technology it is used to make such things as mechanical toys, housings for electronic circuits and in pattern making for vacuum forming plastics.

**Deciduous trees** include hardwoods such as beech and oak. Deciduous trees nearly all have broad leaves. During the winter these leaves fall off.

**Conifers** include softwoods such as pine and cedar. Softwood trees have needles instead of broad leaves. Most softwood trees are evergreens which means they keep their needles all the year round.

**Figure 4.1** *Hardwood tree*

### From trees to planks

#### *Felling*

Trees are growing, living structures. They take in water and nutrients from the soil and transport it to the leaves. In the leaves, energy from sunlight converts water and carbon dioxide from the air into plant food. As this process happens during the summer months, trees are usually cut down in the non-growing season.

The tree is felled and the trunk cut into logs 4–6 m long. The logs are then transported to the sawmill where the bark is removed and they are cut into planks.

**Figure 4.2** *Softwood tree*

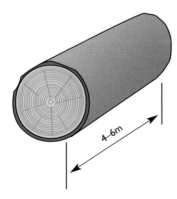

**Figure 4.3** *Logs 4–6 m long*

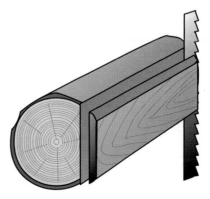

**Figure 4.4** *Logs are cut into planks*

### Seasoning

The planks are left to dry before they are finally sawn into planks for sale to the public. The drying process is called seasoning and can take between 6 months and 2 years if the timber is left outside. The process can be speeded up if the wet planks are placed in a hot building called a kiln. Kiln drying takes 1–3 weeks.

### Conversion

Conversion is the term given to sawing logs into planks. There are two main methods of doing this:

1. plain sawing
2. quarter sawing.

**Plain sawing** is quick and cheap to do but some planks will warp more than others. Figure 4.5 shows two planks; the centre one is the most desirable, as it tends to warp very little, while the lower plank will warp a lot. Wet planks have a tendency to bend away from the heart as they dry out.

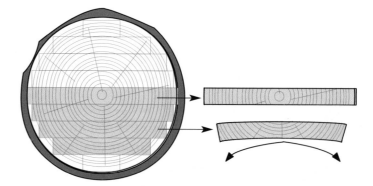

**Figure 4.5** *Plain sawn log*

**Quarter sawing** is slow and expensive to do and is usually only used for expensive hardwoods such as mahogany. Planks cut in this way tend to warp less than plain sawn ones because the growth rings are across the plank, as shown in Figure 4.6. Quarter sawing refers to either of the two methods shown in Figure 4.6. The lower, radial, method is the most expensive and tends to be reserved for special hardwoods such as oak.

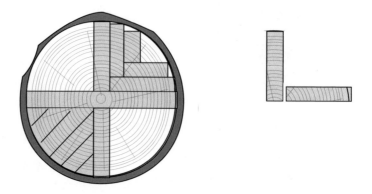

**Figure 4.6** *Two methods of quarter sawing*

### Common sizes of planks

Planks can be purchased in common sizes. This means that if you a buy a plank today, next week, next month or next year it will always have the same dimensions. Planks are sold as either rough or finished (planed) planks. Some of the common finished sizes are shown in Table 4.1.

**Table 4.1** *Common sizes of planks*

| Width (mm) | Finished thickness in millimetres | | | | |
| --- | --- | --- | --- | --- | --- |
| | 12 | 16 | 19 | 32 | 44 |
| 19 | x | x | x | | |
| 32 | x | x | x | x | |
| 44 | x | x | x | x | x |
| 69 | x | x | x | x | x |
| 94 | x | x | x | x | x |
| 119 | | x | x | x | x |
| 144 | | | x | x | x |
| 169 | | | x | x | x |
| 194 | | | x | x | x |
| 219 | | | x | x | x |

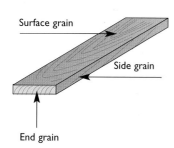

**Figure 4.7** *Grain lines*

### Grain

Grain is the term given to the pattern of the wood. These patterns are made by the growth rings of the tree. Figure 4.7 shows the end grain, surface grain and side grain on a piece of wood.

## Properties of wood

The structure of a tree as it grows allows nutrients to travel up and down the trunk to keep it alive. This structure is a series of short bonded tubes called cells. If you looked at them under a microscope they would look like small drinking straws. It is this tubular structure that gives timber its strength.

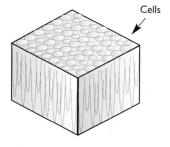

**Figure 4.8** *Structure of wood*

The tubes or cells are larger towards the outside edges of the trunk, so during seasoning they shrink more than the cells in the middle. This is why timber tends to warp.

### Mechanical properties of timber

Because timber has cells arranged in bundles, it may help you to think of a plank as a bundle of straws, and imagine how it will react to different forces.

**Figure 4.9** *Timber is good in tension*

### Tension along the grain

Timber will be strong in tension along its length, that is, it can resist large pulling forces (Figure 4.9).

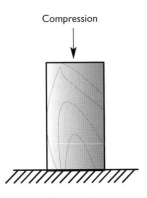

Compression

**Figure 4.10** *Resisting compression*

## Compression down the grain

While timber is good at resisting compression forces applied to each end it is not as good in compression as it is in tension. A piece of timber could be up to 50% weaker in compression than in tension.

## Compression and tension across the grain

Timber is weakest when a compression or tension load is applied across the grain.

## Bending

Timber will bend when a load is applied to it. You can reduce the bending and increase the strength of your project by turning planks on their edge. This is shown in Figure 4.11.

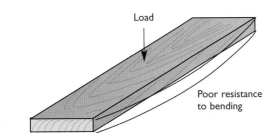

Load

Poor resistance to bending

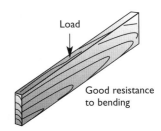

Load

Good resistance to bending

**Figure 4.11** *Resisting bending forces*

## Man-made boards

The term 'man-made board' is given to wood that has been cut and glued to form a board or sheet.

**Advantage:** One advantage of a sheet is its size. While solid timber is rarely more than 300 mm wide, sheets can be up to 1500 mm wide. Many of the man-made boards such as plywood can be much stronger than solid timber because of the arrangement of the grain.

**Disadvantages:** Prolonged exposure to moisture can often cause man-made boards such as MDF and chipboard to become weak. They are difficult to join using normal wood joints and often require special fixings. Nailing and screwing into the edge can be a problem, as the boards tend to split apart as the screw or nail goes in.

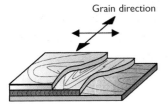

Grain direction

**Figure 4.12** *Plywood*

## Plywood

Plywood is made from layers of thin wood glued one on top of the other to form a sheet. Plywood is extremely strong and it gets this strength from the arrangement of the glued layers, which have grain directions at right angles (Figure 4.12).

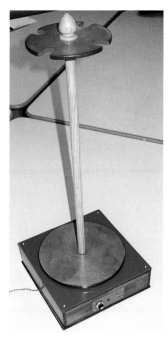

**Figure 4.13** *A rotating display with its base made from mahogany*

## MDF

MDF stands for medium density fibreboard. It is made from small particles of wood chips glued and compressed to form a sheet. While MDF is not as strong as plywood it is cheaper and very useful for making projects such as mechanical toys and boxes.

## Chipboard

This is made from chips of wood compressed and glued together. It tends to be weaker than MDF and plywood. Chipboard is also a difficult material to cut, join and finish because the chips can separate when you try to screw or nail into the edges.

## Timber used in technological products

### Mahogany

This is an expensive, imported decorative hardwood. It is often used in those products that require a decorative finish.

### Beech

This is a close-grained hardwood and is suitable for mechanical products such as children's toys, as it is non-toxic. It is also used in situations where the product is to be exposed to a lot of wear and tear.

**Figure 4.14** *Beech pull-along toy frog*

### Pine

There are a number of pines you can use. Most pines are inexpensive locally grown softwoods from managed forests. As they tend to be pale and have very little grain marking they are often used when appearance is not important, for example making patterns when vacuum forming. Pine has also become very popular for furniture. Figure 4.15 shows a security box made from pine, designed to hold valuables.

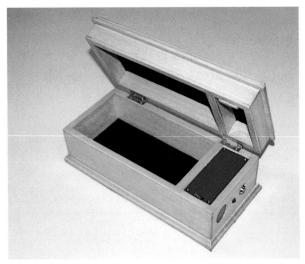

**Figure 4.15** *Pine security box*

**Figure 4.16** *Cedar garden swing*

### Cedar

This is a softwood that comes from North America. It is excellent for use outdoors. It contains a natural chemical that protects the timber from decay.

## Manufacturing in permanent form using wood

### Wood joints

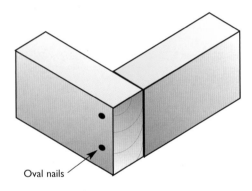

Oval nails

**Figure 4.17** *Butt joint*

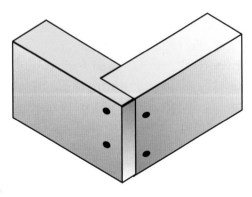

**Figure 4.18** *Lapped joint*

### Butt joint

The butt joint can be used on the corner of boxes and frames. It is the simplest of all the joints to make but it is also the weakest. The joint is simply two pieces of wood glued, butted and nailed together. A typical butt joint is shown in Figure 4.17. To improve the appearance, the nails should be punched below the surface.

### Lapped joint

The lap joint is similar to the butt joint but one of the pieces has a rebate cut out for the other to fit into. The lap joint is much stronger than the butt joint because of the increased gluing surface. On joints deeper than 100 mm it is common practice to nail the joints from both sides. On small-sectioned timber, modern glues make nailing unnecessary. A lap joint is shown in Figure 4.18.

### Halving joint

The halving joint is used for making frames. As its name implies, both pieces of wood used in the joint have half their thickness removed to allow the other piece to sit down in. There are three main types of halving joint:

- 'T' halving
- cross halving
- corner halving.

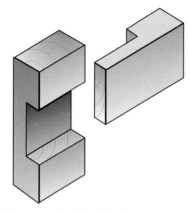 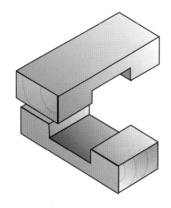 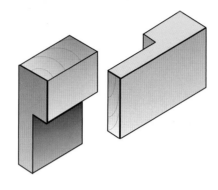

**Figure 4.19** *'T' halving joint*  **Figure 4.20** *Cross halving joint*  **Figure 4.21** *Corner halving joint*

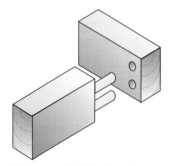

**Figure 4.22** *Dowel joint*

### Dowel joint

Dowel joints consist of two pieces of wood jointed together with two or more round dowels. The joint is glued and cramped and left to set before the cramps are removed. Dowel joints are frequently used when making frames and joining man-made boards.

A dowel joint used on the corner of a frame is shown in Figure 4.22.

#### Cramping frames and boxes

When making a frame or box, it is important to glue and cramp it correctly to ensure that all four corners are square (at 90 degrees). One method for doing this is shown in Figure 4.23. This method has four stages:

1. Apply a good quality PVA wood glue to the joints.
2. Use sash cramps to pull the joints together.
3. Make sure the diagonals are equal. If the diagonals (corner to corner) are equal the frame or box has to be square.
4. Finally, to prevent twisting make sure you leave your job on a flat level surface to dry.

**Figure 4.23** *Ensuring a box has all corners at 90°*

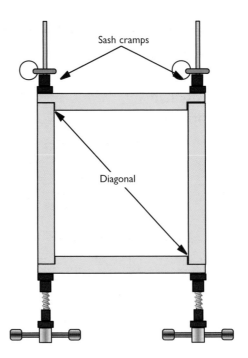

**Manufacturing in semi-permanent form using wood**

### Nails

Nailing is the quickest way to join two pieces of wood. Nails can be used on their own as a fixing or they can be used to cramp two pieces of wood together until the glue dries.

The three main types of nail are:

- panel pins
- oval nails
- wire nails.

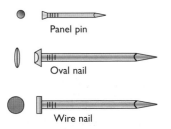

**Figure 4.24** *Types of nails*

The different types of nails are shown in Figure 4.24.

The heads of panel pins and oval nails are usually punched below the surface and the hole filled in with filler. The tool used to do this is called a **nail punch**.

### Screws

Wood screws will give a strong fixing between two pieces of material as the threads pull one piece of wood against the other.

There are two main types of head used on wood screws:

- countersunk
- round-head.

**Figure 4.25** *Nail punch*

Countersunk head screws are used when you want the head to be below the surface of the wood. Round-head screws are used with thin material where there is a danger of the head pulling through the material. Types of screw heads are shown in Figure 4.26.

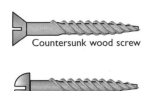

**Figure 4.26**
*Countersunk and round-head screws*

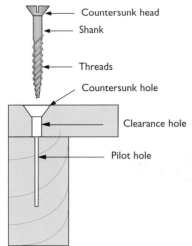

- Countersunk head
- Shank
- Threads
- Countersunk hole
- Clearance hole
- Pilot hole

**Figure 4.27** *Preparing the wood for countersunk screws*

## Preparing the wood to receive a screw

It is important to prepare the wood correctly so that the screw acts as a cramping device pulling the top piece of wood down onto the bottom. To do this you should:

1. Drill a clearance hole in the top piece of wood just slightly larger in diameter than the shank of the screw.
2. Drill a hole, half the diameter of the shank, in the second piece of wood to act as a pilot hole for the screw. This is shown in Figure 4.27.

## Wood cutting saws

There are three main types of saws for cutting wood. These are:

- hand saws
- back saws
- coping saws.

**Figure 4.28** *Wood cutting saws. Coping saw (a), hand saw (b), back saw (c)*

**Figure 4.29** *The correct use of a hand saw*

The saw you use will depend on the type of cut you wish to make. Some typical saws are shown in Figures 4.29 to 4.32.

### Hand saws

These are used to cut large pieces of wood to size. The correct use of a hand saw is shown in Figure 4.29.

### Back saws

These are used to make accurate cuts in wood, for example when making joints. Back saws get their name because they have a heavy strip of metal on the top edge of the blade to keep it straight during sawing. There are a number of types of back saws, the most popular being the tenon saw. Figure 4.30 shows a tenon saw being used to cut a joint. Figure 4.31 shows the correct way to hold the saw.

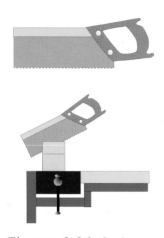

**Figure 4.30** *Back saw (tenon saw)*

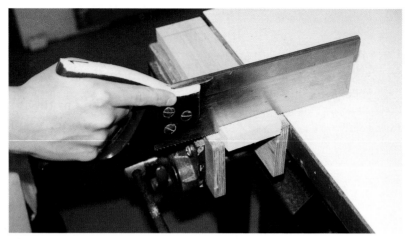

**Figure 4.31** *Correct way to hold a back saw*

### Coping saws

The coping saw is designed to cut curved shapes out of wood.

**Figure 4.32** *Coping saw*

## Woodwork marking-out tools

The main marking-out tools are the:

- try square
- marking gauge
- steel rule.

### Try square

This has a blade and handle fixed at an angle of 90° for marking and checking 90° angles. The square should be held firmly against the side of the wood while marking out.

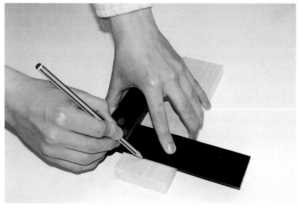

**Figure 4.33** *Using a try square*

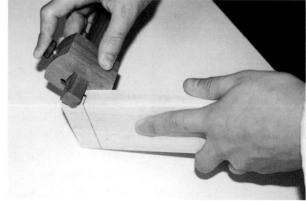

**Figure 4.34** *Using a marking gauge*

### Marking gauge

This is used to mark parallel lines on your wood. It has a steel pin that you use to scratch the parallel line.

### Steel rule

This will be marked out in millimetres only.

## Wood cutting tools

### Bevel-edge chisels

These come in different widths and are used for cutting joints and general woodwork. If you need to strike the chisel, use a mallet as shown in Figure 4.35.

### Smoothing plane

A smoothing plane is used either to prepare the surface of the wood for finishing after sawing or to reduce the wood in size. The correct way to use a smoothing plane is shown in Figure 4.36.

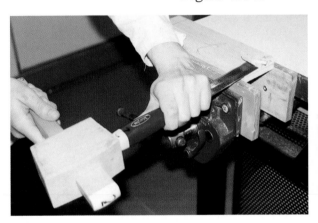

**Figure 4.35** *Using a bevel-edge chisel*

**Figure 4.36** *Using a smoothing plane*

# Metals

There are a number of different metals available for you to use in your projects. These can be categorised into two main groups:

- ferrous metals
- non-ferrous metals.

## Ferrous metals

The most commonly used ferrous metal is **mild steel**. Mild steel is an alloy. An alloy is a metal made by mixing two or more metals together. By doing this you can change the working properties of the metal to suit your particular needs.

Mild steel has good tensile and compressive strength. It is hardwearing and, if heated to a dull red, it can be bent and shaped easily. It can be joined by mig welding, soldering, brazing, riveting and bolting. The main disadvantage of mild steel is it will rust when exposed to the air and moisture. To prevent this you will have to treat the surface of the metal with a coating such as paint.

## Non-ferrous metals

Non-ferrous metals will not rust and can be finished by cleaning and polishing. The only disadvantages are they are not as hardwearing as mild steel and they cost considerably more.

The most popular non-ferrous metals for technological projects are brass, copper and aluminium.

**Brass:** Easily worked, joined and very good for lathe turning. Good surface finish. Brass is an alloy made from copper and zinc.

**Copper:** Easily worked and joined. Can be softened by annealing, then shaped with a wooden mallet. Good surface finish.

**Aluminium:** Easily worked but difficult to join. You can bond aluminium sheet without annealing it. However, round or flat bar must be annealed before bonding. To anneal, a good tip is to rub a bar of soap along the annealed surface when heat is applied, and as this melts the metal is annealed.

## Size and section of metals

Both ferrous and non-ferrous metals are available in a range of tubular sections, solid bars and sheets.

### Sheet metal

Sheet metal comes in a range of sizes from 600 mm × 600 mm to 2000 mm × 1000 mm. You can buy most of the sheet sizes in a range of thicknesses from 0.6 mm to 3 mm.

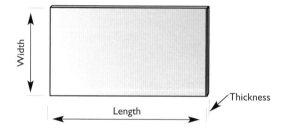

**Figure 4.37** *Sheet metal*

### Solid metal bar

You can buy solid bars of both ferrous and non-ferrous metals in a range of sections and sizes. The most common sections are shown in Figure 4.38.

**Figure 4.38** *Solid metal bar*

### Solid sections

You can buy solid sections of metal in both ferrous and non-ferrous metals although stockholders usually only carry these sections in mild steel. When ordering solid sections of metal you must specify the sectional width and the thickness.

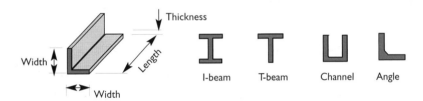

**Figure 4.39** *Solid sections*

### Tubular sections

You can buy both ferrous and non-ferrous metals in tubular sections (Figure 4.40).

**Figure 4.40** *Tubular sections*

# Manufacturing metal products in permanent form

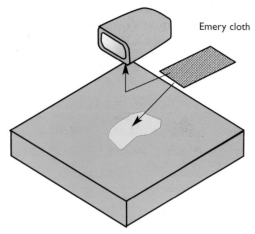

**Figure 4.41** *Clean both surfaces with emery cloth*

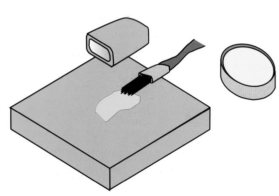

**Figure 4.42** *Apply flux to the joint*

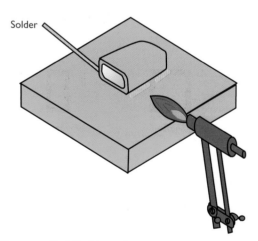

**Figure 4.43** *Heat the material before applying additional solder*

## Soft soldering

Soft soldering is a quick and easy method of permanently joining two pieces of metal. Copper, brass and mild steel can all be joined using soft solder, but aluminium cannot be joined in this way.

While a soft solder joint is permanent, it tends to be weak, which will limit its use.

To soft solder:

1. Clean both surfaces of the joint with emery cloth until they are free of dust and dirt (Figure 4.41).
2. Coat both cleaned surfaces of the joint with flux to keep the metal clean during soldering (Figure 4.42).
3. If necessary hold the joint together using wire to prevent movement.
4. Place the job on a heat resistant surface such as fire bricks.
5. Apply small pieces of solder along the joint.
6. Heat the two pieces of metal to approximately 230 °C using a gentle gas flame (Figure 4.43). The correct temperature is when the heated metal melts the small pieces of solder and solder starts to flow into the joint. Do not overheat the joint.

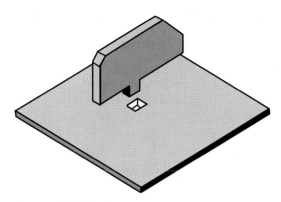

**Figure 4.44** *Close fitting joint to be brazed*

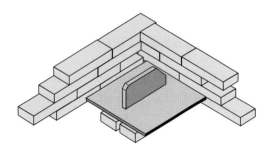

**Figure 4.45** *Containing the heat*

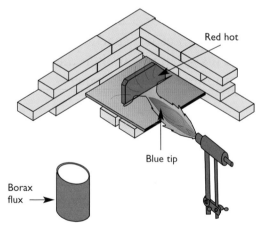

Red hot

Blue tip

Borax flux →

**Figure 4.46** *Use the blue tip of the flame for greatest heat*

*Brazing*

Brazing provides a permanent joint in metal. Because of the high temperatures needed in this process it is mainly used for joining mild steel and is not suitable for joining copper and brass.

To braze two pieces of metal together:

1. Make a close fitting joint (Figure 4.44).
2. Clean the metal with emery cloth until it is brightly polished.
3. Place the assembled job on a heat resistant surface.
4. Heat the metal with a gas and air flame until the metal is bright red (850 °C). The correct temperature will be difficult to achieve unless you contain the heat. To do this use a brazing hearth and surround your work with firebricks (Figure 4.45). The correct flame is also important. This is one where the gas is fully on and the air is increased until the blue inner part of the flame extends three-quarters of the way along the flame (Figure 4.46).
5. Dip the brazing rod into borax flux and offer it to the heated joint.
6. Keep the flame on the job but not on the joint during this stage of brazing and allow the melting rod to flow into the joint.
7. Allow the joint to cool slowly, as sudden quenching in water will cause the joint to fracture.
8. Any excess brass or flux should be cleaned off using a file or emery cloth, as excess flux will cause corrosion of the metal and prevent paint from taking to it.

Generally the brazing rod used in school workshops is a mixture of copper and zinc, which makes brass alloy. Because of the high temperatures involved it is important to wear safety glasses, a leather apron and gloves while brazing.

**Figure 4.47** *Mig welder*

**Figure 4.48**
*Countersunk rivet*

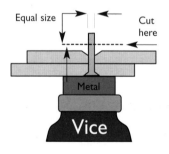

**Figure 4.49**
*Countersunk rivet*

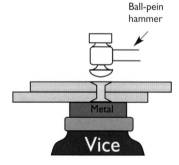

**Figure 4.50** *Filling the countersunk hole*

## Mig welding

Mig welding provides a permanent method of joining two pieces of metal. It is generally used for welding mild steel, although by using a special wire you can weld other metals such as aluminium.

To use mig welding:

1. Clamp the two pieces of metal to be joined.
2. Fix an earth clamp to your job.
3. A large current is passed along a thin steel wire. Bring the wire close to the joint so that an electric arc jumps across the joint. This arcing heats the immediate area to a high temperature causing the surface of the metal and the wire to melt and fuse together.
4. Fusing of the molten wire and the mild steel is only possible because of the flow of argon gas around the welded joint during welding. The argon shield keeps the surface clean, preventing oxidisation of the metal and allowing fusion to take place.

The temperatures involved in mig welding are lower than those associated with electric arc welding with the result that much thinner material can be welded using this process.

It is important to wear a mig welding mask during welding, as the bright arc will damage your eyesight. It is also important to wear long leather gloves and an apron as hot sparks, called splatter, can jump off the job. This splatter is molten metal and will burn your clothes and skin unless you take proper precautions.

### Riveting

Rivets are used to permanently join two or more pieces of metal. They are made from soft malleable metals such as soft iron, brass, copper and aluminium.

### Countersunk rivets

To rivet two pieces of metal using countersunk rivets:

1. Drill a hole in both pieces of metal the same diameter as the rivet.
2. Use a countersink drill to form a countersink in both pieces of metal.
3. Cut the rivet to length. The length of the rivet should be the thickness of the metal plus the diameter of the rivet.
4. Use a ball-pein hammer to drive the rivet in and fill the countersink hole.
5. File the rivet head to remove excess metal.
6. Finish by draw filing.

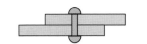

Figure 4.51 *Snap-head rivet*

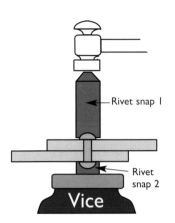

Figure 4.52 *Using rivet snaps*

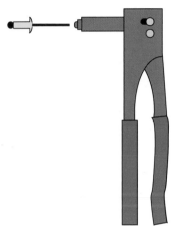

Figure 4.53 *Pop rivet tool*

### Snap-head rivets

The technique of riveting using snap-head rivets is similar to that used with countersunk rivets. In snap-head rivets the head of the rivet is formed using the ball end of a ball-pein hammer. Two rivet snaps are used to create the final shape. The technique is shown in Figure 4.52.

### Pop riveting

Pop rivets are used to permanently join two or more pieces of sheet metal together.

The pop rivet has a hollow centre into which a hardened pin is located. The pin has a ball at one end. It is this ball that forms the second rivet head during the riveting process.

To join sheet metal by pop riveting:

1. Select a rivet made from the same material as you are joining.
2. Drill a hole in both pieces of sheet material equal to the diameter of the rivet.
3. Open the jaws of the pop rivet tool and slide in the pin of the rivet.
4. Slide the rivet through the two pieces of material.
5. Squeeze the two handles together.
6. The ball at the rivet end of the pin will pull into the rivet forming the second head before the ball breaks off.

While pop riveting is quick and easy to do, the mechanical joint is not very strong. The technique of pop riveting is shown in Figures 4.54 and 4.55.

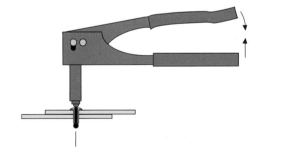

Figure 4.54 *Assembling the rivet in the material*

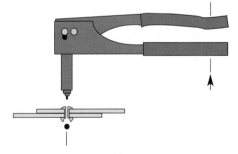

Figure 4.55 *The ball breaks off when the rivet is formed*

## Manufacturing metal products in semi-permanent form

### Nuts and bolts

Nuts and bolts are used to create a mechanical fixing between two pieces of metal. The most common type of nut and bolt is

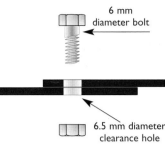

6 mm diameter bolt

6.5 mm diameter clearance hole

**Figure 4.56** *Hexagon-head nut and bolt*

Washer          Spring washer

**Figure 4.57** *Types of washer*

**Figure 4.58** *Antivibration nut and washer*

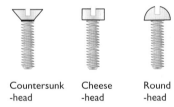

Countersunk -head     Cheese -head     Round -head

**Figure 4.59** *Machine screws*

**Figure 4.60** *Self-tapping screw*

the hexagon-head (Figure 4.56). This enables you to tighten the nut and bolt using a spanner.

## Washers

The purpose of a **washer** is to spread the load from the nut and avoid mechanical damage to the work during tightening.

A problem that can occur with nuts and bolts is that the nut can come loose as a result of vibration. To overcome this problem you should use either an antivibration washer or antivibration nut or both. The most common antivibration washer is the **spring washer**. When the nut is tightened down it compresses the spring washer. It is this force that prevents the nut from working loose. Two different types of washer are shown in Figure 4.57.

**Antivibration nuts** are special nuts that are prevented from working loose by a piece of nylon added to the top of the nut. The bolt has to cut its own threads as it passes through the nylon part of the nut. It is this action that provides the resistance and prevents the nut from working loose. These nuts are often referred to as nylock nuts. An antivibration nut and washer are shown in Figure 4.58.

## Machine screws

Machine screws are used to create a semi-permanent fixing between two or more pieces of metal. They are similar to bolts except they are tightened using a screwdriver. The three main types, which are shown in Figure 4.59, are:

- countersunk-head screw
- cheese-head screw
- round-head screw.

## Self-tapping screws

These are similar to wood screws except they are made from hardened steel and the threads are cut all the way to the head of the screw. They are used to fix two pieces of sheet metal.

# Metalwork fabrication

Fabrication is the term given to making products by joining pieces of metal together.

Many fabrication methods use sheet material. An example of a fabricated sheet mild steel tray and the specialist tools used to make it is shown in Figures 4.61 to 4.64.

Once the shape is marked out, use **tinsnips** to cut the profile (Figure 4.61).

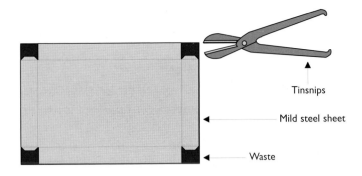

**Figure 4.61** *Using tinsnips to cut the profile*

**Folding bars** are used to hold the sheet material and keep it straight during folding (Figure 4.62).

Holding the folding bars in the vice, place a block of hardwood on top of the side to be folded. Bend this side over to form the side of the tray (Figure 4.63).

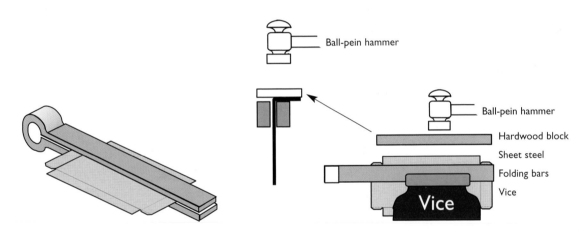

**Figure 4.62** *Folding bars*

**Figure 4.63** *Folding the tray*

The corners could be joined using a number of different methods. The one shown in Figure 4.64 is pop riveting. Soft soldering could also be used, especially if the tray was designed to hold a liquid.

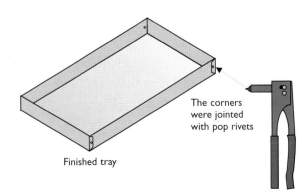

**Figure 4.64** *Pop rivet joints*

**Go-kart platform**

### Design situation

In his spare time a student was involved in racing go-karts and the kart required regular maintenance between races.

### Solution

The solution was a servicing platform on which the kart would sit. The platform was designed to rise and fall quickly and safely to a height of 800 mm, saving time on servicing.

The platform jack was fabricated from tubular steel bolted together. The pivot joints had antivibration nuts and washers to prevent the nuts from working loose. Aluminium chequered plate was used on the platform. This was pop riveted to the tubular frame. A hydraulic ram was used to lift the platform to its maximum height, at which point safety pins were inserted into the joints to prevent the platform from collapsing should the ram fail. The finished project is shown in Figure 4.65.

**Figure 4.65** *A fabricated go-kart servicing platform*

## Making metalwork projects by wasting

The term 'making by wasting' means the product or part of the product is cut from a solid piece of metal. The gearwheel shown in Figure 4.66 was cut on a milling machine from a solid piece of round steel bar.

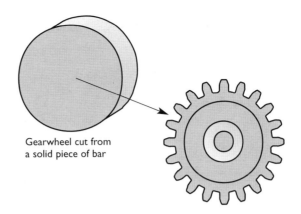

Gearwheel cut from
a solid piece of bar

**Figure 4.66** *Making by
wasting*

**Figure 4.67** *Sliding
bevel*

## Making a sliding bevel by wasting

Not all wasting operations require a milling machine or centre lathe. The sliding bevel shown in Figure 4.67 was cut from flat bar.

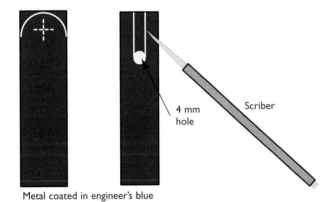

4 mm
hole

Scriber

Metal coated in engineer's blue

**Figure 4.68** *Marking out*

### Marking out

The main body was made from 25 mm × 12 mm flat bar. This was first coated in engineer's marking blue so that the scriber lines could be easily seen (Figure 4.68).

### Making the body

1. A 4 mm hole was drilled at the base of the slot while the bar was still flat and square.
2. A second-cut file was used to remove the waste material at the corners. The final shape was achieved with a smooth-cut file.
3. The waste material was removed from the slot using a hacksaw (Figure 4.71).
4. The slot was finished with a file.

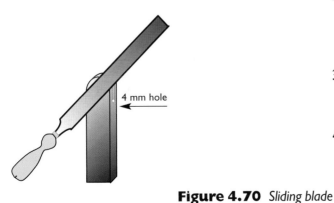

4 mm hole

**Figure 4.69** *Removing
the waste by filing*

**Figure 4.70** *Sliding blade*

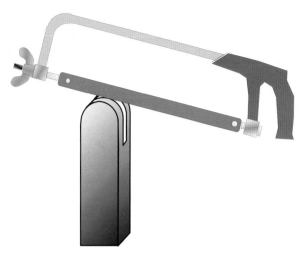

**Figure 4.71** *Hacksaw to remove the waste*

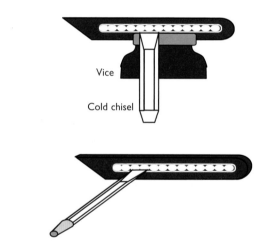

Vice

Cold chisel

**Figure 4.72** *Cutting the slot*

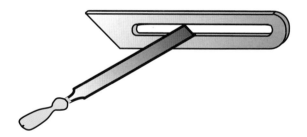

**Figure 4.73** *Warding file*

### *Making the sliding blade*

The sliding blade was made from 25 mm × 3 mm mild steel flat bar.

1. The waste material at both ends was removed with a hacksaw and second-cut file and finished with a smooth-file (Figure 4.71).
2. A series of holes was drilled along the slot using a twist drill and a drilling machine.
3. A cold chisel was used to remove the waste material between the holes. To do this the material was held firmly in the vice with the cutting line down level with the jaws of the vice. A sharp cold chisel and ball-pein hammer were used to chisel away the waste (Figure 4.72).
4. Finally the slot was filed to shape using a thin file called a warding file (Figure 4.73).

## Tapping and threading

### *Tapping*

The term tapping refers to the process of cutting internal threads into which a screw will fit. The tool used to cut the threads is called a **tap** and it is made from high carbon steel. By holding it in a **tap wrench** you can turn the tap.

Turn the tap wrench in a clockwise direction for half a revolution to cut the threads. Then turn it in reverse for half a turn to release the cuttings. This will prevent the tap from becoming clogged.

### Tapping a hole in mild steel

To tap a hole you first need to drill a hole in the material just smaller than the diameter of your tap. The correct hole sizes for each metric thread to be cut are shown in Table 4.2. Next apply cutting paste to the tap. Now enter the taper tap in the hole and press down to start the cut. This is shown in Figure 4.74.

**Table 4.2** *Drill sizes*

| Thread size | Tapping hole | Clearance hole |
|---|---|---|
| M3 | 2.5 mm | 3.5 mm |
| M4 | 3.3 mm | 4.5 mm |
| M5 | 4.2 mm | 5.5 mm |
| M6 | 5.0 mm | 6.5 mm |
| M8 | 6.8 mm | 8.5 mm |
| M10 | 8.5 mm | 10.5 mm |

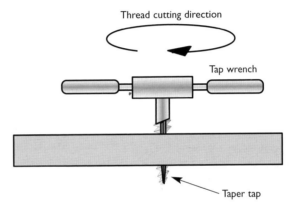

**Figure 4.74** *Cutting threads using a taper tap*

### Threading

The term threading refers to the process of cutting external threads on the outside of a round bar. When cutting external threads a tool called a **die** is used. The die is held in a die stock. The same technique of forward and reverse cutting action is used for cutting external threads.

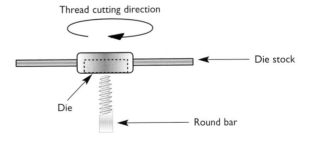

**Figure 4.75** *Cutting external threads*

**Example**　　　**Portable desk lamp**

### Design situation

A student studying for exams works at a desk in her bedroom. The desk is in a corner away from the window. The location provides poor natural light and the nearest plug socket is across the room.

**Figure 4.76** *Portable reading lamp*

### Solution

The solution was a small table lamp powered by its own 3 volt battery that was fixed along with the PCB (printed circuit board) to the underside of the shade. The final design is shown in Figure 4.76.

### Stem

The final design used 8 mm diameter aluminium rod for the vertical stem and supporting arm. Both were cleaned with 00 gauge wire wool and polished on the polishing machine.

The supporting arm had external threads cut using an M8 die.

### Counterweight

The counterweight was made from 30 mm aluminium rod. The rod was drilled for tapping on the centre lathe to a depth of 25 mm. Internal threads were cut using an M8 taper tap, second tap and plug tap.

### Base

The base was made from beech. This is a close grain hardwood that enabled the threaded stem to cut its own threads into the wood as it was screwed in.

### Plastic shade

The shade was vacuum formed over a wooden pattern made from pine. It was fixed to the supporting arm with an M8 antivibration nut and washer as shown in Figure 4.77.

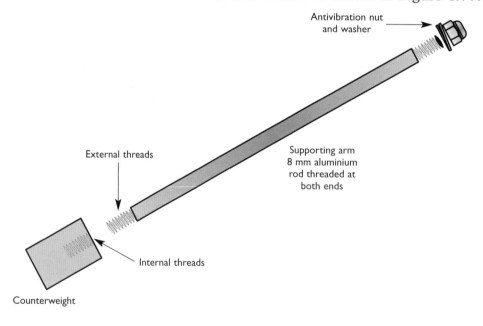

**Figure 4.77** *Threaded bar*

# Plastics

The three most commonly used plastics in the manufacture of technological products are:

- acrylic
- high impact polystyrene (sometimes called rigid polystyrene)
- melamine.

Plastics have the advantage over wood and metal because they have pre-finished surfaces. If care is taken not to scratch or damage these surfaces you will only need to dress and polish the edges when manufacturing plastic products.

## Acrylic

This comes in sheets, tubes and solid bars. Sheets will have a protective film top and bottom to protect them against scratches. This film should be left on until the very last minute during manufacture.

If heated to 165–175 °C acrylic will become flexible, allowing you to bend and reshape it. The two most common methods of reshaping acrylic are:

- line bending
- press forming.

### Line bending acrylic sheet

This is a process where you heat a narrow strip along a sheet of plastic until it becomes elastic, at which point you can bend it to the required angle. A hot wire strip heater or element heater is used to heat the narrow strip on the material. Figure 4.78 shows a typical hot wire strip heater.

*(a)*

*(b)*

**Figure 4.78** *A hot wire strip heater*

When line bending it is advisable to use a jig to hold your work in place until it cools. This will ensure the final angle is correct. The jig shown in Figure 4.79 is adjustable so that you can set the desired angle. This jig is made from wood so it will retain the heat. The trapped heat will slow down the cooling of the bend so it is good practice to have an air gap at the corner to allow the heat to escape.

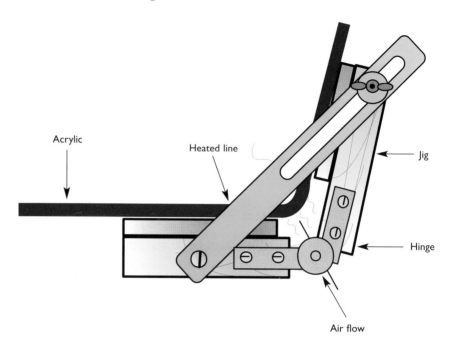

**Figure 4.79** *Line bending jig*

### Vacuum forming acrylic sheet

The technique used for vacuum forming acrylic sheet is similar to the technique used for vacuum forming high impact polystyrene sheet (see page 119). The only difference is that you need to pre-dry the sheet. A vacuum forming station is shown in Figure 4.80.

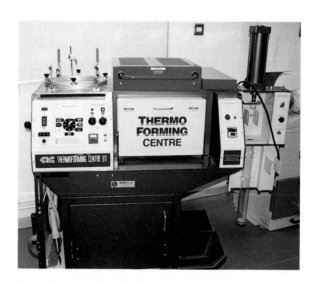

**Figure 4.80** *Forming station*

### Pre-drying acrylic sheet

If you wish to vacuum form or blow mould acrylic, it is necessary to pre-dry the sheet to allow any moisture trapped in it to evaporate. If you fail to dry your sheet, air bubbles will appear in the finished product as moisture turns to steam during the heating of the sheet.

To pre-dry your sheet, place it in an oven for 1.25 hours per mm thickness at 40 °C.

When vacuum forming or blow moulding, the material must then be heated to 165–175 °C.

There are two forms of sheet acrylic – cast and extruded. Extruded must be used for vacuum forming, while cast sheet is better for blow moulding.

### Blow moulding acrylic sheet

The technique of blow moulding is used to form a semi-circular dome in acrylic. The process involves pre-drying the sheet in an oven at 40 °C then increasing the temperature of the oven to 170 °C. At this temperature the sheet will become elastic. The sheet is quickly moved into a suitable blow moulding jig and air pressure applied under it. The air pressure forces the sheet up into a dome. At this point the air pressure should be reduced so that the shape is kept constant. The reduced pressure should be maintained until the sheet has cooled. Figure 4.81 shows a dome being formed using the blow moulding technique.

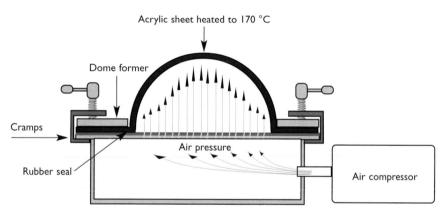

**Figure 4.81** *Blow moulding machine*

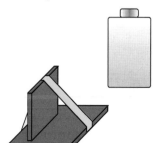

**Figure 4.82** *Permanent fixing using tensol cement*

### Fabricating with acrylic in permanent form

Acrylic can be joined using either tensol cement or fusion cement.

When using **tensol cement** it is good practice to pour a small amount of cement on to a piece of metal. Then dip the edge to be cemented into the liquid before locating it on the job. Finally, hold the joint secure with an elastic band or masking tape until it hardens (Figure 4.82).

**Fusion cement** is sometimes referred to as capillary cement because of the method of application. When using fusion cement the pieces are held in position with masking tape or a rubber band. The cement is dropped with a fine dropper needle into the corner of the joint. The cement is then drawn into the joint by capillary attraction (Figure 4.83).

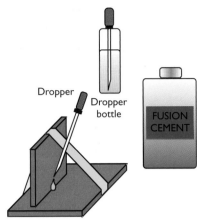

**Figure 4.83** *Permanent fixing using fusion cement*

Care should be taken to avoid getting cement on any part of your job except the joint as it dissolves the surface of the plastic and will permanently mark your work. Also avoid clamping your joint too tightly as this will cause crazing around the joint.

### *Fabricating with acrylic in semi-permanent form*

If the pieces you are fabricating are to be taken apart or the material is to be used as part of a moving joint, then you can fix acrylic in the same way as you would metal. Solid bar and thick sheets can be threaded and screwed together. Or machine screws, nuts and bolts can be used to join two or more pieces of acrylic (Figure 4.84).

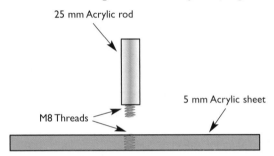

**Figure 4.84** *Threading solid acrylic*

## High impact polystyrene sheet

High impact polystyrene sheet is mainly used for vacuum forming. It is a pre-finished sheet that will become elastic at 90–100 °C. At this temperature it can be vacuum formed over a suitable pattern. It is also possible to line bend polystyrene sheet, but care should be taken not to overheat the material. If your strip heater has a temperature control you should start by setting it at the lowest setting and increase the temperature gradually until the material becomes elastic.

### *Vacuum forming patterns*

A pattern is a temporary model of the final shape. The sides of the pattern should be slightly tapered so that the top of the pattern is smaller than the bottom (Figure 4.85). This will allow the pattern to release more easily after the sheet has been vacuum formed over it. Wood is a suitable material from which to make a pattern, as it is easily cut and shaped. Wooden patterns will also retain heat and allow the plastic to cool more slowly. This helps prevent stress cracks appearing in your work. To avoid excess thinning of the plastic sheet during the vacuum forming process, the height of the pattern should not exceed the length or the breadth of the pattern.

### *Pattern release*

While taper on the sides of your pattern will help the release of the pattern from the vacuum formed shape, you will also need to apply a release agent to the pattern before you start to vacuum form. This will make it even easier to get the pattern out of the plastic. There are a number of release agents you can buy for this job. Talcum power is also an effective release agent for wooden patterns (Figure 4.86).

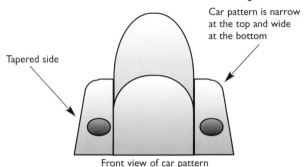

Car pattern is narrow at the top and wide at the bottom

Tapered side

Front view of car pattern

**Figure 4.85** *Adding taper to the wooden pattern*

**Figure 4.86** *Add a release agent to the wooden pattern*

### Vacuum forming

The technique of vacuum forming requires a machine that will heat a plastic sheet before pulling the air out from below it, causing a vacuum. The soft plastic sheet will now be pressed down over the pattern by atmospheric pressure. This process, like many others, requires experience to know when the material is elastic enough and ready for forming over the pattern.

The following are the stages in this process.

**Figure 4.87** *Place the wooden pattern on the vacuum forming machine*

1. Place the wooden pattern on the machine as shown in Figure 4.87.
2. The pattern is lowered in the machine and the sheet fixed and clamped to the top of the machine.
3. Heat is applied to the sheet until it becomes elastic and starts to drape.
4. The heat is removed and the pattern moved up into the soft plastic (Figure 4.88).
5. The vacuum is now turned on and the soft plastic will be pressed down over the pattern.
6. Allow a few seconds for the mould to cool before turning off the vacuum.
7. Remove the sheet from the machine and pull or tap out the pattern.
8. Remove the excess material. There are a number of machines available to trim plastic, one is shown in Figure 4.89.

**Figure 4.88** *Wooden pattern raised into soft plastic sheet*

119

**Figure 4.89** *Trimming off the waste plastic*

## Cutting and shaping plastic

Plastic can be cut and shaped in a similar way to metal, using many of the same tools.

### Sawing plastic

Plastic can be cut to shape using either a hacksaw or a coping saw. Thin sheet can also be scratched with a craft knife and broken along the scratch. Figure 4.90 shows acrylic being cut with a coping saw.

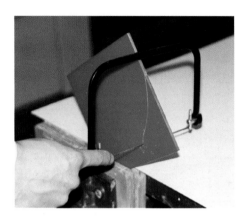

**Figure 4.90** *Using a coping saw to cut acrylic*

### Filing plastic

After sawing you can use metalwork files to shape and smooth your work. There is a range of different files available for this purpose. Some of these are shown in Figure 4.91.

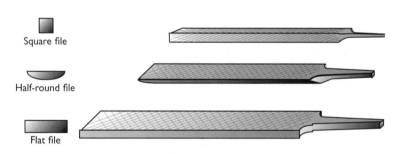

Square file

Half-round file

Flat file

**Figure 4.91** *Common types of files used to shape plastics*

**Figure 4.92** *Hold the scraper away from you and push*

### Finishing plastic

If you have taken care during manufacture not to damage the front and back surfaces you will only have to dress the edges. For most plastics you can finish the edges as follows:

1. Draw file the edges smooth.
2. Use a cabinet scraper to remove file marks (Figure 4.92).
3. Use wet and dry abrasive paper to remove any scratches. The abrasive paper may be wrapped around a small

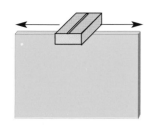

**Figure 4.93** *Wet and dry abrasive paper*

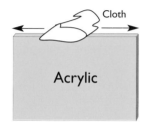

Cloth

Acrylic

**Figure 4.94** *Polish with a soft cloth*

wooden block to keep the edge of the acrylic flat and square. This is shown in Figure 4.93.

4. Polish with acrylic polish (or Brasso) on a soft cloth (Figure 4.94).

The edges of acrylic can be polished on a **polishing machine** but care must be taken not to press too hard against the mop otherwise the acrylic will melt. The polishing machine is not suitable for dressing softer plastic such as high impact polystyrene sheet.

The correct mop is also important, so make sure the machine has a stitched mop design for plastics before you turn it on. If in doubt ask your teacher and under no circumstances should you use this machine until you have been fully trained.

**Figure 4.95** *Polishing machine*

### Melamine

Unlike acrylic or polystyrene, melamine cannot be reshaped by heating. It is very hard wearing and is good at resisting scratching and impact. It is used in plastic products that may be exposed to high temperature. High quality kitchenware, kitchen work surfaces, cups and plates are all made from melamine. It is also used in many electrical products such as electric kettles and plug sockets.

---

### *Questions on timber*

1 Which of the following must be worn when drilling wood on the drilling machine?

   a pair of gloves

   b face visor

   c blazer

2 Which of the following should you do when drilling a very small piece of material?

   a Hold with both hands

   b Hold it in a hand vice

   c Have someone else hold it while you drill it.

3 Which of the following precautions must be practised when using the sanding machine?

   a Hold the wood at an angle

   b Never place the wood on the table

   c Hold the work firmly down on the table keeping both hands clear of the sanding belt.

4 Copy out and complete the following sentences.

   a Trees that lose their broad leaves in winter are called
      d_____trees.

   b Trees that have needles and are green all year are called
      c_____.

   c We get hardwoods from _____trees.

   d We get softwoods from _____.

5 What does the term seasoning timber mean?

6 What does the term timber conversion mean?

7 Draw the end view of a log showing the difference between quarter sawing and plain sawing.

8 Draw a plank of wood and label the:

   a end grain

   b side grain

   c surface grain

9 Man-made boards refer to boards that are made from wood veneers, chips, etc.

   a Write down the name of three man-made boards and give a use for each.

   b Write down two advantages and two disadvantages man-made boards have over solid timber.

10 Mahogany is a timber used in the design and manufacture of products. Name one product that you are familiar with that is made from mahogany.

11 Beech is a close-grained timber. Write down the name of one product made from beech and give one reason why beech was selected.

12 Pine is a commonly used softwood. Write down the name of one product made from pine and give one reason why pine was selected.

13 Draw a butt joint and give one use for this joint.

14 Draw a lapped joint and give one use for this joint.

15 Draw a dowel joint and give one use for this joint.

16 Write down the names of three different types of halving joint.

17 When using wood screws to pull two pieces of wood together it is

important to prepare the wood correctly to receive the screw. Write down the sequence you would use when preparing two pieces of wood to receive a wood screw.

18 Figure 4.96 shows a tool you would use when nailing.

**Figure 4.96**

a Write down the name of this tool.
b Write down what this tool is used for.

19 Figure 4.97 shows a saw.
a Write down the name of this saw.
b Write down one use for this type of saw.

**Figure 4.97**

20 Figure 4.98 shows a saw.
a Write down the name of the saw.
b Write down one use for this type of saw.

**Figure 4.98**

### Questions on metal

1 What is the difference between solid metal bars and tubular bars?
2 Sheet metal can be bought in different-sized sheets. Write down two common sheet sizes.
3 The engineer's sliding bevel shown in Figure 4.99 is to be made from mild steel flat bar.
   a The tool shown in Figure 4.100 was used in the making of the engineer's sliding bevel. Write down the name of this tool and explain its use.
   b The tool shown Figure 4.101 was used in the cutting out of the slot. Write down the name of this tool.

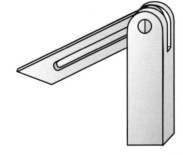

**Figure 4.99**

**Figure 4.100**

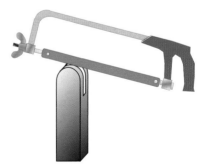

**Figure 4.101**

4 Figure 4.102 shows a tool used when working with metal. Write down the name of this tool.
5 Riveting is a process used to join sheet metal. Explain how you would rivet two pieces of sheet metal together.
6 Write down the name of three different metals that rivets are made from.
7 The tray shown in Figure 4.103 is 150 mm long, 100 mm wide and 30 mm high and is to be made from mild steel sheet. Using sketches and notes, explain how you would make this tray.

8 The terms ferrous metals and non-ferrous metals are used in metalwork. Write down what each of these terms means.

9 The bracket shown in Figure 4.104 is to be made from a mild steel alloy. What is an alloy?

10 The two parts of the mild steel bracket shown in Figure 4.104 have to be joined permanently by brazing. Explain how you would braze the two pieces of metal together.

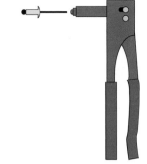

**Figure 4.102**

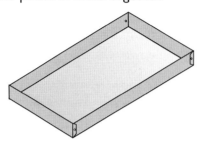

**Figure 4.103**

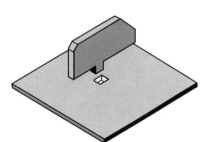

**Figure 4.104**

### Questions on plastics

1 Name two plastics commonly used in the manufacture of technological products.

2 Acrylic has a thin plastic film covering the surface of the sheet.
   a What is the purpose of this thin plastic film?
   b When should you remove this thin plastic film?

3 Acrylic can be made into different shapes by heating. Name a common method of reshaping acrylic.

4 At what temperature will acrylic become flexible?

5 Explain how you would, using only hand tools:
   a Cut a 150 mm disc out of a sheet of 3 mm acrylic.
   b Finish the edges of the disc.

6 Vacuum forming is a process used when forming a shape in plastic.
   a Name the machine you would use when vacuum forming.
   b Patterns are used in vacuum forming. What is the function of a pattern?

7 A plastic box is needed to house an electronic timing circuit. The box is to be vacuum formed over a timber pattern.
   a Write down why rigid polystyrene sheet would be a suitable material for this process.
   b Write down two main features of a well-designed pattern for vacuum forming.
   c There are eight stages in the vacuum forming process. Write down four of these stages.

8 Figure 4.105 shows a sketch of a child's night-light.
   a Write down the name of the material you would use to make the top and give a reason for your choice.
   b Explain how you could produce one of the geometrical shapes shown in the top part of the light.
   c The top is made from four separate pieces of plastic. Explain how you would join the four corners to form the top.

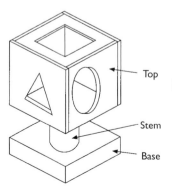

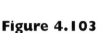

Top

Stem

Base

**Figure 4.105**

### Questions on products using composite materials

1 Figure 4.106 shows an exploded view of a box, which is to hold an electronic counter display circuit. The cover is made from aluminium and the inside from wood.

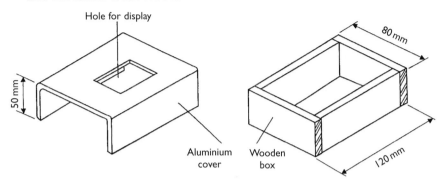

**Figure 4.106**

a State how the aluminium cover could be bent to the required shape.

b By means of a sketch, show a suitable method of attaching the aluminium cover to the wooden box so that the cover could be removed to replace the battery.

c Explain how the rectangular hole could be cut from the aluminium cover.

d Show by means of a sketch how the circuit and battery could be positioned and held securely inside the box.

e By means of a sketch, show a suitable wood joint for the corner of the wooden box.

2 Figure 4.107 shows a display stand 200 mm long, 60 mm high and 60 mm wide, that must be manufactured from one piece of acrylic bent to shape and then attached to a mahogany base.

a Name the equipment you would use to heat the acrylic for line bending.

b Suggest two safety precautions you would take when using this equipment.

c Sketch a suitable former that could be used to help shape the acrylic cover.

d Explain how the acrylic cover may be joined to the mahogany base to enable it to be taken apart if required.

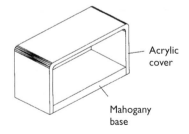

**Figure 4.107**

# CHAPTER FIVE

**Electronics**

## Basic concepts

Electronics is based on the flow of electrons in a circuit. You may be wondering what electrons are. Well everything in the universe is made from atoms. These atoms consist of even smaller particles called electrons, protons and neutrons. The neutrons and protons make the centre or nucleus of the atom, while the electrons move around the nucleus, a bit like a planet and its moons. These electrons have a negative charge. The attraction between the positive nucleus and the negative electrons holds the atom together and the electrons in place.

Figure 5.1 shows a helium atom, which has two electrons moving around its nucleus. A copper atom has 29 electrons moving around the nucleus. The electrons furthest from the nucleus are not so tightly held and so can move from atom to atom. This movement of electrons is what we call electric current. Some materials are better at conducting an electric current than others.

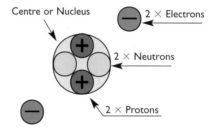

**Figure 5.1** *Electrons in an atom of helium*

**Conductors** are materials with a structure that allows electrons to move within them with relative ease. Metals such as copper, silver, gold and aluminium are all good conductors of electrons.

**Insulators** are materials with a structure that doesn't allow electrons to move freely within them. Materials such as rubber and plastic make good insulators.

**Semiconductors** have only a few electrons free to move. Their conductivity is somewhere betweeen that of conductors and insulators. Silicon and germanium are semiconductors.

The force that makes electrons flow in a conductor is called **voltage** (symbol $V$) and it is measured in volts (symbol V).

An **electric current** is a flow of electrons. When we measure current ($I$) in a circuit we are measuring the number of electrons passing a given point in one second. Current is measured in amps (A).

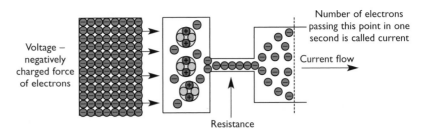

**Figure 5.2** *Voltage, current and resistance*

Scientists who first studied electricity assumed that a current was a flow of *positive* charges. So in diagrams we still show current flowing in circuits from the positive to the negative side of the power supply. However, the *negatively* charged electrons are actually flowing from the negative terminal through the circuit to the positive terminal on a battery.

**Resistance** is a measure of how easily electrons can flow through a conductor. The greater the resistance, the more the flow of electrons is reduced. If voltage is kept constant, increasing resistance decreases the current. Resistance is measured in ohms ($\Omega$).

# Resistors

**Resistance** is present in a circuit when the flow of electrons is reduced. This is usually caused by a **resistor**. A resistor is a circuit component designed to reduce the flow of electrons by a specific amount. The reduction in the flow of electrons is determined by the value of the resistor. The value of a resistor is its resistance in ohms ($\Omega$) or kilo-ohms (k$\Omega$ – often shown simply as 'k' on circuit diagrams).

The circuit symbol for a resistor is shown in Figure 5.3.

**Figure 5.3** *Resistor symbol*

## Types of resistor

### Fixed-value resistors

There are a number of different types of fixed-value resistor which you can buy. The most commonly used is the **four-band resistor** (Figure 5.4).

**Resistor values**

Because resistors are so small it would be difficult to write their value on the side. Instead they have colour bands. The first two bands represent numbers, the third the number of zeros and the fourth the tolerance or accuracy of the resistor.

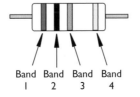

Band Band Band Band
  1     2     3     4

**Figure 5.4** *Four-band resistor*

Table 5.1 can be used to find the value of a resistor.

**Table 5.1** *Resistor values*

| Colour of the band | Band 1<br>1st digit | Band 2<br>2nd digit | Band 3<br>Number of zeros after the 2nd digit | Band 4<br>Tolerance |
|---|---|---|---|---|
| Black | 0 | 0 | – | |
| Brown | 1 | 1 | 0 | 1% |
| Red | 2 | 2 | 00 | 2% |
| Orange | 3 | 3 | 000 | |
| Yellow | 4 | 4 | 0000 | |
| Green | 5 | 5 | 00000 | |
| Blue | 6 | 6 | 000000 | |
| Violet | 7 | 7 | 0000000 | |
| Grey | 8 | 8 | | |
| White | 9 | 9 | | |
| Gold | | | | 5% |
| Silver | | | | 10% |

## Example

To find the value of the resistor shown in Figure 5.4 you would consult Table 5.1.

1st band: red = 2
2nd band: black = 0
3rd band: orange = 000 (3 zeros)
4th band: gold = 5%

So the value of the resistor in Figure 5.4 is 20 000 ohms or 20k (5% tolerance).

### Variable resistors

A variable resistor can be adjusted to alter its resistance. A preset variable resistor is set to the desired value and then left at that setting. The symbol for a variable resistor is shown in Figure 5.5.

**Figure 5.5** *Symbol for a variable resistor*

### Light-dependent resistors (LDRs)

These are semiconductor devices whose resistance decreases when light shines on them. They are useful in light-sensing circuits. The symbol for an LDR is shown in Figure 5.6.

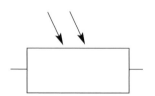

**Figure 5.6** *Symbol for an LDR*

### Calculating the resistance of more than one resistor

#### Resistors in series

The total resistance of resistors in series (as in Figure 5.7) can be found by using the following formula:

$$R_{total} = R_1 + R_2$$

**Example**

Find the total resistance of the two resistors in Figure 5.7.

$$R_{total} = 1k + 1k$$
$$= 2k$$

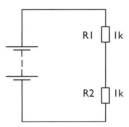

**Figure 5.7** *Resistors in series*

#### Resistors in parallel

The total resistance for resistors in parallel (as in Figure 5.8) can be calculated by using the following formula:

$$\frac{1}{R_{total}} = \frac{1}{R_1} + \frac{1}{R_2}$$

**Example**

Find the total resistance of two resistors in parallel.

$$\frac{1}{R_{total}} = \frac{1}{2k} + \frac{1}{3k}$$

$$\frac{1}{R_{total}} = \frac{3 + 2}{6}$$

$$\frac{1}{R_{total}} = \frac{5}{6}$$

$$R_{total} = \frac{6}{5} = 1.2k$$

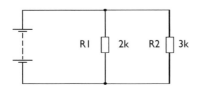

**Figure 5.8** *Resistors in parallel*

Switches turn a circuit on or off by making or breaking a connection.

## Types of switches

### Push switches

These are switches that make or break the connection when they are pressed. There are two main types:

- push-to-make
- push-to-break.

The symbols for these are shown in Figure 5.9.

### Toggle switches

Toggle switches have a lever that is thrown to make or break the connections. The example shown in Figure 5.10 is a single-pole-single-throw (SPST) switch.

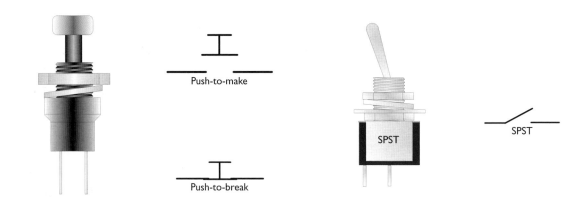

**Figure 5.9** *Push switch and symbol*

**Figure 5.10** *Toggle switch and symbol*

### Micro-switches

Micro-switches are designed for situations where the connection has to be broken by a moving object. The switch has a common contact (COM), one contact that is normally closed (NC) and one that is normally open (NO). When the contacts are arranged in this way they are called single-pole-double-throw switches (SPDT). A SPDT switch is shown in Figure 5.11.

### Slide switches

Double-pole-double-throw switches (DPDT) are used to switch on and off two or more circuits simultaneously. They are often used in motor-reversing circuits (Figure 5.12).

**Figure 5.11** *Micro-switch and symbol*

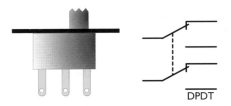

**Figure 5.12** *Slide switch and symbol*

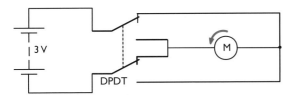

**Figure 5.13** *Anti-clockwise rotation*

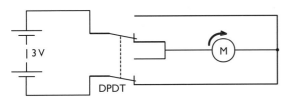

**Figure 5.14** *Clockwise rotation*

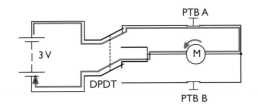

**Figure 5.15** *Limit switches*

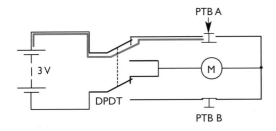

**Figure 5.16** *Cutting the power*

## Reversing circuit for a motor

### Anti-clockwise rotation

You can use a double-pole-double-throw switch to reverse the rotation of a d.c. motor. The circuit in Figure 5.13 uses a DPDT slide switch to change the polarity at the motor, that is, which side of the motor is connected to the positive terminal of the battery. When the positive supply comes in at the right-hand side of the motor it rotates in an anti-clockwise direction.

### Clockwise rotation

When the switch is changed as shown in Figure 5.14 the positive supply arrives at the left-hand side of the motor, causing it to rotate clockwise.

### Adding limit switches

The circuit shown in Figures 5.13 and 5.14 will run continuously. If you were using this circuit to open a window it would be important to have the motor stopping when the window was fully open or closed. To achieve this you would need push-to-break limit switches. Figure 5.15 shows the position of the limit switches in the circuit.

When the power is turned on the motor turns anti-clockwise until it reaches its limit and pushes open a limit switch. This cuts the power to the motor as shown in Figure 5.16.

Only when the DPDT switch is changed over will the power flow in the bottom half of the circuit enabling the motor to turn clockwise. It will continue to turn until the bottom limit switch is pressed, at which point the power will be cut to the motor.

Electronics

131

# Transistors

Transistors are semiconductor devices. This means that they have a resistance to the flow of electrons (current). However, they become conductors when a small voltage is present at one of the legs, called the base leg. The leg closest to the tag is the emitter (e).

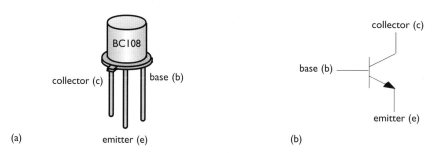

**Figure 5.17** (a)

*Drawing of a transistor*

*(b) Graphic symbol for an NPN transistor*

(a)

(b)

You can use the transistor as a high-speed switch. If a small voltage of 0.6–1.6 V is applied to the base leg it will at once enable a larger current to flow through the transistor from the collector to the emitter. A typical transistor circuit is shown in Figure 5.18, which is an automatic light-sensing circuit.

During the day the resistance of the LDR is low so most of the current flows through this part of the circuit and the voltage at the base leg of the transistor is only 0.59 V. This is less than the 0.6 V required to turn it on, therefore the bulb remains off.

In darkness the resistance of the LDR will increase, forcing more current down to the base of the transistor. When the voltage at point A reaches above 0.6 V the transistor will turn on.

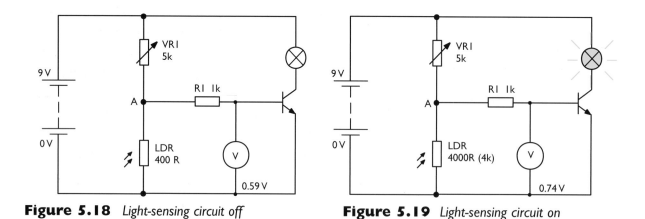

**Figure 5.18** *Light-sensing circuit off*

**Figure 5.19** *Light-sensing circuit on*

In Figure 5.19 the voltage has reached 0.74 V and the transistor is on. When the transistor is on current can flow in the outer part of the circuit, switching on the bulb.

# Capacitors

Capacitors are electronic devices that can be used to give a time delay in a circuit.

They have the ability to store a quantity of electrons, called the charge, and in some ways are like a small rechargeable battery in that they can be charged and then release this charge. The main difference is the amount of charge (electrons) they can store and the release rate. Batteries will release their charge over a long period of time, whereas capacitors release their charge almost instantly.

## Capacitor values

The value of a capacitor is expressed in farads (F). A 1 farad capacitor would be the size of an aluminium soft drink can, just a little too large to use in your electronic circuits. The value of a capacitor is usually less than 1 F. Table 5.2 shows the common units used when working with capacitors.

**Table 5.2** *Capacitor units*

| farad | F | I | |
|---|---|---|---|
| millifarad | mF | 1 000 | $\times 10^{-3}$ |
| microfarad | μF | 1 000 000 | $\times 10^{-6}$ |
| nanofarad | nF | 1 000 000 000 | $\times 10^{-9}$ |
| picofarad | pF | 1 000 000 000 000 | $\times 10^{-12}$ |

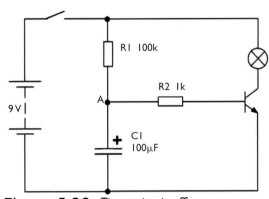

**Figure 5.20** *Timer circuit off*

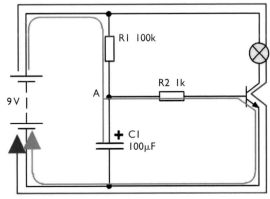

**Figure 5.21** *Timer circuit on*

## Capacitors in circuits

The diagrams in Figures 5.20 and 5.21 are of a timer circuit that uses a capacitor to give a small time delay before the lamp comes on.

When the circuit is turned on, the electrons flow through the left-hand loop of the circuit to fill the capacitor. When the capacitor is full the electrons must flow from A through R1 to the base of the transistor (red line in Figure 5.21). This switches the transistor on so that a current flows through the lamp (blue line) and the lamp is illuminated. The time it takes to fill the capacitor will depend on the value of R1 × C1.

The capacitor does not need to be 'full'. The capacitor will charge through the resistor and as it does so the voltage across the capacitor will rise. When the voltage at point A reaches 0.6 V a base current will flow and the transistor will switch on. This is shown in Figure 5.21.

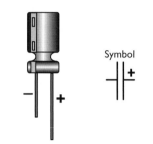

**Figure 5.22** *Axial electrolytic capacitor*

**Figure 5.23** *Radial electrolytic capacitor*

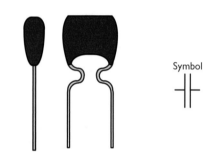

**Figure 5.24** *Metallised polyester capacitor*

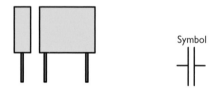

**Figure 5.25** *Miniature polyester capacitor*

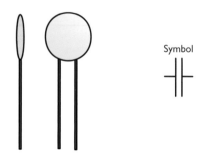

**Figure 5.26** *Ceramic disc capacitor*

The problem with this type of circuit is the time delay you are likely to get. Time delays of more than a few minutes are impractical because large capacitors have poor tolerances. An electrolytic capacitor over 1000 μF will allow charge to leak through it. This will prevent it from providing enough overflow electrons to turn on the transistor.

## Types of capacitors

There are a number of different types of capacitors you can use in your circuit. The choice will depend on the value and the accuracy required.

### Electrolytic capacitors

There are two main types of electrolytic capacitor, axial and radial. These are polarised capacitors and must be connected the correct way round.

These are large-value capacitors and are used for long time delays or as smoothing capacitors in circuits.

Typical value range: 1 μF–4700 μF
Tolerance: ±20%

### Metallised polyester capacitor

These are non-polarised, which means they may be connected either way round. They tend to have a higher degree of tolerance and accuracy than the electrolytic capacitors.

These are medium-value capacitors.

Typical value range: 10 nF–470 nF
Tolerance: ±10–20%

### Miniature polyester capacitors

Typical value range: 1 nF–1 μF
Tolerance: ±10%

### Ceramic disc capacitor

These are non-polarised, so may be connected either way round.

Up to 4.7 nF they tend to have a higher degree of tolerance and accuracy than both polyester and electrolytic capacitors.

Typical value range: 100 pF–4.7 nF
Tolerance: ±10%

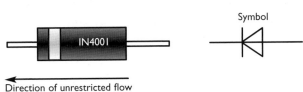

Direction of unrestricted flow

**Figure 5.27** *Diode*

Symbol

### Diodes

Diodes are semiconductors that allow electrons to flow through them in one direction only.

## LEDs

LED stands for Light Emitting Diode. An LED gives off light when current flows through it in one direction. LEDs are often used in electronic products in place of bulbs as they consume much less power. They are often used in hi-fi systems as stand-by indicator lights. An LED and its symbol are shown in Figure 5.28.

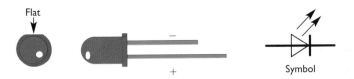

Flat

Symbol

**Figure 5.28** *An LED and its symbol*

The drawing in Figure 5.29 shows an LED used in a key fob torch. The LED must be connected the correct way round or it will not work. The leg nearest the small flat on the rim must be connected to the negative supply.

It is necessary to protect LEDs from too much current. If any type of battery other than a button cell is to be used then you must put a resistor in series with the LED. The following are suggested resistor values for different voltages.

3 V – 120 Ω
5 V – 220 Ω
9 V – 470 Ω
12 V – 560 Ω

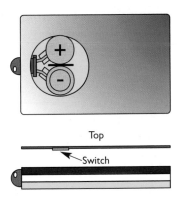

Top

Switch

**Figure 5.29** *Key fob torch which uses an LED as the light source*

Figure 5.30 shows the circuit diagram of a key fob torch. The two 1.2 volt button cell batteries are connected in series to give a total voltage of 2.4 volts. Small button cell batteries like this can be used with LEDs without a current-limiting resistor as they only give out a small current that will not damage the LED.

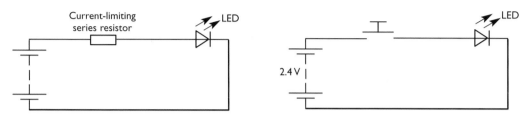

**Figure 5.30** *Current-limiting resistor*

## Types of LEDs

The most popular LED is the 5 mm round. You can also buy 3 mm round. Less popular but still very useful are the rectangular, triangular and square LEDs. All types of LEDs mentioned can be bought in a range of colours.

**Figure 5.31** *Types of LEDs*

---

**Example**     **Torch circuit**

### How it works

When the push-to-make switch is pressed the current flows out of the battery through the protective resistor to the LED. As it passes through the LED it makes it glow and you see this as light. The circuit was made using a PCB.

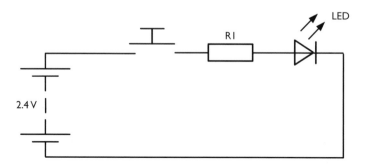

**Figure 5.32** *LED circuit*

### PCBs

PCB stands for Printed Circuit Board. This is a plastic board with a copper layer on one or both sides. Circuits in this book will be made on boards with copper on one side only (single sided).

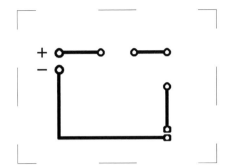

**Figure 5.33** *PCB artwork*

### Making a PCB

To make a PCB you must remove most of the copper, leaving a strip that will become the conductor between components on your board. This is achieved by making a suitable artwork to place on top of a copper board coated with photosensitive film. The film is exposed to ultraviolet light. Areas of the film unprotected by the dark lines on your artwork become unstable. The board is then placed in a developing solution for a short period of time to remove the unstable areas of film. You are now left with a developed board that is ready for etching. Etching is the term given to the process of placing the developed board in a tank containing a chemical heated to 40 °C. The chemical dissolves any unprotected copper, leaving you with a PCB that has a copper track on one side. Holes are now drilled in the copper track and the components passed through from the top side. The components are permanently fixed to the copper track by soldering.

### Silkscreen

This is a drawing showing where the components are placed on the PCB. It will also give the value of each component.

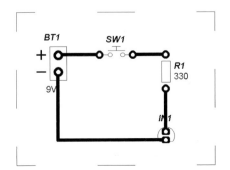

**Figure 5.34** *Silkscreen view of the PCB*

### Top view of the board

This is what you will see when you look at the top of the finished PCB.

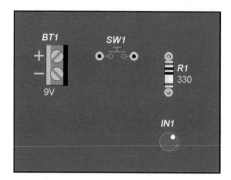

**Figure 5.35** *Top view of the board*

**Note:** If you plan to use button cell batteries it is not necessary to use a current-limiting resistor.

# Light-sensing circuits

Electronic circuits can be made to come on or off when the light level falls. The most common sensor used in these circuits is the LDR (light-dependent resistor).

Example

## Night-light

### Design situation

Young children are often frightened of the dark. There is a need for a small battery operated light which will come on automatically when it becomes dark.

### Solution

The final solution this student designed was the toadstool-shaped night-light shown in Figure 5.36.

### How it works

The LDR sensor at the base of the lamp detects the light level. When it is dark a small bulb under the dome comes on. The bulb will stay on until it is light again.

**Figure 5.36** *Automatic night-light*

### The circuit

The circuit is powered by a 9 volt PP3 battery. When the on/off switch (SW1) is closed power goes to the circuit.

The LDR (light-dependent resistor) is the sensor and its resistance increases with darkness. The variable resistor allows you to set how dark it will be before the lamp comes on.

The transistor is a high-speed switch that turns on when a voltage of 0.6–1.6 V is present at its base leg.

The lamp will only come on if the transistor is on. The bulb must have at least 10 ohms resistance for this circuit to work.

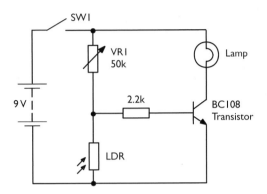

**Figure 5.37** *Night-light circuit*

## Block diagram for the night-light

Circuits can be divided into three main building blocks. These are **input**, **process** and **output**.

The automatic light circuit can be divided into these three main building blocks:

**Input:** LDR with its variable resistor. This is the sensor part of the circuit
**Process:** Transistor with its protective resistor
**Output:** Lamp

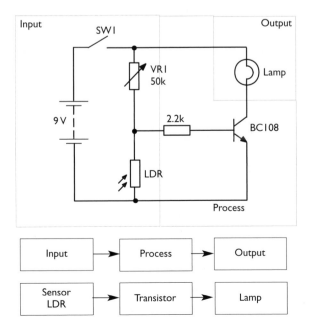

**Figure 5.38** *Block diagram for light-sensitive circuit*

## How the dark-activated circuit works

When you close the on/off switch during the day, current flows from the battery down through the variable resistor to the LDR (red line in Figure 5.39). As light is falling on the LDR it will have a very low resistance and act as a conductor. Current flows through it back to the battery.

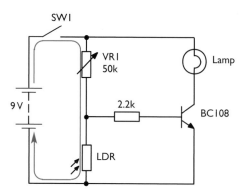

**Figure 5.39** *Path of current during the day*

In the dark the LDR will have a very high resistance. This means the current cannot pass through it and must find another route back to the battery. It flows through the 2.2k resistor to the base of the transistor. If the voltage is greater than 0.6 V the current will flow into the transistor, switching it on (Figure 5.40).

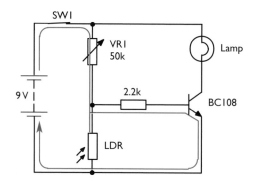

**Figure 5.40** *Path of current at night*

As the transistor switches on, electrons flow around the output part of the circuit (blue line in Figure 5.41). Electrons flowing through the filament of the bulb make it glow white-hot. In this process there will be four energy changes:

- chemical energy
- electrical energy
- heat energy
- light energy.

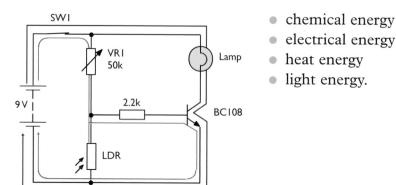

**Figure 5.41** *Path of the current through the output part of the circuit (blue)*

## How the light-activated circuit works

This circuit works the opposite way to the dark-activated circuit in that it is designed to come on when light falls on the LDR. An automatic daylight circuit could be used in a security box.

In this circuit the LDR would be above VR1. This is shown in Figure 5.42.

When the switch is in the on position the alarm would sound if the box was opened, allowing light to shine on the LDR.

If it is dark the LDR will have a high resistance. In this state the current cannot pass through it. The circuit remains off (green line in Figure 5.42).

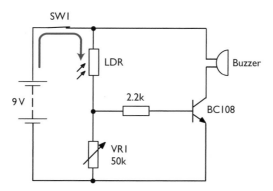

**Figure 5.42** *Path of current when the circuit is in darkness*

When light falls on the LDR its resistance falls so that the voltage at the mid-point of the potential divider rises. When this reaches 0.6 volts, current will flow to the transistor. When the transistor is on the current can pass through it and return to the battery. As the transistor is now on (red line), the current can now flow through the output part of the circuit (blue line). When this happens, the buzzer will come on (Figure 5.43).

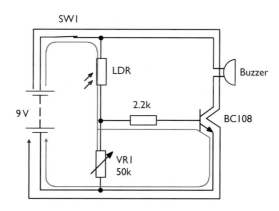

**Figure 5.43** *Path of the current when the circuit is in light*

# Notes on the dark-activated circuit night-light

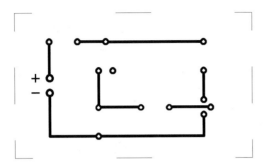

**Figure 5.44** *PCB mask for dark-activated circuit*

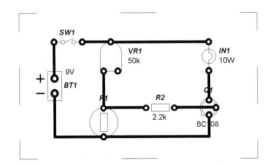

**Figure 5.45** *Silkscreen for dark-activated circuit*

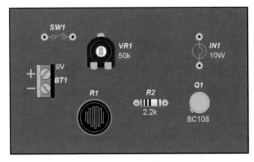

**Figure 5.46** *Top view of the PCB for dark-activated circuit*

### LDR

The LDR worked well as a sensor but would only respond to large changes in light levels.

### Variable resistor

Values of 22k–47k worked well.

### Transistor

The BC108 transistor was used as a simple high-speed electronic switch. Problems occurred with the BC108 when the output was changed to one requiring a flow of current larger than 300 mA (e.g. an electric motor). This caused the transistor to overheat and shortened its life span. If you wish to drive this type of output the BFY51 was slightly better but there was a marked drop in sensitivity.

### Bulb

The choice of bulb was very important. It was found that most low-cost bulbs had an internal resistance of 1–3 ohms. This is too low. Try to purchase bulbs with a resistance of 9–11 ohms. Low-value bulbs cause the transistor to overheat and burn out.

### Power supply

The battery had a life of only a few days if left on all the time. A better solution was a sealed power supply with a matching jack plug socket. This replaced the battery. Most students had a sealed power supply at home as part of an electronic game and were able to use these with their project.

### Components

1 × 2.2k resistor
1 × 50k horizontal miniature preset (variable resistor)
1 × 9 V battery connector
1 × BC108 transistor
1 × board (76.2 mm × 55.9 mm)
1 × ORP12 LDR
1 × 6 V bulb
1 × bulb holder

# Notes on the light-activated circuit security alarm

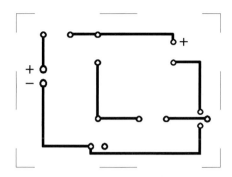

**Figure 5.47** *PCB mask for light-activated circuit*

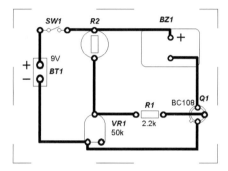

**Figure 5.48** *Silkscreen for light-activated circuit*

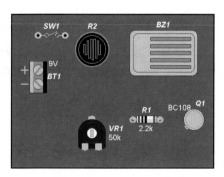

**Figure 5.49** *Top view of the PCB for light-activated circuit*

### LDR

When the LDR was placed in the top part of the circuit it worked well as a sensor, but as with the night-light would only respond to large changes in light levels.

### Variable resistor

It was found that the value of VR1 had to be increased to 100k.

### Buzzer

It was found that most low-cost 6 volt buzzers work fine.

### Key switch

SW1 was changed to a low-cost key switch. These were easily obtained from most of the major suppliers.

### Transistor

The BC108 transistor was used as a simple high-speed electronic switch. As the alarm tended to be on for short periods there was no real problem with the BC108.

### Power supply

It was found that when the circuit was in a waiting state, it consumed very little power from the battery. Unlike the night-light circuit this battery lasted a long time and there was no real need for a separate power supply.

### Components

1 × 2.2k resistor
1 × 100k horizontal miniature preset (variable resistor)
1 × 9 V battery connector
1 × BC108 transistor
1 × board (76.2 mm × 55.9 mm)
1 × ORP12 LDR
1 × 6 V buzzer

# Latched alarm circuit

Electronic circuits can be designed so that they will sound an alarm. The alarm can be made to stay on until you reset it. This is called latching the circuit.

## Example — Burglar alarm

### Design situation

Homes are at constant risk from burglars. Many of these burglaries happen during the night while the people who live in the house are in bed. There is a need for a small individual alarm which could be fixed to a bedroom door.

### Solution

The final solution was a latched alarm that was turned on/off by using a personal key switch (Figure 5.50).

### How it works

The box is fixed to the door frame and the key switch is turned on. If the door is opened the alarm inside the box will sound. It is the key holder who resets the alarm.

The door sensor is a magnetic reed switch. The reed switch is fixed to the side of the box and the magnet is fixed to the edge of the door.

**Figure 5.50** *The latched door alarm*

### Circuit diagram

The circuit is powered by means of a PP3 9 V battery. When the on/off key switch is closed power goes to the circuit.

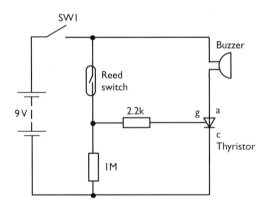

**Figure 5.51** *Latched alarm circuit*

A **reed switch** was used as the sensor. This is a switch that has two fine wires that come together when a magnet is placed close to them.

The **thyristor** is a latching device. It comes on when a small voltage is present at the gate leg (g). It can only be turned off again by cutting the power to the anode leg (a). The buzzer will sound when the thyristor is on.

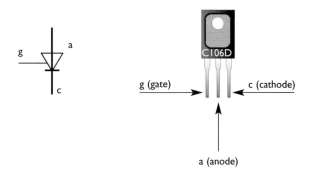

**Figure 5.52** *A thyristor and its symbol*

## Block diagram

Circuits can be divided into three main building blocks. These are input, process and output.

**Input:** Reed switch. This is the sensor part of the circuit
**Process:** Thyristor with its protective resistor
**Output:** Buzzer

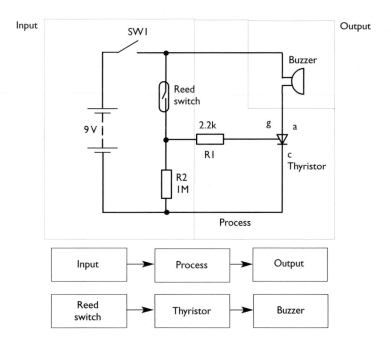

**Figure 5.53** *Block diagram for the latched alarm circuit*

## How it works

When the key switch (SW1) is turned to the on position the alarm is set. The current cannot flow past the open reed switch (Figure 5.54).

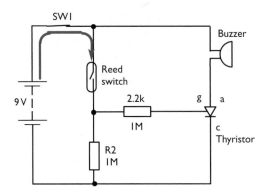

**Figure 5.54** *Path of the current when the reed switch is off*

The alarm is activated by an intruder when the magnet on the door moves past the reed switch as the door is opened. When this happens the fine wires inside the reed switch close.

At this point the current will flow down to the gate leg of the thyristor (g) and cause it to switch on. Figure 5.55 shows the path of the current through the thyristor. The current is now able to return to the battery.

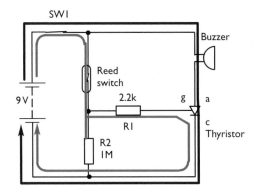

**Figure 5.55** *Path of the current when the reed switch is on*

The thyristor is a latching device. This means that once it is on it will stay on, until you turn it off. To turn off the thyristor you must cut the power to its anode leg (a). You can do this by opening the key switch (SW1).

When the thyristor is on current can flow through the output loop of the circuit making the buzzer vibrate and giving out sound.

## Notes on the latched alarm circuit

### Reed switch: SW1

The standard proximity switch used in commercial house alarms worked well as the sensor. These are available from most electronic suppliers and come as a set. The permanent magnet fits into a 9 mm hole drilled in the edge of the door while the reed switch is enclosed in a plastic housing with flying leads.

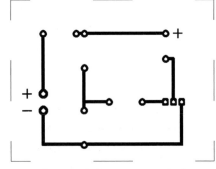

**Figure 5.56** *PCB for the latched alarm circuit*

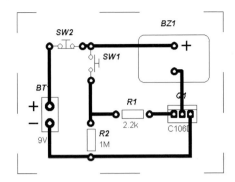

**Figure 5.57** *Silkscreen for the latched alarm circuit*

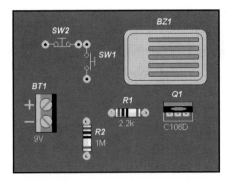

**Figure 5.58** *Top view of the latched alarm PCB*

### Buzzer: BZI

Problems were experienced with buzzers that pulsed as these would cut off the power to the anode side of the thyristor. When this happened the thyristor would reset, effectively cancelling the alarm. The problem can be overcome by adding an LED and current-limiting resistor in parallel with the buzzer.

PCB-mounted buzzers were found to be more secure in the casing.

### Switch: SW2

A low-cost circular key switch was used and this was found to be a good choice as the key could be removed after setting the alarm.

### Thyristor: C106D

A C106D was used but care should be exercised when handling and soldering, as certain types are sensitive to static.

### Power supply: PP3 battery

It was found that when the circuit was in a waiting state, it consumed very little power from the battery.

### Components

1 × 1M resistor
1 × 2.2k resistor
1 × 9 V battery connector
1 × C106D thyristor
1 × board (73.6 mm × 55.9 mm)
1 × PCB-mounted buzzer
1 × proximity switch (compact set in a plastic housing)

# Temperature-sensing circuit

Electronic circuits can be designed so that they will detect changes in temperature and then activate an alarm.

**Example**

## Frost alarm

### Design situation

During the winter freezing temperatures can cause problems for the old or infirm. Problems can arise when a room becomes too cold for living in. There is a need for a warning device that would sound an alarm or a flashing light when the temperature falls below the recommended level.

### Solution

The final solution was a plastic box with a drawing of a person dressed for the cold (Figure 5.59).

**Figure 5.59** *Drawing of the frost alarm*

### How it works

The black sensor on the sleeve of the coat is a thermistor. This is a sensor that detects changes in temperature. If the temperature falls too low, the circuit sounds an alarm.

The circuit has a manual switch so that the alarm can be turned off. The thermistor (sensor) comes out through the case so that it can detect the room temperature.

### Circuit diagram

The circuit is powered by means of a PP3 9 volt battery. When the on/off switch is closed power goes to the circuit. The temperature sensor is a **thermistor**. This is a type of variable resistor whose resistance increases as it becomes cold. When this happens the current flows to turn on the transistor. When the transistor is on the buzzer will be on. The variable resistor allows you to set the sensitivity of the circuit.

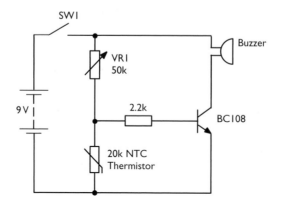

**Figure 5.60**

*Temperature-sensing circuit*

## Block diagram

The temperature-sensing circuit can be divided into these three main building blocks.

**Input:** Thermistor. This is the sensor for the circuit
**Process:** Transistor with its protective resistor
**Output:** Buzzer

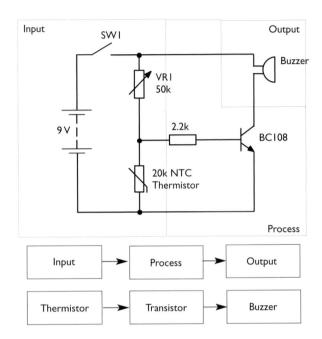

**Figure 5.61** *Block diagram for the temperature-sensing circuit*

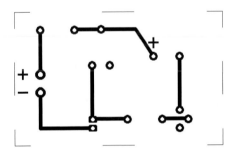

**Figure 5.62** *PCB for the temperature-sensing circuit*

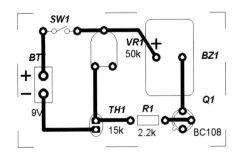

**Figure 5.63** *Silkscreen for the temperature-sensing circuit*

## Notes on the temperature-sensing circuit frost alarm

### Sensor thermistor

There are a number of thermistors available in most good catalogues. NTC (negative temperature coefficient) thermistors are the most common and decrease their resistance with temperature. If a 20k thermistor at 25 °C is used, it will work fine with the 50k variable resistor above it.

### Variable resistor

VR1 was a 50k miniature preset.

### Buzzer

It was found that most low-cost 6 volt buzzers work fine but the PCB-mounted type was found to be more secure in the casing.

### Switch

SW1 was a SPST toggle switch.

### Transistor

The BC108 transistor was used as a simple high-speed electronic switch. As the buzzer tended to be on only for short periods there were no real problems with the BC108. As the buzzer described only draws 25–30 mA, it could be on permanently without causing problems for the transistor which can handle 600 mV.

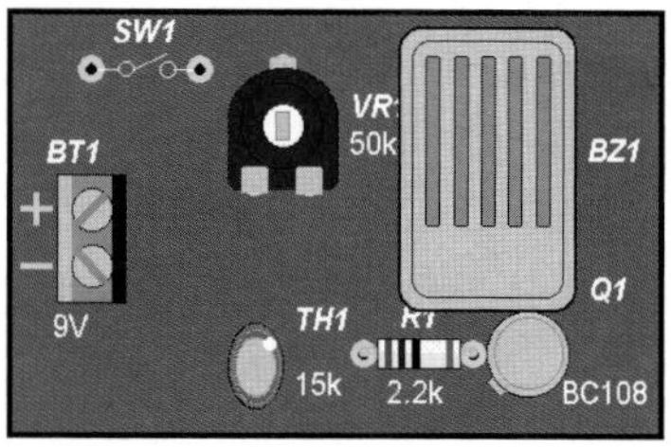

**Figure 5.64** *Top view of the temperature-sensing PCB*

### Power supply

It was found that when the circuit was in a waiting state it consumed a lot of power from the battery. A small external power supply connected by means of a jack plug socket solved this problem.

### Components

1 × 100k horizontal miniature preset
1 × 2.2k resistor
1 × 9 V battery connector
1 × BC108 transistor
1 × board (61 mm × 38 mm)
1 × PCB-mounted buzzer
1 × 20k disc NTC thermistor

# Moisture-sensing circuit

Electronic circuits can be designed so that they will detect moisture and sound an alarm.

**Example** | **Bath level indicator**

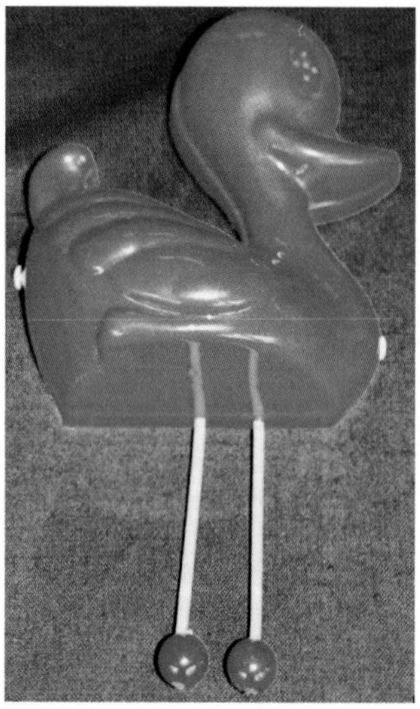

### Design situation

A mother running the bath for her baby found it took a long time to fill. During this time she had to stay in the bathroom and wait until the water had reached the required level. This meant a lot of time wasted while the bath filled. There is a need for a warning device that would let her know when the bath water was at the correct level.

### Solution

The final solution was in the shape of a vacuum-formed plastic duck with two moisture probes in the feet. The duck was fixed to the bath at the correct height using double-sided tape (Figure 5.65).

**Figure 5.65** *Picture of the bath level indicator*

### How it works

The two legs of the duck are metal probes. When the water in the bath reaches these a buzzer sounds inside the duck.

## Circuit diagram

The circuit is powered by means of a PP3 9 volt battery. When the on/off switch is closed power goes to the circuit. The moisture sensors are two metal probes set 25 mm apart. When these are put in water the water acts as a conductor and current flows between them. When this happens a small amount of current also flows down to the base leg of the transistor, turning it on. The buzzer will sound when the transistor is on. The variable resistor allows you to set the sensitivity of the probes.

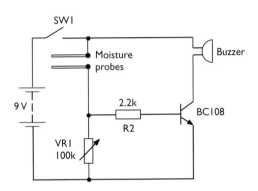

**Figure 5.66** *Moisture-sensing circuit*

## Block diagram

Circuits can be divided into three main building blocks. These are input, process and output.

**Input:** Moisture probes with the variable resistor. This is the sensor part of the circuit
**Process:** Transistor with its protective resistor
**Output:** Buzzer

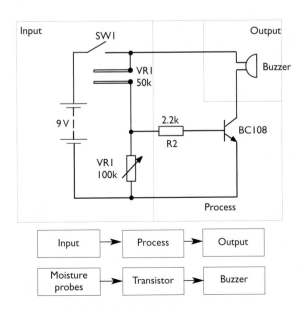

**Figure 5.67** *Block diagram for the moisture-sensing circuit*

## Notes on the moisture-sensing circuit bath level indicator

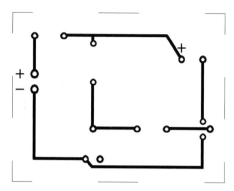

**Figure 5.68** *PCB for the moisture-sensing circuit*

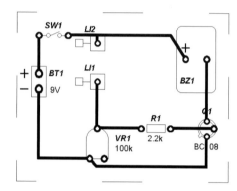

**Figure 5.69** *Silkscreen for the moisture-sensing circuit*

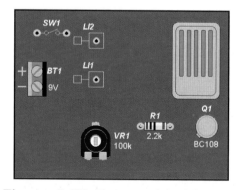

**Figure 5.70** *Top view of the PCB*

### Probes

These were made from 3 mm brass rod threaded at the end. Heat shrink cable was used to insulate the probes, leaving only that part of the rod that passed through the balls to act as conductors. Solder tags were used to secure the wires from the PCB to the probes. When the probes were placed in the top part of the circuit they worked well as sensors. The probes were held to the casing with 3 mm brass nuts and washers.

### Variable resistor

VR1 was a 100k miniature preset.

### Buzzer

It was found that most low-cost 6 volt buzzers worked fine but the PCB-mounted type was found to be more secure in the casing.

### Switch

SW1 was a SPST toggle switch.

### Transistor

The BC108 transistor was used as a simple high-speed electronic switch. As the buzzer tended to be on for short periods there were no real problems with the BC108. As the buzzer described only draws 25–30 mA, it could be on permanently without causing problems for the transistor which can handle 600 mV.

### Power supply

It was found that when the circuit was in a waiting state it consumed very little power from the battery.

### PCB

It is important to apply a coat of insulating varnish to the back of the PCB to protect it against moisture which might cause a short circuit.

### Components

1 × 100k horizontal miniature preset
1 × 2.2k resistor
1 × 9 V battery connector
1 × BC108 transistor
1 × board (73.6 mm × 55.9 mm)
1 × PCB-mounted buzzer
2 × 120 mm × 3 mm diameter brass rod

2 × 100 mm heat shrink cable
2 × 15 mm diameter plastic beads

# Darlington pair transistor

The Darlington pair is two transistors arranged so that the first one is used to turn on the second. By doing this you will have a circuit that is more responsive to small changes in the base current. This means that the output device will change from off to on more sharply.

The circuit shown in Figure 5.71 turns on a bulb when the temperature drops below a certain level. By using a Darlington pair the bulb will glow brightly with a slight decrease in temperature. If a single transistor were used then the bulb would increase in brightness more slowly as the temperature fell.

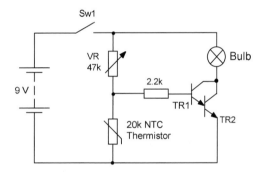

**Figure 5.71** *Darlington pair circuit*

## How it works

When the temperature falls, the resistance of the thermistor increases. This forces the electrons down to the base of the first transistor TR1. TR1 is a BC109 and was selected because it has a high gain (hFE) of 200. This means, for every electron coming in at the base leg, 200 will pass through the collector-emitter. The 200 electrons are then offered to the base leg of the second transistor TR2. This has a gain of 40. You now have a total gain hFE of 200 × 40 = 8000.

A gain of 8000 will enable the small flow of electrons (current) coming in at the base of TR1 to be amplified twice causing a large flow of electrons through TR2. It is this large flow that makes the bulb glow brightly.

TR2 is a BFY51. This was chosen because, while it has a small gain in relation to TR1, it allows a large current, up to 1 amp, to pass through its collector-emitter.

It is possible to buy Darlington pair transistors in a single package such as the TIP121 that has a gain of 1000 and will allow up to 5 amps to pass through its collector-emitter.

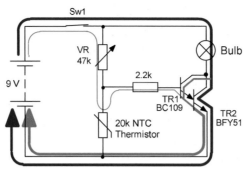

**Figure 5.72** *Flow of current through a Darlington pair circuit*

A cheaper option is the BCX38B which has a greater gain (hFE) of 2000. The drawback with the BCX38B is the amount of current it will allow to pass through it. This is only 800 mA. An advantage of using a single Darlington pair transistor is that the manufacturing of circuits is made easier. Also, the two transistors will be a matched pair for best results.

## Transistor base voltage

The voltage at the base of the BC109 required to turn on the Darlington pair transistors must be between 1.2 volts and 1.6 volts. This is due to the arrangement of both transistors. The first transistor requires a force of 0.6 volts for the electrons to penetrate its base layer. The base of the second transistor is fed from the emitter of the first and requires the same force of 0.6 volts for the electrons to penetrate the base layer, making a combined force of 1.2 volts.

# 555 timer circuits

The 555 timer is an integrated circuit (IC). It is used in electronic circuits when a precise timing period is required. Circuits incorporating the 555 IC will be consistently accurate. However, the maximum practical time period for these circuits will be 20–25 minutes. If timing periods greater than this are attempted you will find that the resistors and capacitors you require become very high values and the poor tolerances of the large value capacitors will result in inaccurate timing periods.

## Pin layout and functions

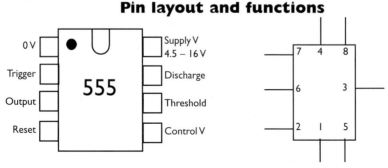

**Figure 5.73** *555 pin layout and functions*

**Figure 5.74** *Graphic symbol for a 555 timer*

The 555 IC is an eight-pin dual-in-line (DIL) IC. Each pin has a precise function to perform. The pin layout can be seen in Figure 5.73 and the functions of the pins are:

1. Pin 1 is the zero volts.
2. Pin 2 is the trigger. When the voltage at this pin falls below ⅓ of the supply voltage the timing cycle will start.
3. Pin 3 is the output. When this pin is on it will give an output voltage close to the supply voltage.
4. Pin 4 is the reset and can be used to reset the timing period back to the start.
5. Pin 5 is the control voltage.
6. Pin 6 is the threshold. When the voltage at this pin reaches ⅔ of the supply voltage it will end the timing period.
7. Pin 7 is the discharge or drain.
8. Pin 8 is the supply voltage pin. Most 555 timers will operate in the range 4.5–16 V.

### 555 monostable/astable circuits

555 timers can be used in two main ways.

- In a monostable circuit. This is a circuit with one stable state, i.e. on or off. A 555 monostable circuit is one that turns on pin 3 for a set period of time before turning off and remaining off until pin 2 is pulled low again.
- In an astable circuit. Astable circuits continually change from off to on. A 555 astable circuit is one that continuously and automatically turns off and on pin 3 for set periods of time.

### 555 timer monostable

The 555 monostable circuit can be used when you want the output to come on for a period of time and then go off.

Figure 5.75 shows a picture of a tablet reminder project designed by a student for his elderly grandparent. The circuit incorporated a 555 monostable. To start the time period the push-to-make switch is pressed. This brings on an LED for the selected time. When the time is up the LED goes out.

The circuit diagram for the project is shown in Figure 5.76.

**Figure 5.75** *555 monostable circuit used in a tablet reminder project*

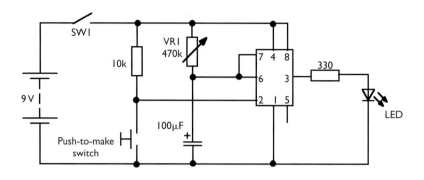

**Figure 5.76** *555 monostable circuit*

### How it works

To explain how it works it is worth considering the function of each of the pins.

### Adding power to the chip

All ICs require power to make them function. The 555 timer is no exception. The positive is connected to pin 8 and the negative to pin 1. Pin 4 is a reset and is not used in this case. However, you will still need to connect it to the positive rail to make the circuit work. This is shown in Figure 5.77.

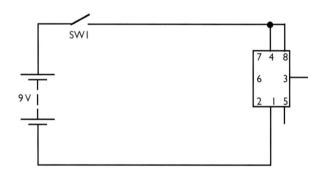

**Figure 5.77** *Connecting the power*

### Connecting the output. Pin 3

The objective of this circuit is to turn on an output device for a set period.

The output in this case is an LED with its 330 ohm current-limiting resistor. These are connected to pin 3. This is shown in Figure 5.78.

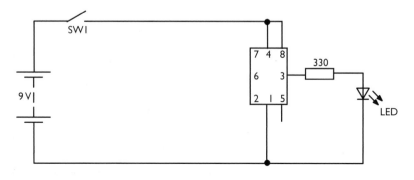

**Figure 5.78** *Connecting the output. Pin 3*

### Starting the timing cycle. Pin 2

When pin 2 is low (less than ⅓ of the supply voltage) the timing cycle will start. The most common way to do this is to connect a push-to-make switch between pin 2 and zero volts. Pin 2 must be tied high through a 10k resistor. This will keep the output low until you press the push-to-make switch. This is shown in Figure 5.79.

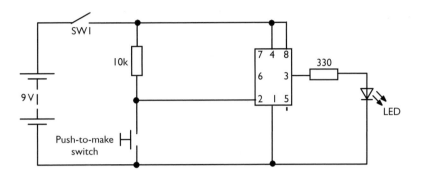

**Figure 5.79** *Starting the timing cycle. Pin 2*

### Achieving the on time. Pin 6

Once the timing cycle has started it should stop after the desired period has passed. To achieve this you will need to connect a resistor and capacitor to pin 6 as shown. The capacitor will fill at a rate determined by the size of the resistor. When the voltage present at pin 6 has reached ⅔ of the supply voltage the time on period will end. This is shown in Figure 5.80.

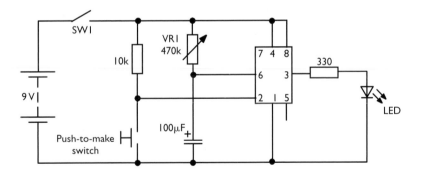

**Figure 5.80** *Achieving the on time. Pin 6*

### Discharging the capacitor. Pin 7

To enable the time cycle to be repeated, it will be necessary to discharge the capacitor through pin 7. This is shown in Figure 5.81.

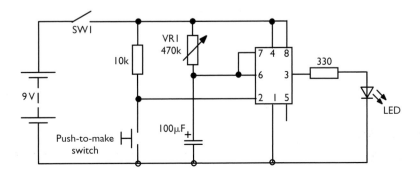

**Figure 5.81**

*Discharging the capacitor. Pin 7*

### Turning the output off for a time period

It is possible to have the output constantly on and then turn off for the time period. To do this, connect your output to the supply rail then down into pin 3.

Once the push-to-make switch is pressed the LED will turn off. This is shown in Figure 5.82.

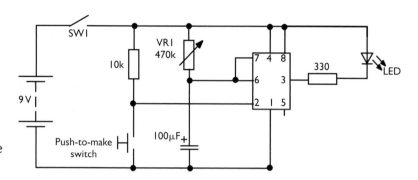

**Figure 5.82** *Turning the output off for a time period*

### Adding a reset

By connecting a push-to-make switch between pin 4 and the supply rail you can reset the 555 timer at any moment in its cycle.

The addition of a reset switch is shown in Figure 5.83. If no reset switch is required, pin 4 must be connected to the supply rail to ensure that the 555 timer resets itself at the end of a timing period.

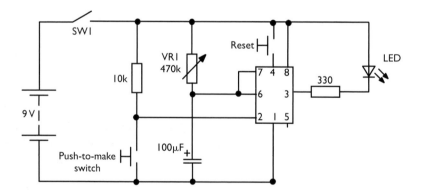

**Figure 5.83** *Adding a reset switch. Pin 4*

### Connecting output devices

If the output device you are connecting to the 555 timer requires a large amount of current the 555 will be unable to operate it directly. The 555, like most ICs, is very good at giving you an output voltage close to the supply voltage but the current will be very small. For outputs other than LEDs and other small current devices you will need to amplify the output current.

The simplest way to amplify the output current is to add a transistor to the circuit and use this to drive your output device. An example of this is shown in Figure 5.84.

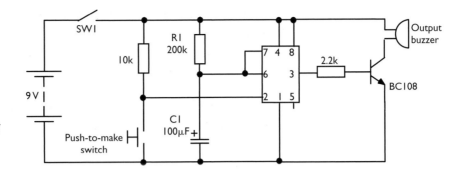

**Figure 5.84** *Amplifying the output current using a transistor*

### Calculating T

Formula for calculating the length of time the LED is on:

$T = R1 \times C1$ seconds

After the 555 has been triggered by pressing the push-to-make switch the buzzer will come on. As $T = R1 \times C1$ then time on will depend on the value of these two components.

The value of $R1$ is given in ohms and the value of $C1$ in farads. If you consider the circuit in Figure 5.84 then:

$R1 = 200\,000$ (200k)
$C1 = 0.0001$ (100 μF)

$T$ can be found by: $T = R1 \times C1$ seconds
$$T = 200\,000 \times 0.0001$$
$$T = 20 \text{ seconds}$$

### 555 astable timer

A 555 astable circuit is one where the output turns on and off continuously.

In this circuit, pin 2 the trigger and pin 6 the threshold are connected together. When the voltage at pin 2 is less than ⅓ of the supply, the output will come on. This will remain on until the voltage present at pin 6 is just greater than ⅔ the supply voltage. At this moment the output will turn off. This happens repeatedly until the circuit is turned off at SW1.

#### How it works

The current flows from the battery down through R1 + R2 to fill the capacitor. At this point the output will be on. Pin 6 will wait until the charge in the capacitor is just greater than 6 volts at which point it turns the output at pin 3 off. It is at this moment the capacitor starts to drain through pin 7 and pin 1. The rate of drain is determined by the value of C1 and R2. Pin 2 is constantly reading the voltage in the capacitor. When the voltage falls below ⅓ of the supply voltage the output at pin 3 will come back on. The circuit is shown in Figure 5.85.

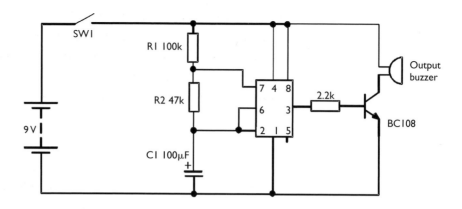

**Figure 5.85** *555 astable timer circuit*

## Waveform for the 555 astable

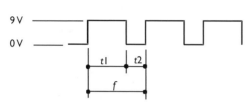

**Figure 5.86** *555 astable timer frequency*

The output waveform for a 555 astable circuit is square wave.

In Figure 5.86, $t1$ will be the time on and $t2$ the time off. $t1 + t2 = f$, the frequency in Hz.

## Calculating frequency

Formula for calculating the frequency:

$$f = t1 + t2$$

$$t1 = 0.7 \times (R1 + R2) \times C1$$

$$t2 = 0.7 \times R2 \times C1$$

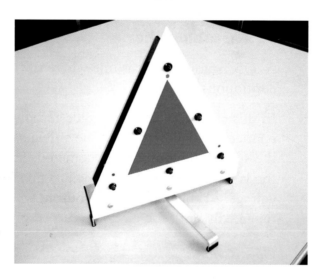

**Figure 5.87** *A 555 astable circuit is used to pulse the LEDs on a warning triangle*

## Notes on 555 timer circuits

There are a number of different types of 555 ICs on the market. The most commonly used is the CMOS ICM7555 type, as they don't draw nearly as much current as the older NE555 type. This should make your battery last longer.

## Accuracy

The problem will be in calculating the timing cycle. The standard resistor will have a 2–5% tolerance while capacitor tolerances could be as poor as 50%. Electrolytic capacitors have the poorest tolerances of all and these tend to be what most students use for long time delays. This makes precise calculations difficult. However once you have your 555 built and have it running the time cycle will be constant every time.

# Ohm's law

Sometimes it is important to know how much current is flowing in your circuit. Too little and the circuit may not work. Too much and the circuit may be damaged. You may wish to know the resistance in the circuit or at a certain point in the circuit. Or you may wish to know the voltage difference at a certain point in your circuit.

If you know two of the three variables resistance, voltage difference or current it is possible to calculate the remaining one. You can do this by using **Ohm's law**.

Ohm's law states that:

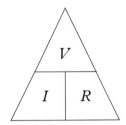

$$\text{the resistance in ohms} = \frac{\text{voltage difference in volts}}{\text{current in amps}}$$

or simply:

$$R = \frac{V}{I} \text{ or } V = I \times R \text{ or } I = \frac{V}{R}$$

# Operational amplifier as a comparator

Operational amplifiers, or op amps as they are called, are ICs used to amplify small differences in voltage. The IC is housed in an 8-pin DIL package (DIL stands for dual-in-line) and because of their wide use in a whole range of applications, millions are produced every year. This mass production makes the operational amplifier a relatively low cost and useful component.

This section considers the op amp as a sensing comparator in control circuits.

There are a number of different makes and types of op amps to choose from. Experience has shown that the CA3140 is a good choice when the op amp has to function as a comparator. Therefore the CA3140 will be used throughout this chapter.

Coming to terms with the CA3140 op amp as a comparator should be relatively straightforward. Its main function is to compare the voltage at pins 2 and 3 and provide the relative

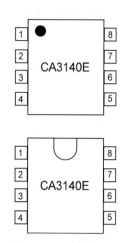

**Figure 5.88**

*Identifying pin 1*

**Figure 5.89** *Graphic symbol for an op amp*

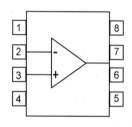

**Figure 5.90** *Package diagram*

output. When pin 2 is higher than pin 3 the output is low but if pin 3 is the highest then the output is high.

## Identifying the CA3140

The CA3140 is housed in an 8-pin DIL package. Pin number one is beside the small dot at the top of the package or at the top left corner if the package has a U-shaped cut-out. The identification of pin 1 is shown in Figure 5.88.

## Graphic symbol for an op amp

This is a small triangle with the two inputs and output drawn on. This is shown in Figure 5.89.

## Package diagrams

Sometimes you may see the package with the symbol drawn on top. This can be helpful to you when identifying the pin layout for a specific IC. This is shown in Figure 5.90.

## Pin identification

Pin 1: Offset null (not required for this module)
Pin 2: Inverting output (−)
Pin 3: Non-inverting input (+)
Pin 4: Negative
Pin 5: Offset null (not required for this module)
Pin 6: Output
Pin 7: Positive supply
Pin 8: Not connected
Pins 1, 5, 8 are not used

## Light-sensing circuit

The circuit in Figure 5.91 shows an op amp used to turn on a bulb when there is a small change in the amount of light falling on the LDR.

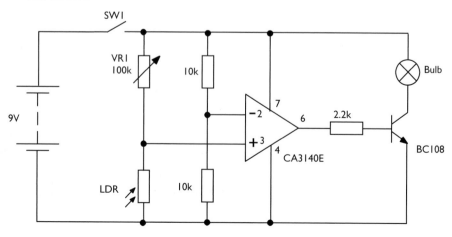

**Figure 5.91** *Light-sensing circuit*

### Designing the op amp circuit shown in Figure 5.91

#### Connecting the output

As with all op amp ICs, the objective is to turn on an output. The CA3140E has pin 6 as its output (Figure 5.92).

When the output is high (on) the voltage will be very close to the supply voltage, but as with most ICs the current will be small. The purpose of the BC108 transistor is to amplify the output current.

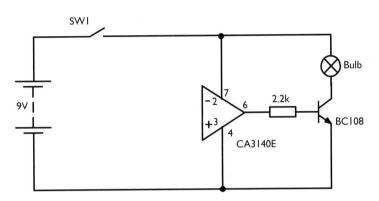

**Figure 5.92** *Output pin 6*

#### Adding the reference voltage to pin 2

When the op amp is being used as a comparator you will need to set a reference voltage at either pin 2 or pin 3. In this example, pin 2 has been set as the reference voltage.

The two 10k resistors act as a potential divider. As both resistors are the same value then the voltage drop across each will be 4.5 V resulting in 4.5 V being present at pin 2. This is referred to as the reference voltage and is shown in Figure 5.93.

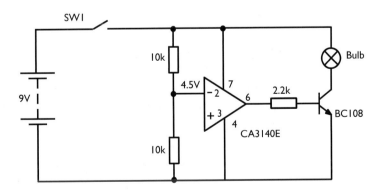

**Figure 5.93** *Setting the reference voltage at 4.5 V*

#### Adding the sensor to the op amp circuit

VR1 and the LDR provide the second potential divider. VR1 is set so that the voltage at pin 3 is just below that of pin 2. This is shown in Figure 5.94. A slight increase in resistance at the LDR due to falling light levels will increase the voltage at pin 3. When this is higher than 4.5 V, pin 6 will go high, turning on the output.

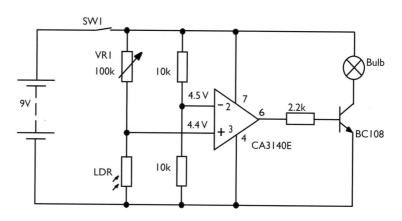

**Figure 5.94** *Adding the sensor*

### Positioning the output device

When the bulb is connected to the circuit it will come on when pin 6 is high.

It is good practice to connect your output device between the emitter and negative rail as the op amp may also be on when the output is low. This is due to the internal structure of the op amp which enables pin 6 to conduct via pin 4 to the negative rail when no output signal is present at pin 6. This is shown in Figure 5.95.

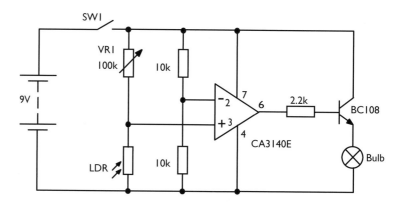

**Figure 5.95** *Placing the output below the transistor*

### Frost alarm circuit

In this circuit a 15k NTC thermistor and 47k variable resistor form the sensing part of the circuit. As the temperature falls the resistance of the thermistor rises, increasing the voltage at pin 3. When this rises above the voltage present at pin 2 the buzzer will sound (Figure 5.96).

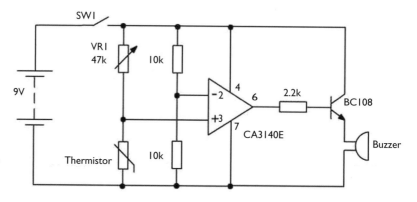

**Figure 5.96** *Frost alarm circuit*

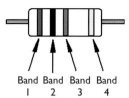
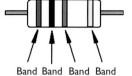

Band Band Band Band
1    2    3    4

**Figure 5.97**

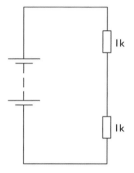

**Figure 5.98**

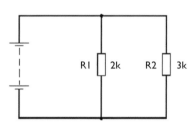

**Figure 5.99**

**Figure 5.100**

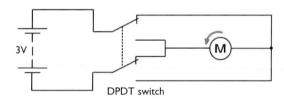

**Figure 5.101** *BC108*
*transistor*

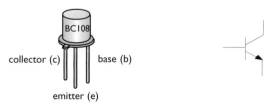

### Questions on electronics

1 Coloured bands are used on resistors.
   a What is the function of these bands?
   b What is the value of the resistor shown in Figure 5.97?

2 Write down the colour codes for the following resistors:
   a 1000 ohms
   b 10 000 ohms
   c 2200 ohms
   d 3.3 k ohms.

3 Figure 5.98 shows two resistors.
   a Are these resistors in series or parallel?
   b Calculate the total resistance of the two resistors.

4 Figure 5.99 shows two resistors.
   a Are these resistors in series or parallel?
   b Calculate the total resistance of the two resistors.

5 Figures 5.9 to 5.11 (pages 130–131) show three different types of switches and their symbols.
   a Write down the name of each switch.
   b What do the initials SPST and SPDT mean?

6 Figure 5.100 shows a motor-reversing circuit with the motor turning anti-clockwise.

   3V

   DPDT switch

   a Copy out this circuit.
   b With reference to the polarity of the circuit, explain how the motor could be made to turn clockwise.

7 Figure 5.101 shows a BC108 transistor.

   collector (c)   base (b)

   emitter (e)

   Copy out the symbol and correctly label the three legs: collector, base and emitter.

8 Figure 5.102 shows an electronic sensing circuit.

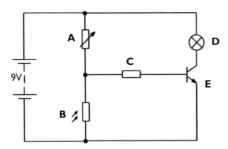

**Figure 5.102**

a Name the components labelled A, B, C, D, E.

b State the function of the components labelled A, B, C, D, E.

c This circuit can be divided into three main building blocks: input, process and output. Copy out the circuit and identify these three building blocks.

d Suggest a possible application for this circuit.

e Explain how the circuit works.

f What would happen if components A and B changed places?

9 Figure 5.103 shows a basic timing circuit.

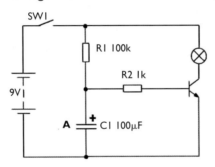

**Figure 5.103**

a Name the component labelled A.

b With reference to this circuit, write down the function of component A.

c Explain how the circuit works.

10 Figure 5.104 is a drawing of a thyristor.
Copy out the symbol and correctly label the three legs: anode, cathode and gate.

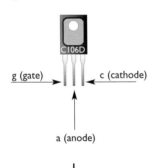

g (gate)     c (cathode)

a (anode)

Symbol

**Figure 5.104** *Thyristor*

11 Figure 5.105 shows a circuit for a burglar alarm.

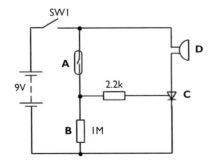

**Figure 5.105**

a Name the components labelled A, B, C, D.

b State the function of the components labelled A, B, C, D.

c Component C enables this circuit to latch. What does the term latch mean?

d Once the circuit has latched it will have to be reset. Explain how you would reset the latched circuit.

12 The incomplete circuit shown in Figure 5.106 is part of a frost alarm circuit.

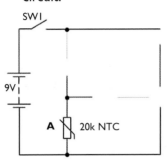

**Figure 5.106**

a Name the component labelled A.

b With reference to component A, what do the letters NTC stand for?

c Complete the circuit diagram so that a buzzer would sound when the temperature falls to freezing.

d Explain how your completed circuit works.

# CHAPTER SIX

**Mechanisms**

## Introduction

A wheel is a round disc that rotates on an axle. The axle is usually an **interference fit** to the wheel. In this case the wheel and axle move as one. If the centre of the wheel is a **clearance fit** then it will rotate on the axle. In this case it is common practice to use a bearing to reduce friction.

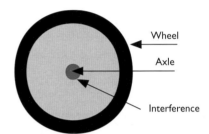

**Figure 6.1** *Wheel and axle*

If a cyclist moves down the road in a straight line this is called linear motion. At the same time the wheels on the bicycle will turn and this is called rotary motion (Figure 6.2).

**Figure 6.2** *Rotary and linear motion*

## Cams

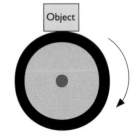

**Figure 6.3** *Rotating wheel*

Cams are mechanisms that change one type of motion into another. The two types of motion are:

- rotary
- reciprocating.

If an object is placed on a turning wheel it will rub on its outer edge but will not go up and down (Figure 6.3). However, if an object is placed on top of a rotating cam it will rise and fall. Cams also change rotary motion to reciprocating motion.

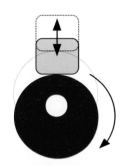

**Figure 6.4** *Plate cam*

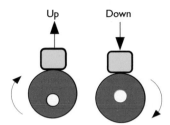

**Figure 6.5** *Circular cam*

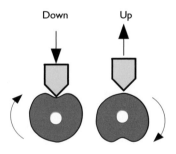

**Figure 6.6** *Heart-shaped cam*

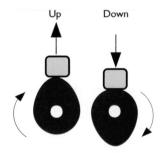

**Figure 6.7** *Pear-shaped cam*

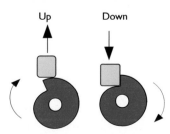

**Figure 6.8** *Snail cam*

Most cams are wheel-shaped flat discs with a bump on them or with the axle positioned off-centre. These are called **plate cams** (Figure 6.4). Plate cams have rotary motion but the object resting on the cam moves up and down in reciprocating motion.

Cams are usually made from hardened steel but small plastic and wooden cams can be used if wear is not going to be a problem.

## Types of cams

These are the four main types of cam used in technological products:

- circular or eccentric cam
- heart-shaped cam
- pear-shaped cam
- snail cam.

**Circular cams** cause the follower to rise and fall at a uniform rate (Figure 6.5).

**Heart-shaped cams** cause the follower to rise to a height which remains constant until the follower reaches the groove, where it falls sharply at a uniform rate before rising again (Figure 6.6).

**Pear-shaped cams** cause the follower to rise rapidly as it comes into contact with the bump part of the cam. This is shown in Figure 6.7. The rise and fall of the follower will happen with equal speed. For half of the revolution of the cam the follower does not move. This is known as dwell.

**Snail cams** cause the follower to rise slowly then fall sharply into the step. This is shown in Figure 6.8.

## Cam followers

The part that rests on the cam and moves up and down is called the follower (Figure 6.9).

Followers can be made from a range of materials; wood, plastic and mild steel are popular for small products where wear is not a design consideration. When wear must be avoided then the follower would be made from hardened steel.

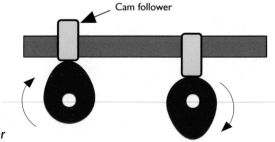

**Figure 6.9** *Cam follower*

There are three main types of followers used with cams:

- flat follower
- knife follower
- roller follower.

**Flat followers** have a large flat surface at the base of the follower. This surface should be hardened steel to prevent wear. In Figure 6.10 the flat follower is resting on a pear-shaped cam. The follower is in reciprocating motion while the plate cam is in rotary motion.

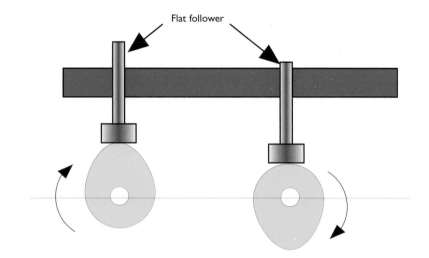

**Figure 6.10** *Flat follower resting on a pear-shaped cam*

**Roller followers** are followers with a small roller bearing at the end. These are used to reduce friction and wear between the follower and the cam. This is shown in Figure 6.11.

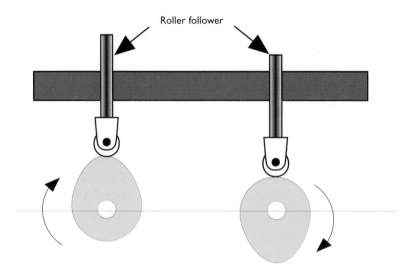

**Figure 6.11** *Roller follower sitting on a pear-shaped cam*

**Knife followers** are mainly used with heart-shaped cams. They have a hardened steel tip and are designed to go into tight curves on the edge of the cams. This is shown in Figure 6.12.

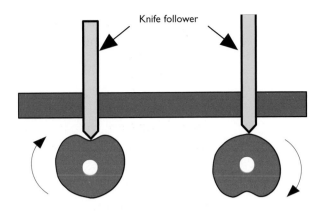

Knife follower

**Figure 6.12** *Knife follower resting on a heart-shaped cam*

| Example | **Cam-operated toy** |
| --- | --- |

### Design situation

As part of GCSE coursework a student wished to design an educational toy for a younger brother. Early in the investigation it was decided to include movement in the toy to make it more appealing.

**Figure 6.13** *Cam toy*

### Solution

The final solution was the cam-operated dog shown in Figure 6.13.

### How it works

As the crank (handle) is turned, the cam on the bottom axle moves round causing the dog's mouth to open and close. Cams are commonly used in this way when movement in one part of the mechanism causes the required movement in another part. Leaving the mechanism open meant the child was able to see how the project worked.

Knowledge of cams and how they work is important in the design and manufacture of this type of product. The following section will explain how the cam and follower were made.

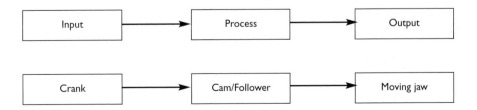

| Input | Process | Output |
| --- | --- | --- |

| Crank | Cam/Follower | Moving jaw |
| --- | --- | --- |

As the crank is turned the cam rotates, making the follower rise and fall. As the follower rises the mouth opens and as it falls the mouth closes. Figures 6.14 and 6.15 show the operation of the cam.

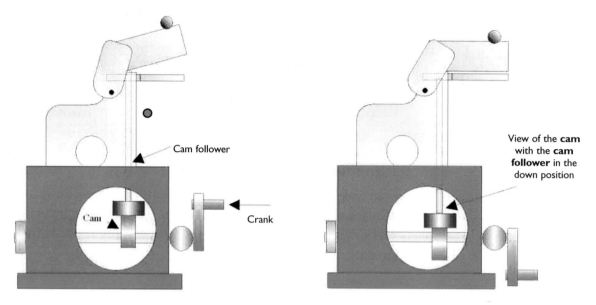

**Figure 6.14** *Cam in the raised position*          **Figure 6.15** *Cam in the down position*

The circular cam was made from a 20 mm beech dowel drilled off-centre. The follower was made from 3 mm and 20 mm beech dowels glued to form a flat follower. Figures 6.16 and 6.17 show the parts of the mechanism.

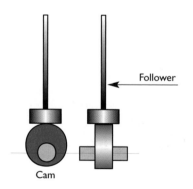

**Figure 6.16** *Cam and flat follower*

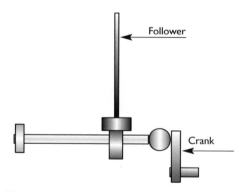

**Figure 6.17** *Cam–flat follower–crank*

# Levers

The lever is possibly the simplest of all mechanisms to understand. It is used in most machines from the simple builder's crowbar to the handle on a door. One of its functions is to enable a small effort to move a large load.

If you want to lift a heavy box you could place a bar or plank under one edge and push down to make the heavy box rise up.

The man in Figure 6.18 is using a bar to lift the box. This bar is called a **lever**. The box is called the **load**.

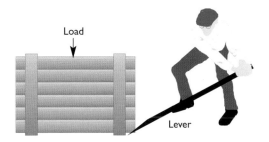

**Figure 6.18** *Lifting a heavy object (the load)*

If you try this you will discover that you need to place a small object like a stone or another piece of wood under your lever to make it work. This is called the **fulcrum** for the lever and is shown in Figure 6.19.

When you push down on the lever this is called the **effort** (Figure 6.20). You should also discover that the longer the lever is from the fulcrum, the less effort you will need to lift the box.

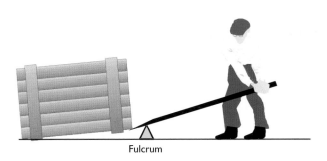

**Figure 6.19** *Fulcrum under the lever*

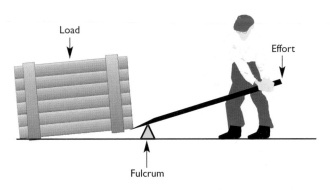

**Figure 6.20** *The effort is being applied near the end of the lever*

## Classes of lever

There are three main types of levers called classes of lever. These are called class 1, class 2 and class 3 levers.

The type of lever will depend on the positioning of the three parts of the lever: fulcrum, load and effort.

### Class 1 lever

This lever has its fulcrum between the load and the effort. It is the most common type of lever (Figure 6.21).

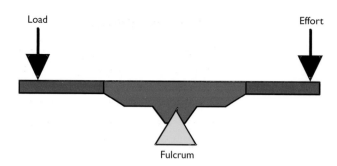

**Figure 6.21** *The see-saw is a class 1 lever*

### Class 2 lever

Class 2 levers have the fulcrum at one end, the effort at the other and the load in between.

A garden wheelbarrow with rubble in it is a class 2 lever. The axle at the front of the barrow is the fulcrum point, the load is the weight of the wheelbarrow plus its contents, acting downwards, and the effort is made by the person pulling upwards on the handles (Figure 6.22).

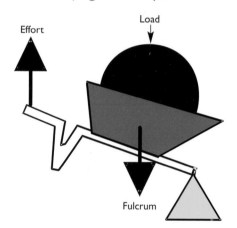

**Figure 6.22** *The wheelbarrow is a class 2 lever*

### Class 3 lever

This is a lever where the fulcrum is at one end, the load at the other end and the effort in between.

A fishing rod is an example of a class 3 lever. The person fishing holds the rod at one end (fulcrum), the weight of the fish is at the other end (load) and the effort is the pulling on the rod to lift the fish out of the water (Figure 6.23).

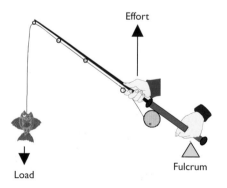

**Figure 6.23** *The fishing rod is a class 3 lever*

## Drawing levers

Rather than making a drawing of a lever every time, you can draw a symbol to represent it.

The screwdriver being used to open a tin shown in Figure 6.24 is a class 1 lever. If you wanted to draw this as a symbol it would look like Figure 6.25.

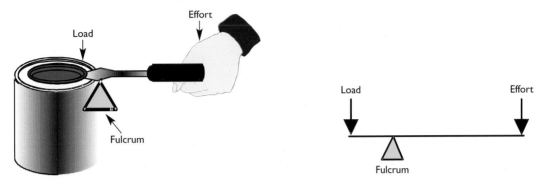

**Figure 6.24** *Lever used to remove a lid*

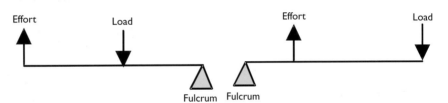

**Figure 6.25** *Class 1 lever*

Graphical symbols for class 2 and class 3 levers are shown in Figures 6.26 and 6.27.

**Figure 6.26** *Class 2 lever*      **Figure 6.27** *Class 3 lever*

A knowledge and understanding of levers can be very useful when designing products. The different classes of levers and the mechanical advantage they can provide will give an insight into levers and what they can do.

| Example | Paint tin lid remover |
|---------|----------------------|

### Design situation

A student's father worked as a painter. Every day the father had the problem of opening tins of paint safely.

### Solution

The final solution was a lever that has a hole in one end for fixing it to a keyring. In this way it also acted as a key fob.

**Figure 6.28** *Opening a tin of paint*

### How it works

The narrow end slides under the lid. The back edge rests on the rim of the tin. When you apply a downward force to the end of the tin opener the tip forces the lid up out of the tin (Figure 6.29).

**175**

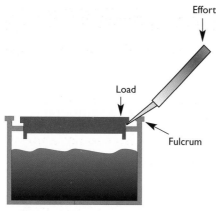

**Figure 6.29** *Paint tin opener*

## Making the project

Cut a piece of 12 mm wide by 3 mm thick mild steel 100 mm long.

### Marking out

Mark a line 30 mm from the end and file the area to form a taper (Figure 6.30).

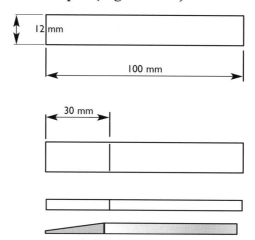

**Figure 6.30** *Marking out*

### Forming the taper

Hold the work in the vice and file to shape. Then, using a hammer, bend the tapered end to form a 30° slope (Figure 6.31).

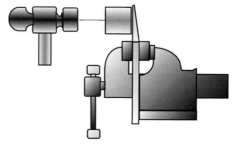

**Figure 6.31** *Bending the lever*

### Finishing the taper

The taper is now finished with emery cloth.

### Finishing

Mask the taper and paint the handle or, better still, if you have access to a plastic fluidisation tank the project can be heated and dipped to form a plastic-coated handle.

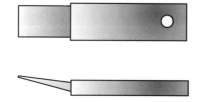

**Figure 6.32** *The finished project*

| **Projects incorporating levers and linkages**

It is difficult to think of mechanism projects that do not include linkages and levers.

The following design solutions are the work of two students who were given the brief of 'design an interesting coat-hook that would encourage a younger brother or sister to hang up their coat'. As a starting point they were asked to consider a basic coat-hook (Figure 6.33).

The two solutions shown are a dog that raises its ears (Figure 6.34) and a clown that raises its arms (Figure 6.35). Both are operated by placing a coat on the hook.

**Figure 6.33** *Basic coat-hook*

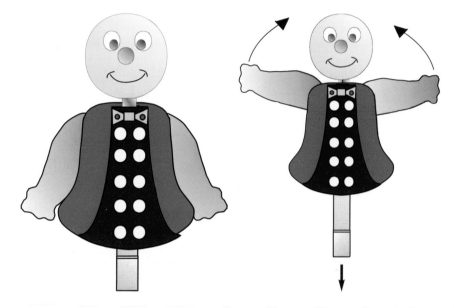

**Figure 6.35** *Clown coat-hook*

**Figure 6.34** *Dog with moving ears*

Each of the designs incorporate levers and linkages to create movement. The arms and ears are the levers. A piece of string fixed to the ends of the levers acts as a linkage between the levers and the metal coat-hook. When the coat-hook is pulled down, the pivoted arms move down at the top, causing the lower arm to move up with a large movement (Figure 6.36).

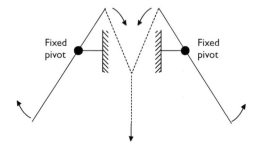

**Figure 6.36** *Symbol diagram of the mechanism*

### Making the coat-hook

Both designs used the same principle of arms or ears at the side that rise when a coat is placed on the hook.

**Figure 6.37** *The body*

### Body

The design used two 6 mm MDF squares for the body. Two 3 mm holes were drilled for the fixed pivots as shown in Figure 6.37.

### Aluminium hook

The hook was made from 12 mm by 3 mm aluminium that had all the sharp edges filed off.

### Guide blocks

The two guide blocks were made from 8 mm square pine cut to a length of 35 mm. The top block was 12 mm long (Figure 6.38).

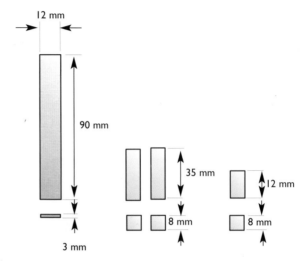

**Figure 6.38** *The hook and guide blocks*

### Locating the hook

By holding the aluminium bar on the centre line the two guide-blocks were glued in place, making sure that the bar would slide between them (Figure 6.39).

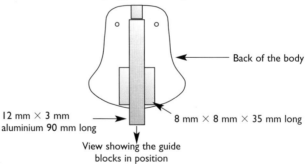

**Figure 6.39** *Locating the hook*

### Bending the hook

The aluminium hook was bent using the cold bending technique, around a 25 mm metal bar (Figure 6.40).

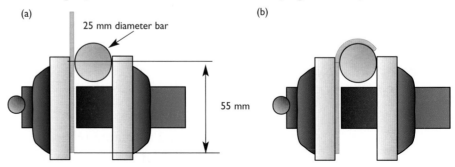

**Figure 6.40** *Plan view of the vice*

### Loose pivot

A 3 mm hole was drilled in the hook, close to the end of the bar, and countersunk on both sides (Figure 6.41). This was to take the linkages.

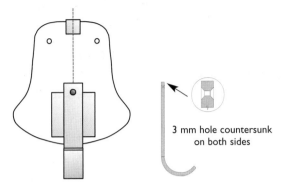

**Figure 6.41** *The loose pivot*

### Moving parts

Figure 6.42 shows the blanks from which the two moving parts were to be formed. Both had 3.5 mm clearance holes drilled in one end. These were to be the clearance holes for the fixed pivots. Figure 6.43 shows how these blanks are fixed to the backboard.

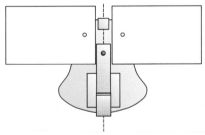

**Figure 6.42** *The moving parts are made from these blanks*

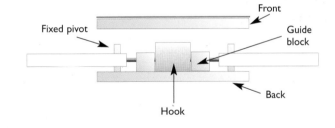

**Figure 6.43** *View of the top edge of the backboard showing the position of the fixed pivots, hook and guide blocks*

### Fixing the linkage

For ease of construction, nylon string was used as the linkage.

A hole was drilled in the top of the levers so that a downward pull would cause the ears to rise. The linkage was passed through the hole in the hook before fixing to the levers.

Two 3 mm dowel rods were glued in with the linkages to give a permanent fixing.

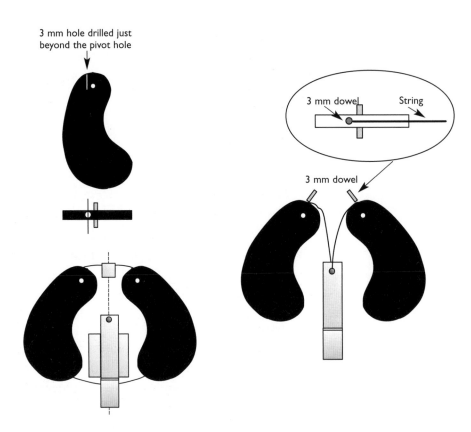

3 mm hole drilled just beyond the pivot hole

3 mm dowel — String

3 mm dowel

**Figure 6.44** *Fixing the string*

The same technique for fixing the string was used with both designs.

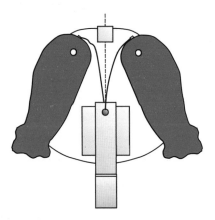

**Figure 6.45** *Assembled clown mechanism*

# Belts and pulleys

Belts and pulleys are used in machines. There are several good reasons for using belts and pulleys when designing products containing mechanisms:

- Belts and pulleys transfer motion from one part of the machine to another.
- They can be used to increase or decrease the relative speeds of two shafts.
- Safety: if the load on the drive belt is too great it can slip on the pulley without causing damage to the machine or operator.

● It is easy to change direction between two pulleys using a belt.

The following are some examples of belts and pulleys used in products in the home and school.

### Pedestal drill

Type of belt: vee

Vee belts are often used on pedestal drills. This can be a major safety feature as the belt can slip on the pulley if the drill bit gets stuck during drilling. If you have the work held firmly in a vice then the slipping action can help prevent you getting injured.

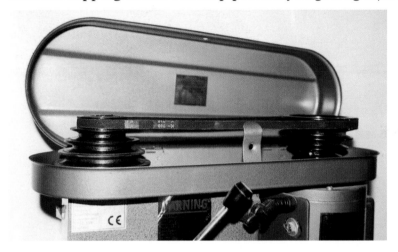

**Figure 6.46** *Vee belt used on a pedestal drill*

### Washing machine

Type of belt: vee or flat

An electric motor is the drive source for a washing machine. The drive between motor and drum is a belt and pulley. This has the advantage that if the machine is overloaded or clothes get caught between the drums then the belt can slip without damaging the machine.

**Figure 6.47** *Flat belt used on a washing machine*

### Vacuum cleaner

Type of belt: round or flat

A vacuum cleaner will use either a round or flat belt to transmit the drive from the motor to the sweeping brushes.

The round belt used on some vacuum cleaners enables the designer to mount the motor at 90° to the brushes. Also, if the brushes catch on the carpet the belt can slip, preventing the carpet and cleaner from being damaged.

**Figure 6.48** *Vacuum cleaner drive belt*

## Drawing belts and pulleys

### Graphical symbol

The graphical symbol for a belt and pulley is shown in Figure 6.49. The centre of the shaft or axle is where the two centre lines in the circles cross.

### Pulley direction

The arrows indicate the direction of the belt and the circles indicate the pulleys.

In Figure 6.49 both pulleys are turning clockwise.

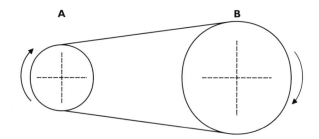

**Figure 6.49** *Symbol for a belt and pulley*

In Figure 6.50, pulley A is turning clockwise while pulley B is turning anti-clockwise. Crossover is only possible with a round belt and pulley system. Flat belts were used extensively in steam-powered agricultural and industrial machinery.

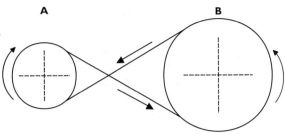

**Figure 6.50** *Pulleys turning in opposite directions*

## Types of belt

### Round belts

Round belts are round in section. They are usually found on light machines where a small drive force is required or when the belt has to turn through 90°.

Vacuum cleaners and CD players often use round belts.

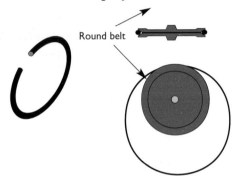

**Figure 6.51** *Round belt*

One of the main advantages of the round belt is its ability to twist between shafts that are at 90° to one another. Figure 6.52 shows how a vertical shaft can be made to turn a horizontal shaft, simply by allowing a round belt to pass over the two pulleys.

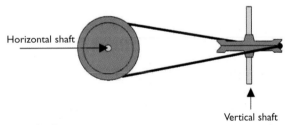

**Figure 6.52** *Shafts at 90°*

### Vee belts

With the vee belt you have a larger area of the belt in contact with the pulley. This increases the friction between the two and enables you to have a greater drive force before the belt starts to slip (Figure 6.53).

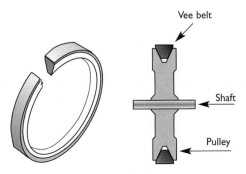

**Figure 6.53** *Vee belt*

## Shaft speed

If pulleys of different diameters are placed on two shafts then the shafts can be made to turn at different speeds. The pulley that provides the power is called the **driver pulley**, while the one on the output shaft is the **driven pulley**. In Figure 6.54 the driver pulley is smaller than the driven pulley. In this case the driver pulley at the motor (10 mm diameter) will have to turn four revolutions before the driven pulley (40 mm diameter) completes one revolution.

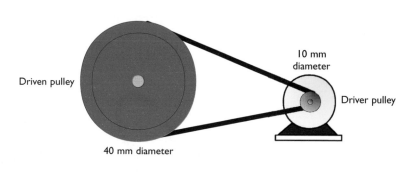

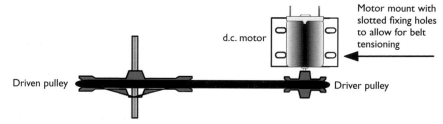

**Figure 6.54** *Shaft speed*

## Stepped cone pulleys

If pulleys of different diameters are placed on the same shaft then the shaft can be made to turn at different speeds. In the example shown in Figure 6.55 a four-stepped cone pulley system is used. An electric motor is the power source. The pulleys on the shaft of the electric motor will be the driver pulleys.

A stepped cone pulley can be found on pedestal drills. It is used to change the speed of the output shaft. By moving the vee belt downward on the pulleys you will make the output shaft run more slowly.

When the vee belt is on the top pulleys the output shaft is at its maximum speed (Figure 6.55).

When the vee belt is on the bottom two pulleys the output shaft is at its slowest speed (Figure 6.56).

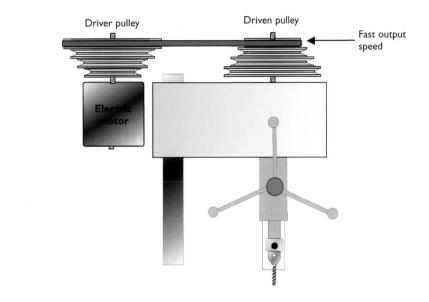

**Figure 6.55** *Pedestal drill*

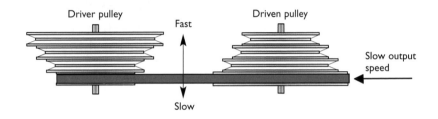

**Figure 6.56** *Changing speed*

## Tensioning belts using motor mounts

When a belt is passed around a pulley you must make sure it is tight. This is called applying tension. The simplest method of doing this is to mount the motor so that it can slide to increase the tension.

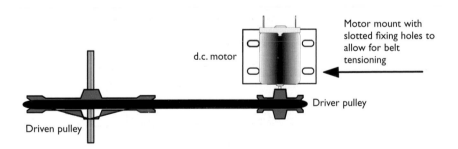

**Figure 6.57** *Motor mounts*

# Gears

Gears are designed to transmit motion from one shaft to another. Unlike belts and pulleys, which enable the belt to slip on the pulley, gears provide precise non-slip motion between shafts.

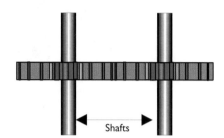

**Figure 6.58** *Gears transmit motion between shafts*

Gears are wheels that have teeth on the outer edge. These teeth are designed to fit together. When two or more gears fit correctly we call this **meshing** (Figure 6.59).

**Figure 6.59** *Meshed gears*

When two or more gears mesh this is called a **gear train**. Two or more gears meshed side by side is called a simple gear train (Figure 6.60).

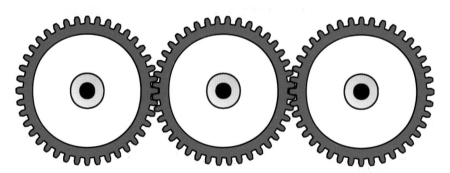

**Figure 6.60** *Simple gear train using three gears*

## Spur gears

Gears like those shown in Figure 6.61 which connect parallel shafts are called spur gears. The smaller wheel is called the pinion. The larger is called the gear wheel.

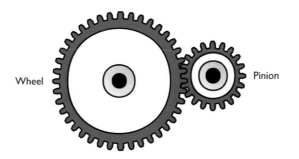

**Figure 6.61** *Spur gears*

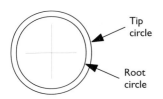

**Figure 6.62** *Graphical symbol for a gear wheel*

## Drawing gears

The graphical symbol for a gear is two circles with a centre cross where the centre of the shaft would be. The outer circle represents the tip of the tooth. The inner circle represents the bottom or root of the tooth (Figure 6.62).

When two or more gears mesh then the symbols overlap so that the tip circle of one gear touches the root circle of the adjoining gear. The graphical symbol is shown in Figure 6.63.

As well as showing the front view of the gears it is sometimes necessary to show gears on their edge. The graphical symbol for meshed gears on their edge forming a simple gear train is shown in Figure 6.64.

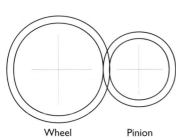

**Figure 6.63** *Meshed spur gears*

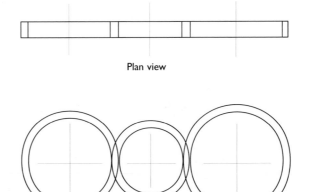

**Figure 6.64** *Symbol for three meshed gears viewed from the front and from the top (plan view)*

## Direction of gears

When you have two gears meshed together, one gear will go clockwise while the other goes anti-clockwise. In the example shown in Figure 6.65, the driver gear is turning anti-clockwise. This makes the driven gear turn clockwise.

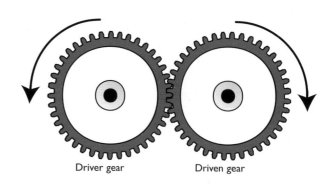

**Figure 6.65** *Direction of rotation*

Driver gear    Driven gear

If you have three gears in the train then the first and last gear will turn in the same direction. In Figure 6.66 the yellow and red gears are turning in the same direction. The centre gear is called an **idler gear**.

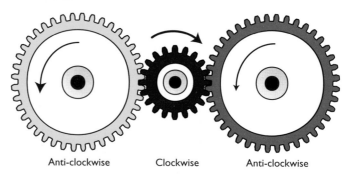

**Figure 6.66** *Changing direction using an idler gear*

Anti-clockwise    Clockwise    Anti-clockwise

## Calculating the gear ratio

Sometimes you will need to know how fast the driven gear is turning in relation to the driver gear. This is called calculating the gear ratio.

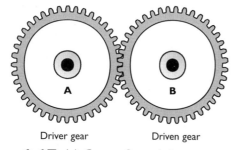

Driver gear    Driven gear

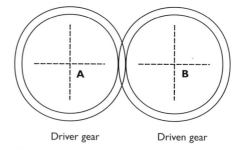

Driver gear    Driven gear

**Figure 6.67** *(a) Gears of equal size*        *(b) Symbol for the two gears*

If you consider the two gears in Figure 6.67, gear A has 40 teeth and gear B has 40 teeth. If gear A turns through one revolution gear B will also turn through one revolution. To calculate the gear ratio we use the formula:

$$\text{Gear ratio} = \frac{\text{number of teeth in the driven gear}}{\text{number of teeth in the driver gear}} = \frac{40}{40} = \frac{1}{1}$$

Gear ratio = 1:1

If you change the size of the driver gear to 20 teeth, as shown in Figure 6.68, then you will change the speed of the driven gear. This can be calculated using the same formula.

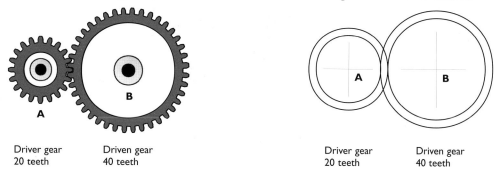

Driver gear          Driven gear                    Driver gear          Driven gear
20 teeth             40 teeth                       20 teeth             40 teeth

**Figure 6.68** *(a) Different size of gears*                  *(b) Symbol for unequal gears*

$$\text{Gear ratio} = \frac{\text{number of teeth in the driven gear}}{\text{number of teeth in the driver gear}} = \frac{40}{20} = \frac{2}{1}$$

Gear ratio  = 2:1

The driver gear will now turn twice for every single turn of the larger driven gear.

### Calculating the gear ratio of a simple gear train

When calculating the gear ratio of a simple gear train incorporating three gears you would use the same formula as for two gears.

$$\text{Gear ratio} = \frac{\text{number of teeth in the driven gear}}{\text{number of teeth in the driver gear}}$$

However, this time you will have to consider the gears in pairs of driven divided by driver, with A as the first driver gear.

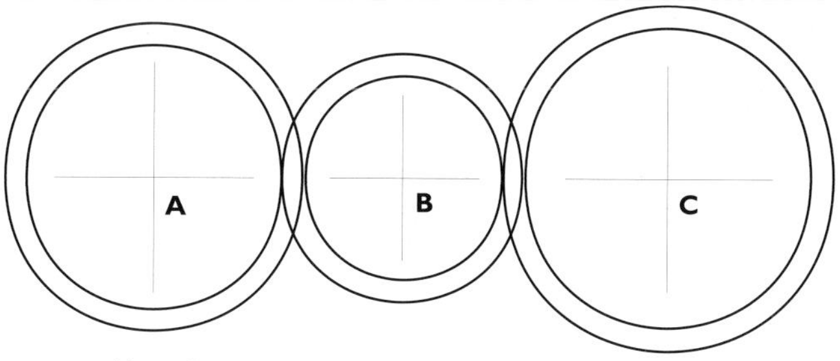

**Figure 6.69** *Calculating the gear ratio for a simple gear train*

30 teeth          20 teeth          40 teeth

$$\text{Gear ratio} = \frac{\substack{\text{number of teeth in} \\ \text{the driven gear B}}}{\substack{\text{number of teeth in} \\ \text{the driver gear A}}} \times \frac{\substack{\text{number of teeth in} \\ \text{the driven gear C}}}{\substack{\text{number of teeth in} \\ \text{the driver gear B}}}$$

$$= \frac{B}{A} \times \frac{C}{B}$$

$$= \frac{20}{30} \times \frac{40}{20} = \frac{800}{600} = \frac{8}{6} = \frac{4}{3}$$

Gear ratio  = 4:3

Notice that this is the same as the gear ratio for A and C if B were not there.

### Idler gear

In a simple gear train the middle gear is called an idler gear. The idler gear does not change the speed of the final driven gear. The function of the idler gear in Figure 6.70 is to enable the rotational direction of the driven gear to change. In the example shown, the idler gear enables the driven gear to turn in the same direction as the driver gear.

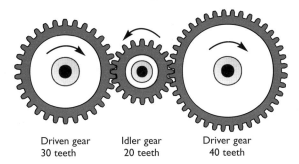

Driver gear
40 teeth

Idler gear
20 teeth

Driven gear
30 teeth

**Figure 6.70** *Idler gear*

# Jockey pulleys

Jockey pulleys are used to apply tension to the belt where it is not practical to move the drive source to increase tension. Timing belts in car engines often use a jockey pulley to give the desired tension. In this case it would not be possible to slide one half of the engine away from the other to tension the belt. There are two main types of jockey pulleys, fixed and sprung.

## Fixed jockey pulley

A fixed pulley will require tightening from time to time. This is achieved by means of a slot on the jockey pulley bracket. By loosening the nut you can slide the jockey pulley to increase or decrease the tension on the belt. The nut would then be tightened to maintain the tension.

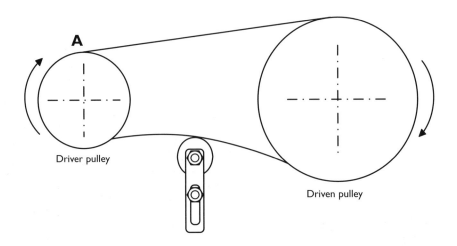

Driver pulley

Driven pulley

**Figure 6.71** *Fixed jockey pulley*

### Sprung self-adjusting jockey pulley

The sprung self-adjusting jockey pulley has a strong spring that keeps the wheel firmly against the belt. This type of jockey pulley is used when stretching of the belt is a problem or when belt slip is desirable.

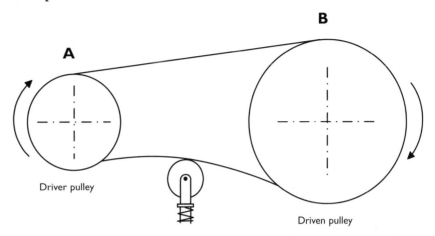

**Figure 6.72** *Sprung self-adjusting jockey pulley*

# Compound gear train

In a compound gear train the shafts will be rotating at different speeds. Consider the three-shaft compound gear train shown in Figure 6.73. As the driver shaft completes one revolution 40 teeth on the outer gear will have passed point A. As the driver gear is in contact with the middle 20-teeth compound gear at point B this gear will also turn through 40 teeth. This will mean that point B will have rotated twice. The outer teeth on the middle gear will also go round twice, which means 80 teeth will pass point D. 80 teeth passing point D will also mean 80 teeth passed point C. The 20-teeth gear on the driven gear will rotate four times to allow 80 teeth to pass point C. Simply, this means that one revolution of the driver gear results in 2 revolutions of the middle gear, which results in 4 revolutions of the driven gear. This results in the shaft of the driven gear rotating 4 times as fast as the driver shaft A.

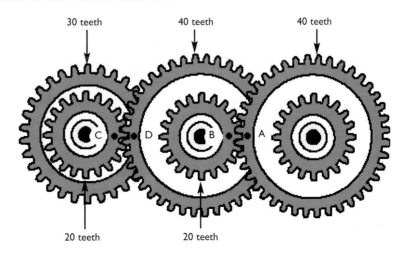

**Figure 6.73** *Compound gear train*

Figure 6.74 shows the graphical symbol for a three-shaft compound gear train.

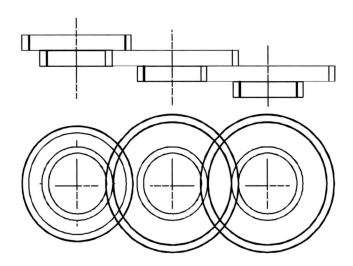

**Figure 6.74** *Graphical symbol for a compound gear train*

## Building a compound gear train with a gear ratio 5:1

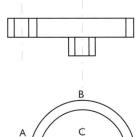

**Figure 6.75** *Symbol for the gear train*

The gear wheel and compound gear shown in Figure 6.75 has the driver gear (A) fixed to the motor and one compound gear (B,C) fixed to the output shaft. This combination will reduce the speed of the output shaft by a ratio of 5:1.

### Calculating the gear ratio

$$\text{Gear ratio} = \frac{\text{number of teeth in the driven gear}}{\text{number of teeth in the driver gear}}$$

$$= \frac{B}{A}$$

$$= \frac{50}{10} = \frac{5}{1}$$

Gear ratio = 5:1

### Calculating the velocity for the gearbox

If the motor is turning at 2800 rev/min. Then:

Velocity of driven gear =

$$\frac{\text{number of teeth on driver gear} \times \text{velocity of driver gear}}{\text{number of teeth on driven gear}}$$

$$\text{Velocity of driven gear} = \frac{A}{B} \times \frac{2800}{1} = \frac{10 \times 2800}{50 \times 1} = \frac{560}{1} = 560$$

Velocity of driven gear = 560 revs/min

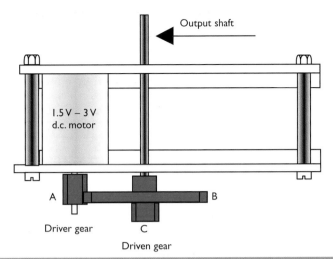

**Figure 6.76** *View of the assembled gearbox for a simple gear train*

| Example | **Building a compound gear train with a gear ratio 625:1** |

Using modular gears and matrix plates it is possible to design and build a gearbox with a gear ratio of 625:1.

This example uses a gear wheel on the motor and four compound gears to reduce the speed of the output shaft by a ratio of 625:1. The motor is still turning at 2800 revs/min.

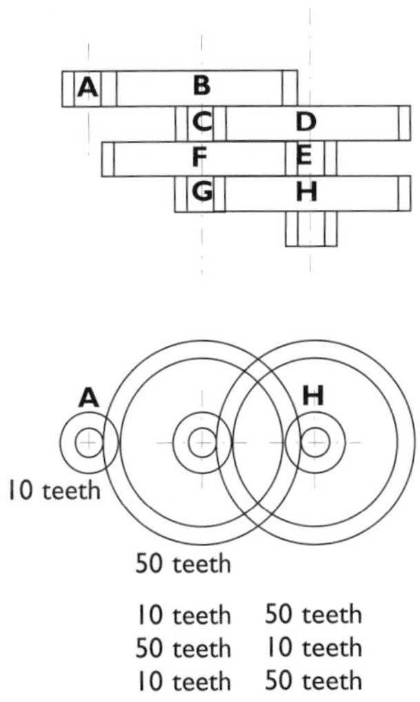

*Calculating gear ratio*

$$\text{Gear ratio} = \frac{\text{number of teeth in the driven gear}}{\text{number of teeth in the driver gear}}$$

$$= \frac{B}{A} \times \frac{D}{C} \times \frac{F}{E} \times \frac{H}{G}$$

$$= \frac{50}{10} \times \frac{50}{10} \times \frac{50}{10} \times \frac{50}{10} = \frac{6\,250\,000}{10\,000} = \frac{625}{1}$$

Gear ratio =    625:1

**Figure 6.77** *Symbol for the compound gear train*

A
10 teeth

50 teeth

10 teeth    50 teeth
50 teeth    10 teeth
10 teeth    50 teeth

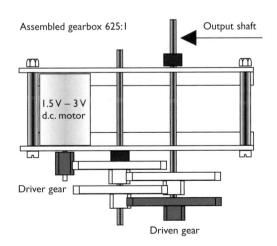

**Figure 6.78** *View of the assembled gearbox for a compound gear train*

### Calculating the velocity of the driven gear

Velocity of driven gear $=$
$$\frac{\text{number of teeth on driver gear} \times \text{velocity of driver gear}}{\text{number of teeth on driven gear}}$$

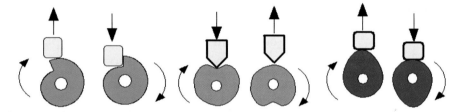

$$\text{Velocity of driven gear} = \frac{A \times C \times E \times G \times 2800}{B \times D \times F \times H \times 1}$$

$$= \frac{10 \times 10 \times 10 \times 10 \times 2800}{50 \times 50 \times 50 \times 50 \times 1}$$

$$= \frac{1 \times 2800}{625 \times 1} = 4.48$$

Velocity of driven gear $= 4.48$ revs/min

---

### Questions on mechanisms

1 Figure 6.79 shows pear, snail and heart-shaped cams.

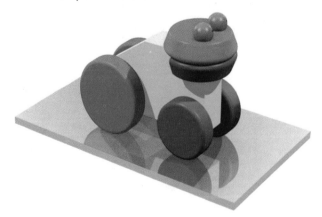

**Figure 6.79** *Cams*

    **a** Copy the three cams and write the correct name against each one.

    **b** What is the part that rests on the top of the cam called?

    **c** The part that rests on top of the cam moves up and down. What type of motion is this?

    **d** What is the function of a cam?

2 Figure 6.80 shows a drawing of a toy frog. The back of the frog has to move up and down.

**Figure 6.80** *Toy frog*

    **a** How would you achieve this?

    **b** When fixing the back wheels, would the wheels be interference fit or clearance fit on the axle?

3 Figure 6.81 shows a cam and follower.

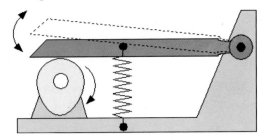

**Figure 6.81** *Cam and follower*

a What is the function of the spring?

b What could happen if the spring was to break?

4 Figure 6.82 shows three products that incorporate the principle of a lever. One product is based on a class 1 lever, one on a class 2 lever and one on a class 3 lever.

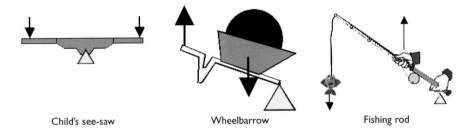

**Figure 6.82** *Class of levers*

Child's see-saw      Wheelbarrow      Fishing rod

a Write down the name of each product and label it either a class 1, class 2 or class 3 lever.

b Draw the graphical symbol for each class of lever.

5 Figure 6.83 shows a lever used to open a tin of paint.

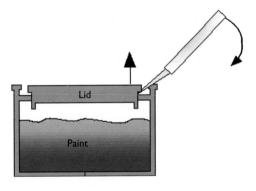

Lid

Paint

**Figure 6.83** *Tin of paint*

a Copy the diagram and show on your drawing the fulcrum (pivot point), where the effort is applied and where the load is applied.

b Write down a suitable material that the lever could be made from.

c On your sketch, show how the lever could be modified so that a smaller effort is needed to remove the lid.

6 Figure 6.84 shows a drawing of a pedestal-drilling machine found in school workshops. The machine has a belt drive and a pulley system to transfer motion from the electric motor to the drill bit.

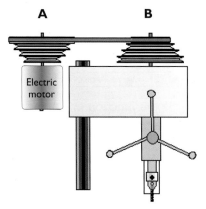

**Figure 6.84** *Pedestal-drilling machine*

a What would happen to the speed of the drill bit if the belt were moved from the top pulleys to the bottom pulleys?

b Which pulley is the driver pulley and which is the driven pulley?

c Why do you think a belt drive is preferred on a pedestal-drilling machine to a chain and sprocket drive?

7 Figure 6.85 shows a chassis for a model car.

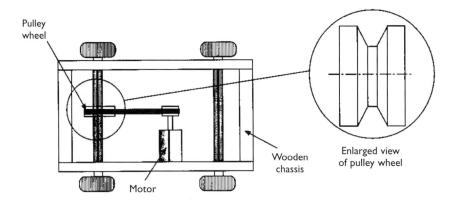

**Figure 6.85** *Model car*

a Write down the type of belt you would use for this pulley wheel.

b Write down one advantage and one disadvantage of using a pulley drive system compared with a chain drive in a mechanical system.

c Suggest an alternative to the pulley or chain drive system for the model car.

d Look at Figure 6.85 again. Explain with the aid of sketches how the belt drive could be modified to provide a range of speeds.

e A student wishes to mount the motor vertically which will mean the belt will have to turn through 90 degrees as shown in Figure 6.86. What would you have to change on the pulley system to allow this to happen?

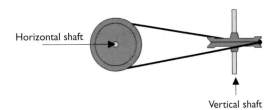

**Figure 6.86** *Shaft at 90 degrees*

Horizontal shaft

Vertical shaft

8 Look at Figure 6.87. It's a symbolic drawing of the pulley wheel for the car shown in Figure 6.85.

   a Calculate the speed of the driven pulley (B) if the driver pulley (A) turns at 80 revs/min.

   b State the velocity ratio of the pulley system.

   c When the car was built it was found that the belt came off because it was loose. Draw a means of keeping tension on the belt.

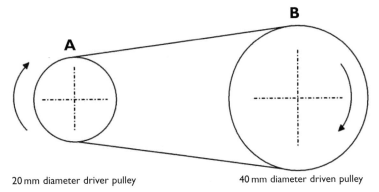

20 mm diameter driver pulley          40 mm diameter driven pulley

**Figure 6.87** *Symbolic drawing of the pulley wheel*

9 Figure 6.88 shows a simple gear train. The driver gear (A) shows the direction of rotation.

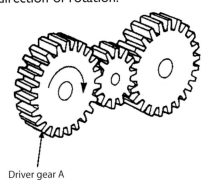

Driver gear A

**Figure 6.88** *Simple gear train*

   a What is the direction of rotation of the other two gears?

   b What is the main function of the middle gear?

   c What is the name of the middle gear?

10 Figure 6.89 shows a simple gear train and its graphical symbol.

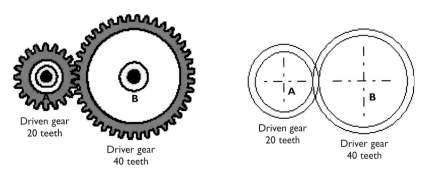

Driven gear
20 teeth

Driver gear
40 teeth

Driven gear
20 teeth

Driver gear
40 teeth

**Figure 6.89** *Simple gear train*

**a** Calculate the gear ratio for this gear train.

**b** If the driver gear rotates at 50 revs/min, what will be the velocity (speed) of the driven gear?

11 Figure 6.90 shows a simple gear train. Gear A is the driver gear.

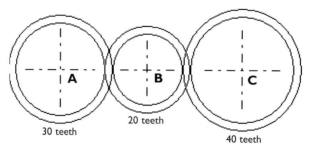

**Figure 6.90** *Simple gear train*

**a** Calculate the gear ratio for this gear train.

**b** If the driver gear (A) rotates at 70 revs/min, what will be the velocity (speed) of the driven gear?

12 Figure 6.91 shows a simple gear train. Gear A is the driver gear.

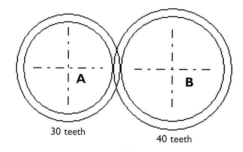

**Figure 6.91** *Simple gear train*

**a** Calculate the gear ratio for this gear train.

**b** If the driver gear rotates at 70 revs/min, what will be the velocity (speed) of the driven gear?

**c** Compare your answer to question 11 with your answers to question 12. Comment on your findings.

13 Figure 6.92 shows a compound gear train.

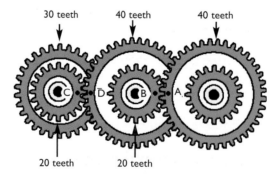

**Figure 6.92** *Compound gear train*

**a** What is the difference between a simple gear train and a compound gear train?

**b** What is meant by the terms driver gear and driven gear?

**c** Draw the graphical symbol for the compound gear train.

**d** Calculate the gear ratio for the compound gear train.

**e** If the driver gear A is rotating at 100 revs/min, calculate the velocity of the output shaft of the driven gear C.

# CHAPTER SEVEN  Computer control

## Introduction

Computer control allows you to use the computer to control external devices. Devices such as electric motors, lamps, buzzers, relays, buggies, robotic arms, LEDs and many others can be connected to the computer. A robotic arm which uses computer control designed by a student is shown in Figure 7.1.

### Control software

This is a program that you can use with your computer to control external devices. There are a number of specially written software packages on the market and these can be purchased through educational supply companies. Alternatively, you could write your own programs and many students still do this using basic or machine code programming language. However, the time you would need to learn the language is considerable.

### Control interfacing

**Figure 7.1** *Robotic arm using computer control*   Under no circumstances should you directly connect external devices to your computer. To do so may, and most likely will, result in you damaging the computer beyond repair. You must always connect your project through an **interface**.

An interface is a device designed to protect your computer. Most will also amplify (increase) the electrical signal coming from the computer. It will also enable you to make physical connections to the computer easily and safely.

### Input–process–output

All but the most basic control systems will have input–process–output and computer control is no different. Consider a computer system in terms of input–process–output:

**Input:** Press a key, this is an input via the keyboard.

**Process:** After the key is pressed the input is processed in the CPU (central processing unit).

**Output:** The signal from the keyboard is processed and the letter is displayed on the screen. Therefore the output device is the monitor.

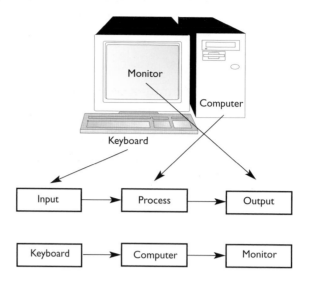

**Figure 7.2** *Computer input–process–output*

## Microprocessor systems

Microprocessors/computers have a number of building blocks that are linked to each other. These are the CPU, ROM, RAM, I/O and A-D. The interconnection between these building blocks is shown in Figure 7.3.

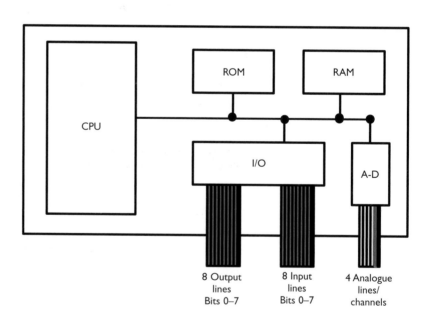

**Figure 7.3** *Micro-processor/computer building blocks*

### CPU (Central Processing Unit)

It is the job of the CPU to handle and process all the information coming into the computer and then do something with it. The CPU can only do its job if it has other supporting ICs (integrated circuits). It is the job of these other ICs to store and handle vital information.

### ROM (Read Only Memory)

The function of the ICs containing ROM is to hold vital information necessary for the running of the microprocessor/computer. The term 'read only memory' means that the CPU can only read this information but cannot add to or remove information from it.

### RAM (Random Access Memory)

When you put information into a microprocessor/computer it is held in the RAM. You can add to and remove information from the RAM. For example, as you type a letter the words are held in the RAM. The CPU can then access this information if and when it is needed, for example to send a completed letter to the printer.

## Input–process–output in computer controlled systems

Here input–process–output usually refers to the system being controlled by the computer. If you consider the set of traffic lights shown in Figure 7.4 the input will be the push switch that starts the sequence. The output will be the lights. The process will happen in two places:

- the CPU
- the interface.

The CPU processes the signal and runs the program. The interface takes the small signal from the computer and amplifies it to turn on the traffic lights.

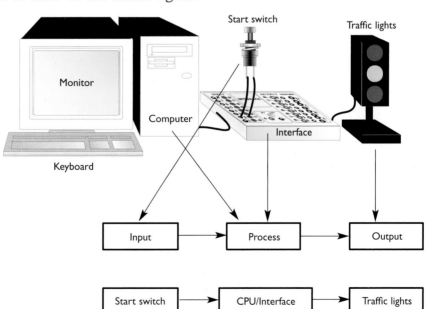

**Figure 7.4**

*Input–process–output for traffic lights*

# Outputs

Most microprocessors/computers can have eight output lines (wires) connected to them (Figure 7.5). These lines can be programmed to come on and off as required using the appropriate software. Each line is called a **bit** and they are numbered 0 to 7. The voltage at each line is 5 volts but the current will be very small so this needs to be increased (amplified) to a meaningful level if you wish to turn on output devices such as lamps, motors and buzzers.

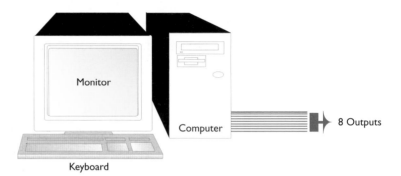

**Figure 7.5** *8 × output lines, bits 0–7*

## Amplifying the output signal

To amplify a signal means to increase either the current or voltage or both. This can be achieved by using a transistor as shown in Figure 7.6.

The output line is bit 0. This comes from the computer at 5 volts. It is used to turn on a transistor that is connected to a 12 volt secondary power supply. It is important to connect both zero volts together.

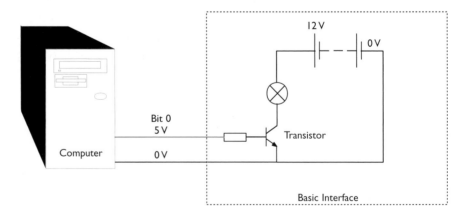

**Figure 7.6** *Amplifying an output signal*

## Connecting output bits 0–7

So far only one output bit is connected to the interface. To connect all eight you would simply repeat the circuit shown in Figure 7.6. The circuit would then be housed in a box for protection. This box is called an interface.

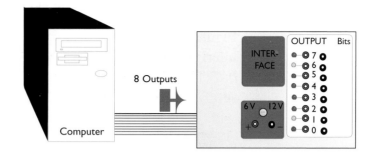

**Figure 7.7** *Housing the outputs*

# Inputs

It is possible for your computer to detect an input signal and respond in some way. Most computers will allow you to connect eight inputs called bits. Each bit is identified by a number from 0 to 7.

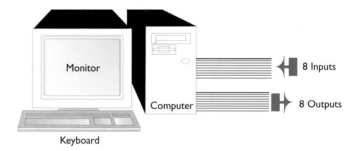

**Figure 7.8** *8 × input lines, bits 0–7*

### Detecting an input signal

The term input would seem to imply that you have to send a signal (voltage) into the computer. This is not strictly true; what you are actually doing is making the computer detect the closing or opening of a switch. The power for the switch comes out of the computer and all you have to do is connect a switch between this line and zero volts. This is shown in Figure 7.9.

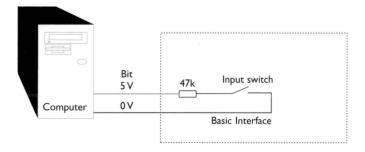

**Figure 7.9** *Detecting an input signal*

A high signal of 5 volts comes out of the computer. A switch is connected between the 5 volts and 0 volts. When the switch is closed the computer will detect the fall in voltage and identify this as a low signal. The 47k resistor is used to prevent a short circuit between 5 volts and 0 volts when the switch is closed.

### Connecting input bits 0–7

Figure 7.9 shows one input line bit 0 connected to a basic interface. This would be repeated for all eight input lines, bits 0–7. The circuit would then be housed in a protective box similar to the one shown in Figure 7.10.

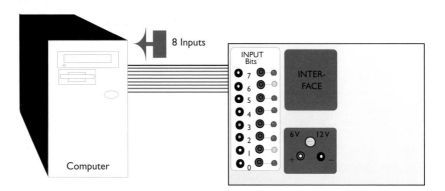

**Figure 7.10** *Housing the inputs*

# Digital input/output interface

The interfaces explained so far have been **digital interfaces**. This means that they can detect an input that is on or off (high or low). They can also turn an output on or off. By combining both the output and input interfaces in one housing you have a digital input/output interface. On commercial interfaces 4 mm sockets are commonly used to enable you to plug in your input switches and output devices. Some commercial interfaces also have status LEDs to indicate when an input/output is high or low.

A typical commercial digital input/output interface is shown in Figure 7.11. It has eight input sockets, eight output sockets, four motor sockets and a switch that allows you to amplify the signal from the computer to either 6 or 12 volts.

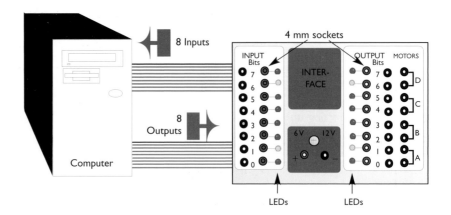

**Figure 7.11** *8 × input/output digital interface*

With this or similar interfaces you can connect up to eight sensors to the inputs and up to eight output devices. D.C. motors can be connected to the motor sockets. This will enable you to make the motors turn both clockwise and anti-clockwise.

If you plan to use the motor sockets you should be aware that the corresponding output sockets will then not be available.

# Flowcharts for digital input/output

You can use a flowchart to help you plan the sequence of your microprocessor/computer control program. There are a number of common symbols used in flowcharts to represent conditions such as start, stop, output, decisions, wait and loops. These symbols are shown below.

**Start/Stop/End**    **Output**    **Decision**    **Process**    **Sub-routine**

Use the Start symbol at the beginning of your program/sub-routine or procedure.

Use the Stop symbol to stop your program.

Use the End symbol to end a sub-routine or procedure.

Use the Output symbol to turn on or off outputs.

Use the Decision symbol for all inputs. Digital input signals, analogue signals, comparing the values of variables in a loop, are all inputs. Decision symbols usually have a yes/no arrow out from them and denote whether or not the decision has happened or not.

Use the Process symbol for time delays and variables.

Use the Sub-routine symbol for calling a sub-routine into your main program. Some software packages call this Macros or Procedures.

An example of the use of flowchart symbols is shown in Figure 7.12.

## Output summary

In addition to using the correct symbols in your flowchart it is necessary to give a summary of what you want to happen at each stage of the program.

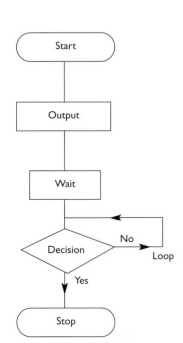

**Figure 7.12** *Flowchart symbols*

If you wished to write a program to turn on bit 0 you would have to give the output cell a name and specify the condition of each bit. This is shown in Figure 7.13. The summary is then shortened to O/P 0 0 0 0 0 0 0 1.

**Figure 7.13** *Output summary*

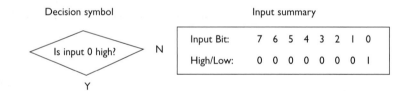

| Output symbol | | | | | | | | | Output summary | | | | | | | | |
|---|---|---|---|---|---|---|---|---|---|---|---|---|---|---|---|---|---|
| 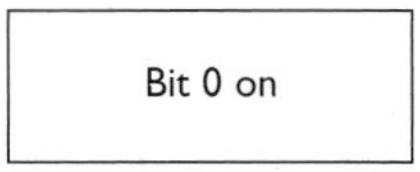 Bit 0 on | | | | | | | | | Output Bit: | 7 | 6 | 5 | 4 | 3 | 2 | 1 | 0 |
| | | | | | | | | | High/Low: | 0 | 0 | 0 | 0 | 0 | 0 | 0 | 1 |

## Decision summary

Decisions are mainly associated with inputs. If you wished to include a decision in your program that waited until input bit 0 was high, then you would give the decision cell a name and specify the condition of the input bit. The program would check to see if this condition was true and if it was, the program would do something; if not it would keep checking until it was true. An example is shown in Figure 7.14. Once again the summary would be shortened to read I/P 0 0 0 0 0 0 0 1.

**Figure 7.14** *Input summary*

| Decision symbol | Input summary | | | | | | | | |
|---|---|---|---|---|---|---|---|---|---|
| Is input 0 high? N | Input Bit: | 7 | 6 | 5 | 4 | 3 | 2 | 1 | 0 |
| Y | High/Low: | 0 | 0 | 0 | 0 | 0 | 0 | 0 | 1 |

## Wait summary

If you want to have a time delay in your program flowchart you would use the wait symbol. It is usual to specify the wait in seconds or parts of a second. An example of the summary for this is shown in Figure 7.15.

**Figure 7.15** *Wait summary*

| Symbol | Wait summary |
|---|---|
| Wait 3 | Wait 3 seconds |

**Programming model racing car start lights**

### Design situation

A student was asked to design a set of start lights for use with model racing cars. The lights had to come on when the input switch was pressed. The light sequence was to be red, red/amber then green.

**Figure 7.16** *Racing track*

### Solution

A set of model traffic lights was made which included a push-to-make switch and three coloured bulbs. Each of the three lights was connected to the output bits 0–2 on the interface. Green was connected to bit 0, amber was connected to bit 1 and red was connected to bit 2. The switch was connected to input bit 0. A photo of the lights is shown in Figure 7.18.

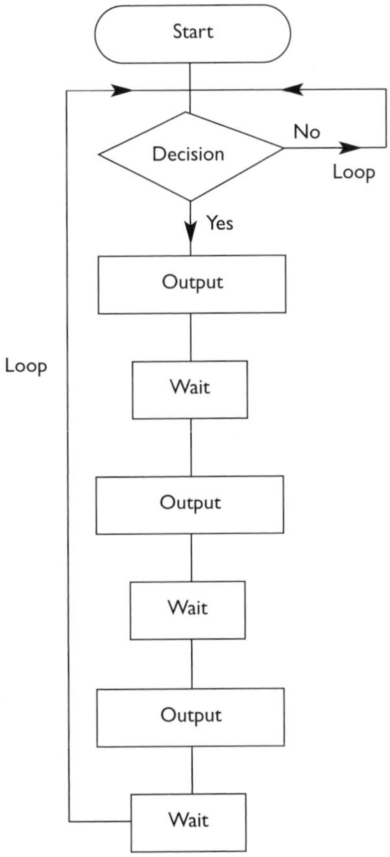

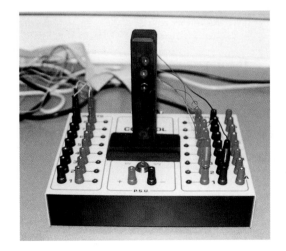

**Figure 7.18** *Lights for model car racing*

**Figure 7.17** *Symbols used in the flowchart*

### Flowchart

Figure 7.17 shows the basic sequence for the lights.

Figure 7.19 shows the final sequence. This was set out so that the program would start, then go round in a loop until the input switch was pressed. Once this input was true then the program moved down to turn on the first output red light. A wait of 1 second was then added so that the light would stay red for one second. Next the red and amber came on together for 2.5 seconds before the green go light came on. The green light remained on for 10 seconds after which time the program looped back to the start to wait for another input.

Figure 7.19 shows what is happening at each stage of the program.

### Final flowchart and summary

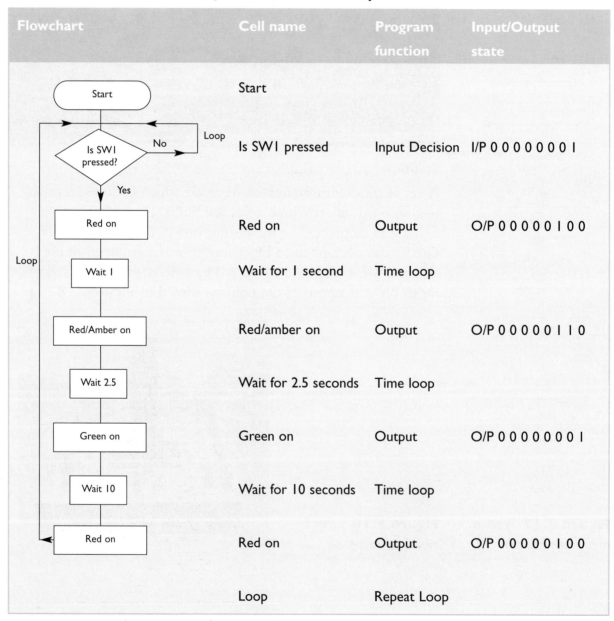

| Flowchart | Cell name | Program function | Input/Output state |
|---|---|---|---|
| Start | Start | | |
| Is SW1 pressed? | Is SW1 pressed | Input Decision | I/P 0 0 0 0 0 0 0 1 |
| Red on | Red on | Output | O/P 0 0 0 0 0 1 0 0 |
| Wait 1 | Wait for 1 second | Time loop | |
| Red/Amber on | Red/amber on | Output | O/P 0 0 0 0 0 1 1 0 |
| Wait 2.5 | Wait for 2.5 seconds | Time loop | |
| Green on | Green on | Output | O/P 0 0 0 0 0 0 0 1 |
| Wait 10 | Wait for 10 seconds | Time loop | |
| Red on | Red on | Output | O/P 0 0 0 0 0 1 0 0 |
| | Loop | Repeat Loop | |

**Figure 7.19** *Flowchart and programming details*

### Design situation

Christmas decorations can become uninteresting if they just sit there doing nothing. There is a need for a Christmas decoration that will be controlled by a computer. This will enable it to be programmed so that the lights come on and off in different patterns.

### Solution

The solution was an electronic Christmas tree with eight lights. The lights were LEDs and each one was connected to an output port on the computer interface. The final solution can be seen in Figure 7.20.

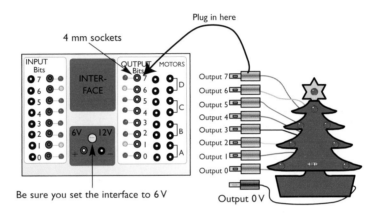

**Figure 7.20** Computer-controlled Christmas tree

### Making the Christmas tree

The tree was made on a PCB. Each LED was soldered to the board with the negative leg to the outside so that there was a common negative (Figure 7.21).

**Figure 7.21** Connecting the LED

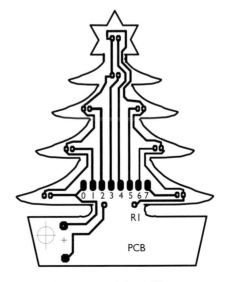

**Figure 7.22** Back of the PCB

209

### Connecting to the computer

The positive leg of each LED was soldered to the inside tracks. Each LED had a wire connected to it and a 4 mm plug joined to the end. These were then plugged into the interface.

The current limiting resistor R1 is 74R and the voltage should be 5–6 volts.

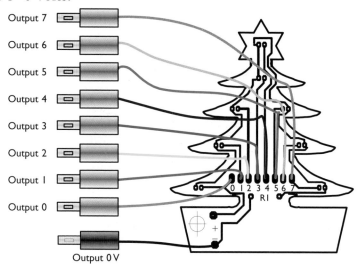

**Figure 7.23** *PCB connected to output lines*

### Final flowchart and summary

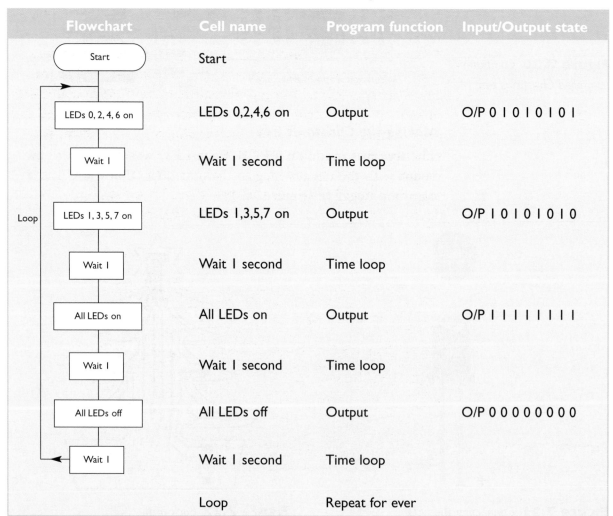

| Flowchart | Cell name | Program function | Input/Output state |
|---|---|---|---|
| Start | **Start** | | |
| LEDs 0, 2, 4, 6 on | LEDs 0,2,4,6 on | Output | O/P 0 1 0 1 0 1 0 1 |
| Wait 1 | Wait 1 second | Time loop | |
| LEDs 1, 3, 5, 7 on | LEDs 1,3,5,7 on | Output | O/P 1 0 1 0 1 0 1 0 |
| Wait 1 | Wait 1 second | Time loop | |
| All LEDs on | All LEDs on | Output | O/P 1 1 1 1 1 1 1 1 |
| Wait 1 | Wait 1 second | Time loop | |
| All LEDs off | All LEDs off | Output | O/P 0 0 0 0 0 0 0 0 |
| Wait 1 | Wait 1 second | Time loop | |
| | Loop | Repeat for ever | |

**Figure 7.24** *Flowchart and programming details*

**Cycle shop display**

### Design situation

A local cycle shop owner wanted a counter-top display that would come on 5 seconds after a customer walked into the shop. The display had to run for just under 1 minute.

**Figure 7.25** *Cycle shop*

### Solution

The solution was a computer-controlled model cyclist. A push-to-make switch fixed to the shop door activated the display. After 5 seconds the display started to turn. A reed switch was fixed to the cycle's rear frame and the magnet inserted in the wheel. This provided a second input that was used to count the revolutions of the rear wheel. Three separate lines were used in the flowchart (Figure 7.27) to determine when the count was equal to or greater than 100. These were: setting A as a variable, increasing the value of A by one each time the program moved past a certain point and by setting up a decision that checked the value of the variable A.

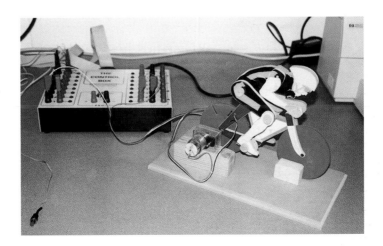

**Figure 7.26** *Picture of the cycle shop display*

## Flowchart summary and programming details

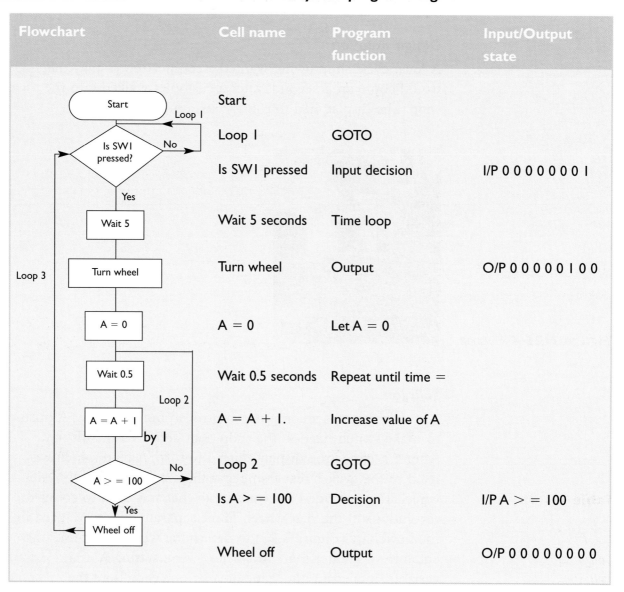

| Flowchart | Cell name | Program function | Input/Output state |
|---|---|---|---|
| | Start | | |
| | Loop 1 | GOTO | |
| | Is SW1 pressed | Input decision | I/P 0 0 0 0 0 0 0 1 |
| | Wait 5 seconds | Time loop | |
| | Turn wheel | Output | O/P 0 0 0 0 0 1 0 0 |
| | A = 0 | Let A = 0 | |
| | Wait 0.5 seconds | Repeat until time = | |
| | A = A + 1. | Increase value of A | |
| | Loop 2 | GOTO | |
| | Is A > = 100 | Decision | I/P A > = 100 |
| | Wheel off | Output | O/P 0 0 0 0 0 0 0 0 |

**Figure 7.27** *Flowchart and programming details*

# PICs

The term PIC stands for Peripheral Interface Controller. It is an IC that can be programmed to respond to one or more inputs and control one or more outputs. It is often referred to as a computer-on-a-chip. This is because it enables you to manufacture computer-control projects without having to leave your project wired to the computer. You simply download your program to a PIC. The PIC is then plugged into your circuit board. The PIC is a mini programmable microprocessor IC that can be repeatedly programmed and reprogrammed. It has within it all the necessary sub-systems to allow it to do this job.

## Internal structure of the PIC

The PIC will have built-in:

- ROM (Read Only Memory)
- RAM (Random Access Memory)
- I/O (Input Output)
- CPU (Central Processing Unit)

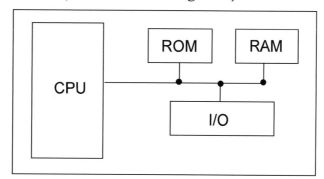

**Figure 7.28** *PIC building blocks*

These are the building blocks of all computers although PCs will have larger ones and sometimes more of these as well as some others.

## PIC types

There are a number of different PICs available for you to purchase and many people will have their favourites but for GCSE project work the ones in Table 7.1 seem to be the most popular.

**Table 7.1** *PIC types*

| PIC Type | Number of pins | I/O pins | Inputs | Outputs |
|---|---|---|---|---|
| PIC12F641 | 8 | 6 | 2 digital | 4 |
| PIC12F675 | 8 | 6 | 2 digital 2 analogue | 2 |
| PIC16F84 | 18 | 13 | 5 digital | 8 |
| PIC16F716 | 18 | 13 | 5 digital 2 analogue | 8 |
| PIC16F873 | 28 | 22 | 8 digital 4 analogue | 8 |
| PIC16F627 | 18 | 15 | 5 digital 2 analogue | 8 |

**Figure 7.29** *PIC16F84*

Once you have mastered one PIC the rest are much the same. Some will have all digital or all analogue inputs. Others will have a mixture of both, so to simplify things a little the 18-pin PIC16F84 will be considered in detail to give you an understanding of digital PICs.

## Connecting the PIC16F84

The PIC16F84 is an 18-pin IC. It has 5 inputs and 8 outputs. You will need to connect it to a stable 6 V supply. Four 1.5 V AA batteries will be fine for this. The IC needs an external clock in the form of a 4 MHz resonator. You will also need to add a reset push-to-make switch to enable you to reset the program.

213

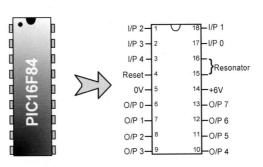

**Figure 7.30** *PIC16F84 pin layout*

### Connecting the power supply

Pin 14 = +6 V. Pin 5 = 0 V. You will also need a 100 nF decoupling capacitor between pin 14 and 0 volts and a 100 μF smoothing capacitor across the supply.

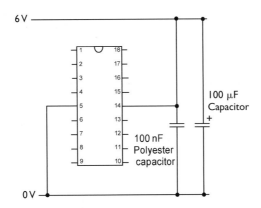

**Figure 7.31** *Power*

### Connecting the reset

Pin 4 = reset. You must keep this high to enable the PIC to work but once the reset switch is pressed the program will reset.

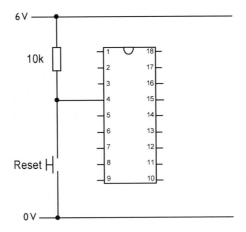

**Figure 7.32** *Reset*

### Connecting the resonator

Pins 15–16 are the resonator pins. The third (middle) leg of the three-pin resonator must be connected to 0 V.

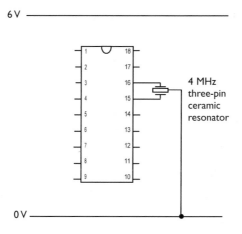

**Figure 7.33** *External clock*

### Connecting the inputs

Pins 1–3 and 17–18 are the inputs. You would tie the inputs low, then by using a switch, offer a high to the pin.

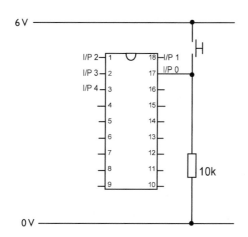

**Figure 7.34** *Inputs*

# PIC16F84

The PIC16F84 has become a very popular choice for Technology and Design students. It is ideal for use in projects that require up to five digital inputs and up to eight outputs. Possible projects include security systems, combination locks, long timers, event counters, buggies, seven-segment displays, traffic light controller and many more. It is important to come to terms with the chip itself as knowing and understanding this will enable you to not only to use the PIC16F84 but also to design, construct and fault-find your circuits. A step-by-step guide to designing a circuit containing the PIC16F84 will now be explained in detail.

### A step-by-step guide to building a circuit using the PIC16F84

#### Graphical symbol

The graphical symbol for the PIC16F84 is shown in Figure 7.35. Each pin is shown as a line with the pin number on it.

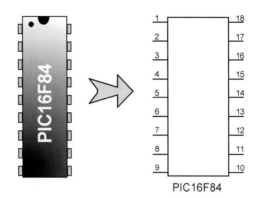

**Figure 7.35** *Symbol for the PIC16F84*

### Step 1: Adding the power supply

Connect the positive to pin 14. Next connect the negative to pin 5.

Add a smoothing capacitor C1, between the positive and negative of the supply.

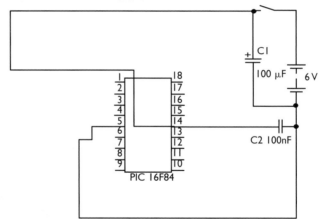

**Figure 7.36** *Adding the power supply to the PIC16F84*

Add a 100 nF decoupling capacitor C2, between pin 14 and negative. This will ensure the smooth operation of the PIC16F84. This is shown in Figure 7.36.

### Step 2: Adding the reset

This is added in two parts. First connect a 10k resistor between positive and pin 4. This keeps pin 4 high. Next connect a push-to-make switch between pin 4 and negative, this will enable you to make a low at pin 4. Each time the push-to-make switch is pressed, a low will be present at pin 4. This low will cause the program inside the PIC to reset to the start. This is shown in Figure 7.37.

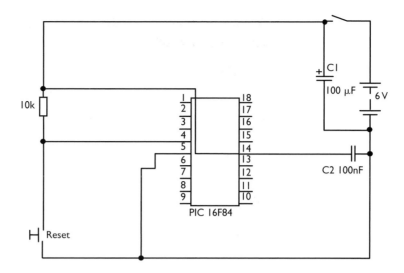

**Figure 7.37** *Adding the reset*

## Step 3: Adding the resonator

You will need a 4 MHz three-pin resonator. The middle pin is connected to negative. The other two legs are connected to pins 15 and 16. These legs can be connected either way round. The purpose of the resonator is to provide a clock pulse. The PIC will need this pulse to keep the program working in real time. This is shown in Figure 7.38.

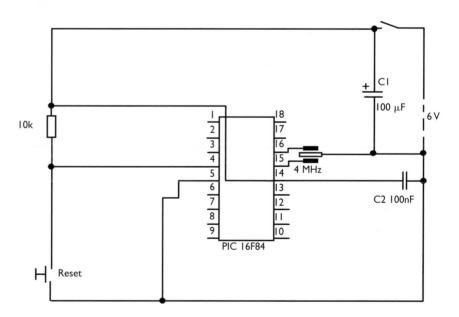

**Figure 7.38** *Adding the resonator*

## Step 4: Adding an input

You have five digital inputs on the PIC16F84. These are labelled input 0–4. An input is detected by the PIC when the input signal (voltage) changes from low (0) to high (1) or vice versa.

### Pull-down resistors

A 10k pull-down resistor is connected between pins 3 and the negative rail. This is shown in Figure 7.39. The 10k resistor holds the input low until you press the push-to-make switch.

When the input is pressed the signal appearing at pin 3 goes high. You can then write a program that will incorporate this change from low to high (from 0 to 1).

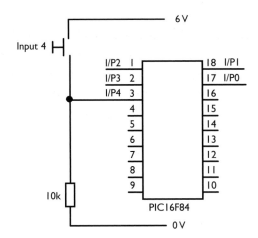

**Figure 7.39** *Connecting inputs*

## Inputs 0–4

It is good practice to pull all the inputs either high or low even if they not being used. This will help prevent false signals appearing at the pins. The circuit shown in Figure 7.40 uses only one input but the other four are pulled low. Table 7.2 shows the input pins and their corresponding bit numbers.

**Table 7.2** *Input pin numbers for the PIC16F84*

| Pin no. | 17 | 18 | 1 | 2 | 3 |
|---------|----|----|----|----|----|
| Input no. | 0 | 1 | 2 | 3 | 4 |

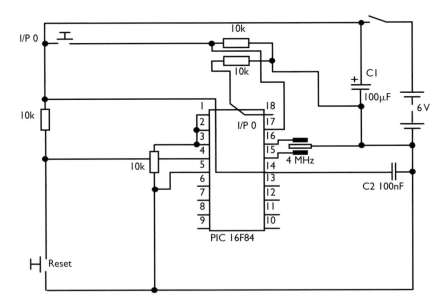

**Figure 7.40** *Connecting the Inputs*

## Step 5: Adding outputs

The PIC16F84 has eight outputs and you can use one or all as required.

The output pins and the corresponding bit numbers are shown in Table 7.3.

**Table 7.3** *Output pin numbers for the PIC 16F84*

| Pin no. | 6 | 7 | 8 | 9 | 10 | 11 | 12 | 13 |
|---------|---|---|---|---|----|----|----|-----|
| Output no. | 0 | 1 | 2 | 3 | 4 | 5 | 6 | O/P 7 |

The PIC is like any other IC in that the output voltage will be close to the supply voltage but the current will be low. This small current is only suitable for low current devices such as LEDs. For all other output devices such as relays, lamps and buzzers, you will need to amplify the current.

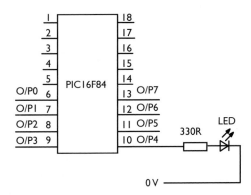

**Figure 7.41** *Adding an output*

### Amplifying an output

The most effective way to amplify the output signal from the PIC16F84 is through a transistor or even better through a Darlington pair transistor. A good low-cost Darlington pair transistor is the BCX38B. Connecting a Darlington pair to an output is shown in Figure 7.42.

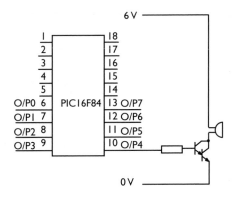

**Figure 7.42** *Amplifying the output signal*

### How it works

The output was required to drive a 6 V buzzer. The buzzer was connected to the 6 V supply rail. An output from pin 10 (output bit 4) is offered to the base leg of the Darlington pair transistor. When this happens, the transistor is on and the larger current from the supply rail can flow through it and the buzzer. This will cause the buzzer to sound. The Darlington pair transistor requires a protective resistor. This can be any value between 1 and 10k.

## Step 6: Adding outputs to the circuit

The circuit diagram for the PIC16F84 using one input and one output is shown in Figure 7.43. The output is an LED and is connected to output 0 (pin 6).

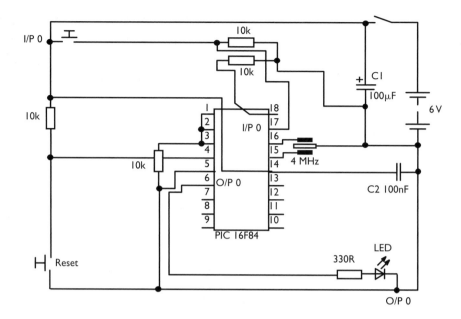

**Figure 7.43** *Connecting an LED to output 0*

## Adding an LED and buzzer to the circuit

The circuit diagram shown in Figure 7.44 incorporates one input and two outputs. The LED and its series resistor are connected directly to the output at pin 6. However, the buzzer is connected to a Darlington pair transistor and draws its current directly from the 6 V power supply.

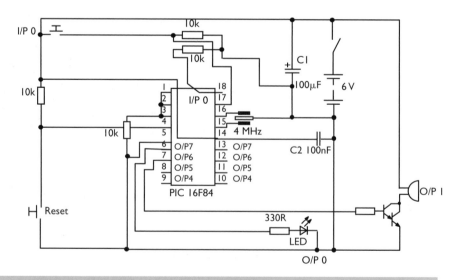

**Figure 7.44** *Connecting an LED and buzzer to outputs 0 and 1*

## Designing a circuit using two inputs and one output

### Design situation

The game of chess requires the player to make a move within a certain period of time. There is a need for a precise timer that would be set by the player once they had completed their move. The opposing player would then have until the light and buzzer came on to complete their move.

### Solution

The solution incorporated the PIC16F84. The circuit used two inputs and one output on the PIC16F84. The output is to a BCX38B that is used to turn on the LED and the buzzer, but these could be changed for any other suitable output device.

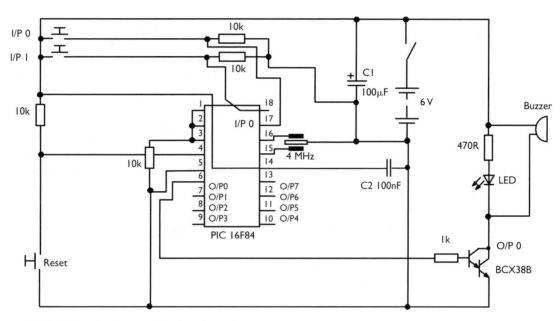

**Figure 7.45** *Circuit diagram for the chess timer*

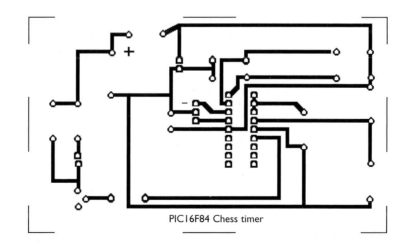

**Figure 7.46** *PCB for the chess timer*

### Bill of materials

1 × PIC16F84
1 × 18-pin DIL socket
1 × 100 μF Electrolytic capacitor
1 × 100 nF capacitor
1 × 470 ohm resistor
1 × 4 MHz 3-pin ceramic resonator

4 × 10k resistors
1 × 1k resistor
1 × BCX38B transistor
1 × green LED
1 × 6 volt buzzer
2 × Push-to-make switch
1 × SPST toggle switch
1 × Board 106.5 mm × 68.5 mm

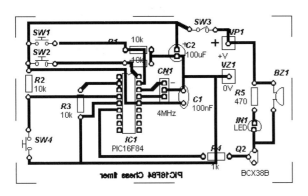

**Figure 7.47** *Silkscreen for the chess timer*

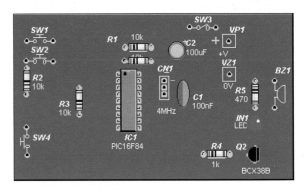

**Figure 7.48** *Top view of the chess timer PCB*

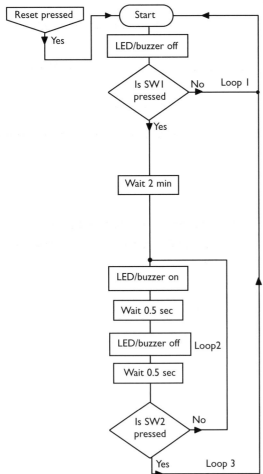

**Figure 7.49** *Flowchart for the chess timer*

## Program sequence for chess timer

- Start.
- LED and buzzer off.
- Press switch 1 to start the game.
- Wait for two minutes for the player to make a move or check whether the reset switch has been pressed. If yes, go to start. If no, go to next line.
- LED and buzzer on and off every 0.5 seconds until switch 2 is pressed.
- Press switch 2 to return to start.

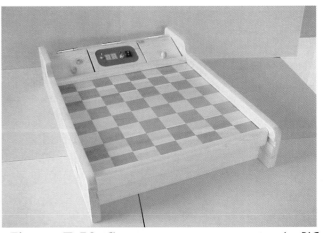

**Figure 7.50** *Chess game timer incorporating the PIC*

## Flowchart summary

| Cell name | Program function | Input/output state |
|---|---|---|
| Start | | |
| LED/buzzer off | Output | O/P 0 0 0 0 0 0 0 0 |
| Loop 1 | GOTO start | |
| Is SW1 pressed? | Input decision | I/P ... 0 1 |
| Wait 120 seconds | Time loop | |
| Is reset pressed? | GOTO state (event) | |
| LED/buzzer on | Output | O/P 0 0 0 0 0 0 0 1 |
| Wait 0.5 seconds | Time loop | |
| LED/buzzer off | Output | O/P 0 0 0 0 0 0 0 0 |
| Wait 0.5 seconds | Time loop | |
| Is SW2 pressed? | Input decision | I/P ... 1 0 |
| Loop 2 | GOTO | |
| Loop 3 | Repeat loop | |

**Figure 7.51** *Summary for chess timer program*

### Questions on computer control

1 The following sentences are incomplete. Copy out the sentences and add in the missing words:

  a Computer control allows you to use the computer to control _____ devices.

  b Devices such as _____, _____, can be connected to the computer.

2 Write down the three main functions of an interface.

3 Within the context of computer control, what is meant by the terms:

  a ROM

  b RAM

  c CPU?

4 Figure 7.52 shows output, start/stop/end, sub-routine, decision and process cells, used in computer-controlled programming. Copy out the cells and correctly label each one.

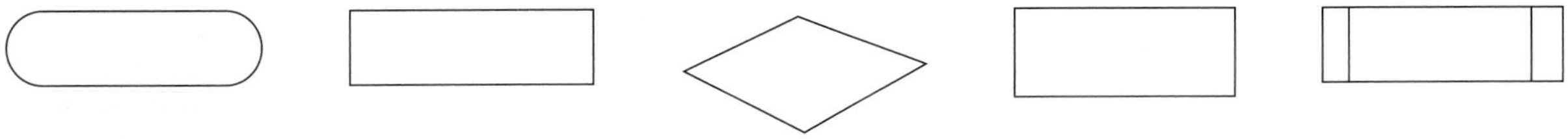

**Figure 7.52** *Flowchart cells*

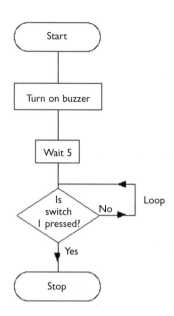

**Figure 7.53**

**Figure 7.54** *Traffic lights*

5 Write down the name given to the diagram shown in Figure 7.53.

6 Figure 7.54 shows a set of traffic lights used as a starting display for a model car racetrack. Draw a flowchart to turn the lights on and off in the following sequence:

  a Switch on the red light, wait for 5 seconds then switch it off.

  b Switch on the amber light, wait for 2 seconds then switch it off.

  c Switch on the green light, wait for 15 seconds then switch it off.

  d Repeat this sequence a, b, c continuously.

  e A modification is required to the sequence a, b, c so that an audio signal will come on when the green light is on.

   i Write down the name of a suitable audio device that could be used.

   ii Redraw your flowchart to include this audio device.

7 Figure 7.20 on page 209 shows a small Christmas tree that has to be connected to a computer through an interface.

  a Into which sockets on the interface would you plug the Christmas tree leads?

  b Write down the name of the output devices used on the Christmas tree.

  c The lights on the tree have to wait until an input switch is pressed before coming on and off in a sequence decided by you. Write down the sequence you would wish these lights to come on and off.

  d Draw a flowchart that would have the lights waiting until the input is pressed before carrying out your sequence.

8 Figures 7.55 and 7.56 show a computer-controlled digger. The two motors A and B can only rotate in the direction shown by the arrows (forward movement).

**Figure 7.55** *Digger*        **Figure 7.56** *Motors A and B*

  a Draw a flowchart to show how the digger might perform the following movements:

   i Start

   ii Wait until the input switch is pressed

   iii Move forward for 5 seconds

   iv Turn to the left through 90 degrees (1 second turns the digger 45 degrees)

v   Move the digger forward for 5 seconds

vi   Turn the digger right through 45 degrees

vii   Move forward for 5 seconds

viii   Turn the digger left through 45 degrees

ix   Move forward for 5 seconds

x   Stop.

b  If motors A and B could rotate both forward and reverse, suggest two ways in which the digger could be made to turn to the left. A flowchart is not required.

9  What do the letters PIC stand for?

10  What is the function of a PIC?

11  Figure 7.57 shows a model sliding door mechanism.

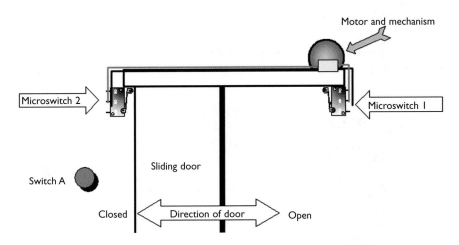

**Figure 7.57** *Sliding door*

An electronic PIC circuit is to be used to control the movement of the door. The sequence of operations is as follows.

Step 1: When switch A is pressed the motor operates, causing the door to open (move to the right).

Step 2: When the door comes in contact with microswitch 1 it stops and remains stationary for 3 seconds.

Step 3: The motor then reverses and the door closes (moves to the left).

Step 4: When the door comes in contact with microswitch 2 the system stops until switch A is pressed once more.

a  Draw a flowchart to operate this system using a PIC.

b  Draw the electronic circuit diagram incorporating a PIC of your choice to control the sliding door. A 12-volt d.c. car battery powers the motor.

# CHAPTER EIGHT  **Pneumatics**

## Introduction

Pneumatics is a system that operates with compressed air. A simple pneumatic device is the compressed air drill used by dentists for drilling teeth. Industry uses pneumatics in the manufacture of a range of components. The car industry uses robots with pneumatic cylinders that open and close to lift and place components onto cars as they are being assembled. Some tennis ball manufacturers use pneumatics to lift and place balls into a test rig.

The main advantage of pneumatics is that it will repeat the operation accurately over and over again. The main disadvantage can be the noise and the need for special compressors.

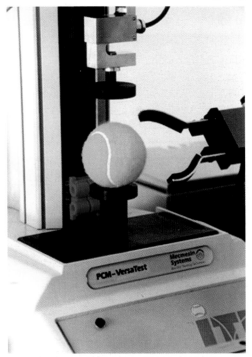

**Figure 8.1** *Rig for testing tennis balls*

### Safety

When working with pneumatic equipment it is important to work safely. Compressed air is a form of stored energy and when released incorrectly it can do serious damage to you and others. So always exercise caution when using it.

**The following are a few simple safety rules you should follow.**

#### Compressor system

**Do** ensure that this is in good working order before you use it. A qualified engineer should check the complete system at least once a year.

**Figure 8.2** *Compressed air system*

**Do not** use equipment if you are in any doubt about its condition.

**Do** ensure the pressure at the compressor is set correctly. Just enough pressure to operate the system should be used, 6–7 bar is adequate for most school use.

**Figure 8.3** *The reservoir pressure gauge*

**Figure 8.4** *The line pressure gauge*

**Do** ensure the pressure in the line is set correctly, 4–5 bar is adequate for school workshops.

### *Workstation*

**Do** ensure the pressure at your workstation is set correctly. Set it as low as is practical to operate your system. For small-bore components used in school for modelling purposes 2–3 bar should be adequate. You can set this by adjusting the air pressure regulator at your station.

**Do not** connect the main air supply to your system until you have checked all components and pipes are connected correctly. Only the operator should turn on the system.

**Do not** continue to operate the system if you notice air leaking from any joint or component.

**Do** turn off the main air supply to your system before making alterations.

### *Moving parts*

**Do** keep your fingers away from all moving parts.

**Do not** blow compressed air at anyone as this can result in serious injury.

**Do** ensure all pipes are connected, as loose pipes will thrash around when the air supply is turned on.

**Figure 8.5** *Manifold, pressure gauge and regulator*

# The pneumatic 3/2 valve

One of the basic components of any pneumatic circuit is the pneumatic valve. Valves act like electrical switches in that they are designed to turn something on. Valves can be used to perform the simple task of switching on or off the main air supply.

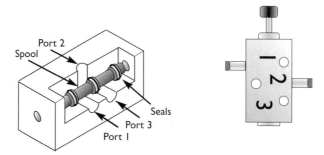

**Figure 8.6** *A 3/2 pneumatic valve*

There are two main types of valves you will use in pneumatics. These are 3/2 valves and 5/2 valves. The 3/2 valve gets its name because it has three ports (holes) and is capable of changing between two states. State one is when it is **actuated**, that is, the air at port 1 passes through the valve and out through port 2. The second state is **un-actuated**; this is when the air is exhausting through port 2 and port 3.

## Air flow through 3/2 valves

The spool in Figure 8.7 is moved by air. These valves are called **pilot/pilot air operated 3/2 valves**. The air moving the spool is called **signal air**.

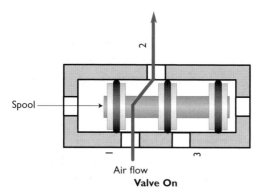

**Figure 8.7** *The air flow through an actuated 3/2 valve (on)*

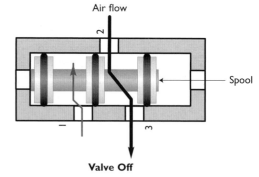

**Figure 8.8** *The air flow through an un-actuated 3/2 valve (off)*

## Drawing 3/2 valves

A 3/2 valve has three ports. Each port has a specific function. Port 1 is where the main air comes in. Port 2 is the output port when the valve is actuated (turned on). Port 3 is the exhaust.

Figure 8.9 shows the symbol for a 3/2 valve in the actuated (on) state. In this state the air comes in port 1 and goes out

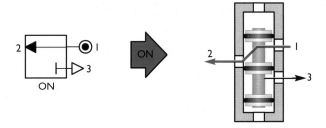

**Figure 8.9** *3/2 valve in actuated (on) state*

port 2. Also shown is a sectional drawing through a 3/2 valve in this state.

Figure 8.10 shows the symbol for a 3/2 valve in the off state. A sectional drawing of the valve is also shown. In this state the valve allows air to pass through port 2 and out port 3.

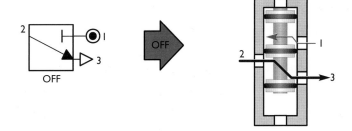

**Figure 8.10** *3/2 valve in un-actuated (off) state*

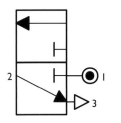

**Figure 8.11** *Symbol for a 3/2 valve*

### Symbol for a 3/2 valve

When you draw the symbol for a 3/2 valve you must show both the on and off states. It is usual to show the actuated (on) position of the valve at the top and the un-actuated (off) position at the bottom. The symbol for a 3/2 valve is shown in Figure 8.11.

## Operating valves

No diagram of a valve is complete without showing the means of operation. The 3/2 valves and 5/2 valves used in pneumatics can be operated using a number of different mechanical or electrical operators.

### Symbol for a push-button/spring return 3/2 valve

Pushing the button on top of the valve operates this valve (Figure 8.12). When the button is released the spring inside the valve makes it return to the off position.

It is common to see this valve labelled as a push-button operated 3/2 valve.

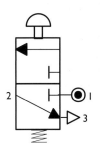

**Figure 8.12** *Push-button/spring return 3/2 valve*

### Symbols for mechanically operated 3/2 and 5/2 valves

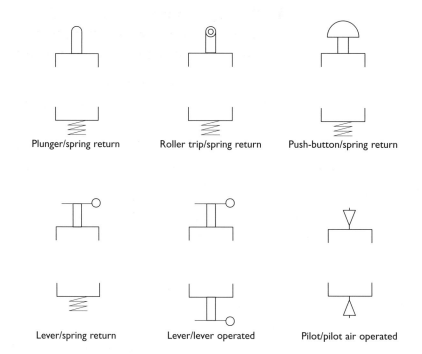

**Figure 8.13**
*Mechanical and pilot air operation*

Plunger/spring return    Roller trip/spring return    Push-button/spring return

Lever/spring return    Lever/lever operated    Pilot/pilot air operated

# Single-acting cylinders

A single-acting cylinder is a pneumatic output device that requires compressed air to make the piston move out. When the air is removed a spring causes the piston to return. The out stroke is called the positive stroke and the return stroke is called the negative stroke.

Figure 8.14 shows a single-acting cylinder with part of the cylinder cut away to let you see inside.

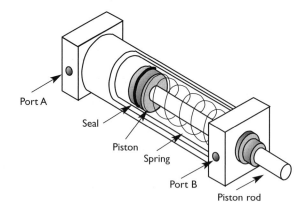

**Figure 8.14** *Cut-away drawing of a single-acting cylinder*

Port A

Seal

Piston

Spring

Port B

Piston rod

### How it works

Air coming in port A will cause the piston to move out. Remove the air pressure and the spring will push the piston back again.

The seal around the piston prevents the air from escaping over the piston. Port B allows the air in front of the piston to escape. This is called the exhaust.

### Symbol for single-acting cylinder

When you want to draw a single-acting cylinder it is not necessary to draw what it looks like. Instead you draw the symbol for it. This is shown in Figure 8.15.

The circuit diagram for a single-acting cylinder being controlled by a 3/2 valve is shown in Figure 8.16.

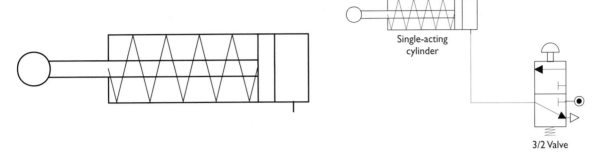

Single-acting cylinder

3/2 Valve

**Figure 8.15** *Symbol for a single-acting cylinder*  **Figure 8.16** *Circuit diagram for a single-acting cylinder*

When the piston and piston rod is moving out we call this **going positive**. When the piston and piston rod is going in we call this **going negative**.

### Cylinder off

When no air is present at the back of the piston the spring keeps it in the negative position (Figure 8.17).

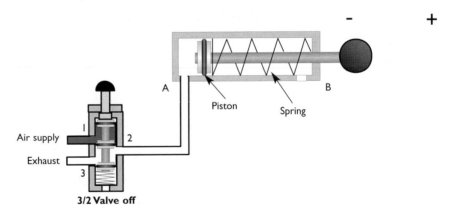

**Figure 8.17** *Cylinder negative*

### Cylinder going positive

Press the 3/2 valve and compressed air arrives at the back of the piston (port A). This makes the piston move out with a certain force.

The air in the cylinder in front of the piston is allowed to escape through a small vent hole at the front of the cylinder (port B) (Figure 8.18).

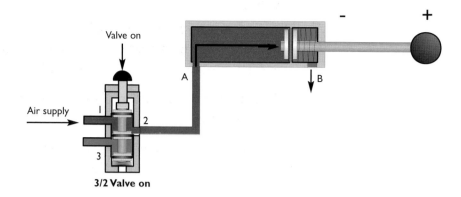

**Figure 8.18** *Cylinder positive*

### Cylinder going negative

When the 3/2 valve is released the spring inside the cylinder forces the piston back to a negative position. The escaping air is called the exhaust and passes through the 3/2 valve via port 2 to port 3 (Figure 8.19).

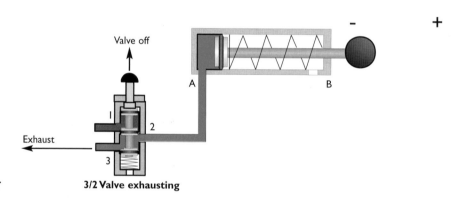

**Figure 8.19** *Exhaust air*

| Example | **Single-acting cylinder used to open and close a bus door** |
|---|---|

### Design situation

A bus company which operates a fleet of school buses would like to change its manually operated doors to pneumatically operated ones. This will allow the driver to remain in his/her seat when opening the door.

**Figure 8.20** *School bus*

### Solution

The final design used a single-acting cylinder actuated by a push button spring return 3/2 valve. A model of the bus was made to show how the system would operate.

The door was pulled open by means of a single-acting cylinder as shown in Figure 8.21.

The spring in the single-acting cylinder caused the door to close automatically when the air was removed from the cylinder (Figure 8.22).

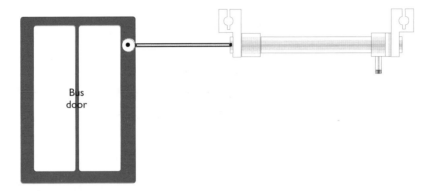

**Figure 8.21** *Door open*

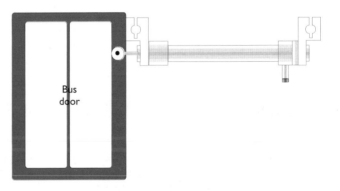

**Figure 8.22** *Door closed*

### Circuit diagram for the bus door

A circuit diagram for the bus door is shown in Figure 8.23. When the push button/spring return 3/2 valve is actuated (on) the main air at port 1 passes through the valve and out port 2. This causes the single-acting cylinder to go positive.

When the button is released the spring inside the cylinder causes it to go negative, closing the door.

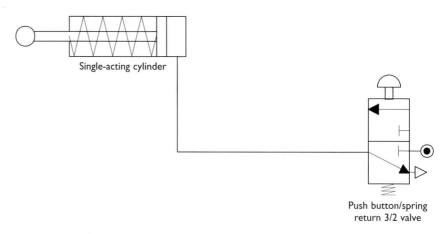

**Figure 8.23** *Symbolic drawing of the circuit*

Push button/spring
return 3/2 valve

Single-acting cylinder

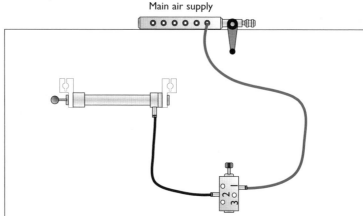

Main air supply

**Figure 8.24** *Real-world view of the circuit before it was fitted to the model bus*

# Valves in 'OR' logic

| Example | Modifying the bus door circuit |
|---|---|

It was decided to modify the circuit for the bus door to include a push button on the outside of the bus, so that pupils entering the bus could also open the door.

Figure 8.25 shows the modified circuit. When either valve **A** or valve **B** is pressed the cylinder will go positive. When valves are arranged in this way they are said to be in an **OR logic** combination. When this is added to the original circuit design the driver inside the bus or the pupils outside the bus can open the door.

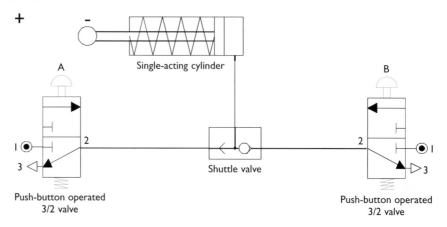

**234**    **Figure 8.25** *Symbolic drawing of an OR circuit*

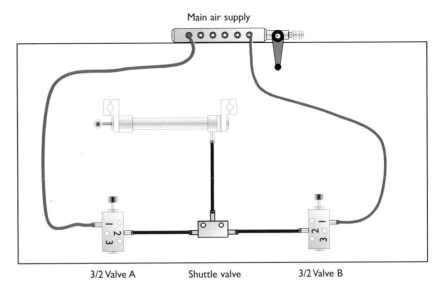

**Figure 8.26** *View of the modified circuit*

3/2 Valve A          Shuttle valve          3/2 Valve B

# Shuttle valves

The shuttle valve is the component that is at the heart of circuits that include the OR logic functions. A shuttle valve is shown in Figure 8.27 and its symbol in Figure 8.28.

**Figure 8.27** *Shuttle valve*   **Figure 8.28** *Symbol for a shuttle valve*

### How the shuttle valve works

Inside the shuttle valve there is a small rubber spool that moves from side to side. In Figure 8.29 the spool in the shuttle valve is forced over to the left by the air flowing through valve B. When this happens air is able to flow through the shuttle valve to the cylinder.

When valve A is pressed first, the spool will move to the right allowing the air to pass through and flow into the cylinder (Figure 8.30).

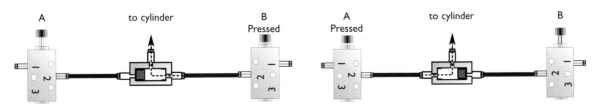

A          to cylinder          B
Pressed

A          to cylinder          B
Pressed

**Figure 8.29** *Valve B pressed*          **Figure 8.30** *Valve A pressed*

# Speed control using a one-way flow restrictor valve

It is good practice where possible to restrict the cylinder's exhaust.

**Improving the bus door design**

When the bus door was operated it was found to open very quickly. It was decided to use a one-way flow restrictor to control the speed of the air going into the single-acting cylinder (going positive). The modified circuit diagram can be seen in Figure 8.31.

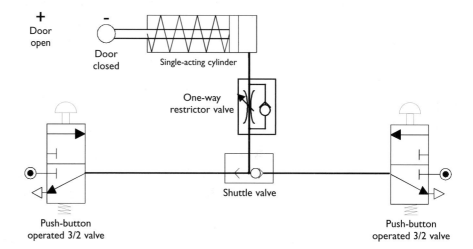

**Figure 8.31** *Circuit diagram of the OR logic circuit with a one-way restrictor valve added*

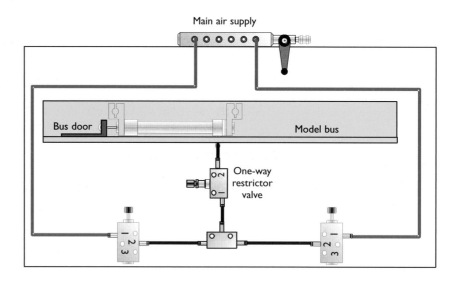

**Figure 8.32** *Modelling the bus door*

# Flow restrictor valves

**Figure 8.33** *A one-way restrictor valve*

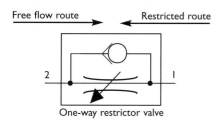

**Figure 8.34** *Symbol for a one-way restrictor valve*

There are two main types of restrictor valve: one-way and two-way (bi-directional).

## One-way flow restrictor

A one-way restrictor valve is shown in Figure 8.33 and its symbol is shown in Figure 8.34. The arrow at the ball shows the direction in which the air is restricted by the valve.

### How it works

The one-way restrictor valve will allow the air to flow freely through it in the direction port 2 to port 1. This happens because the ball is pushed back, compressing the spring. This enables the air to flow freely in the direction of the arrow (Figure 8.35).

When the air is flowing in the direction of port 1 to port 2 then it must pass through the narrow chamber at the tip of the screw. The size of the opening can be increased or decreased by turning the adjuster screw. The air coming in port 1 forces the ball against the seals to prevent the air going down this free-flow route (Figure 8.36).

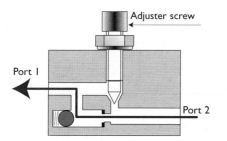

**Figure 8.35** *Sectional view showing the free-flow route*

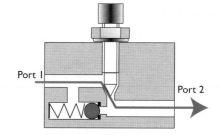

**Figure 8.36** *Sectional view showing the restricted route*

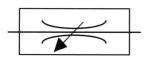

**Figure 8.37** *Symbol for a two-way flow restrictor*

## Two-way restrictor

A two-way restrictor valve will control the speed of the cylinder going positive and negative by restricting the flow of air passing down the pipe. The restriction is equal in both directions. The symbol for a two-way restrictor is shown in Figure 8.37.

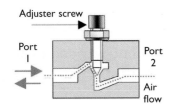

**Figure 8.38** *Sectional view of a two-way restrictor*

## How it works

The air passing through the restrictor valve has to flow past a cone-shaped chamber. The adjuster screw can be raised or lowered to open or close this chamber. A small opening will restrict the flow of air in both directions (Figure 8.38).

# Valves in 'AND' logic

You can arrange two valves in series to create an AND logic function. Figure 8.39 shows a circuit designed to operate with **AND logic** function. Only when both valves are pressed will the single-acting cylinder go positive.

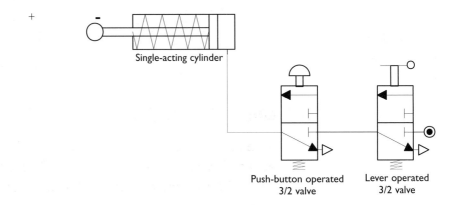

**Figure 8.39** *Symbolic drawing of an AND circuit*

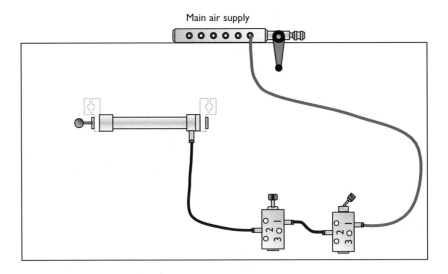

**Figure 8.40** *Modelling the circuit*

The main use for the AND arrangement of two valves is in situations where safety is important.

In Figure 8.41, AND logic is used to ensure the guillotine's safety guard is down before the machine comes on. The single-acting cylinder will only come down to cut the paper (positive stroke) when the guard is down and the manual button is pressed.

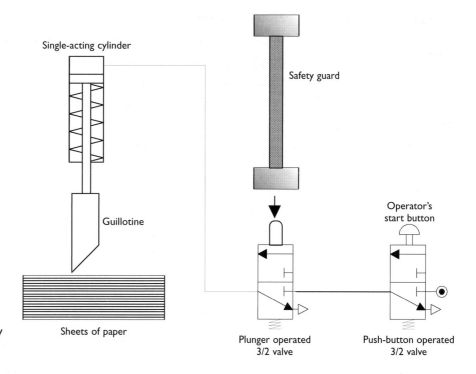

**Figure 8.41** *Circuit diagram for guillotine safety guard*

Single-acting cylinder

Guillotine

Sheets of paper

Safety guard

Operator's start button

Plunger operated 3/2 valve

Push-button operated 3/2 valve

---

| Example | Bus door circuit |
|---|---|

The AND logic function could be added to the bus door circuit as a safety feature for the driver (Figure 8.42). It could be part of the handbrake system so that the bus must stop and the handbrake be put on before the driver can open the door.

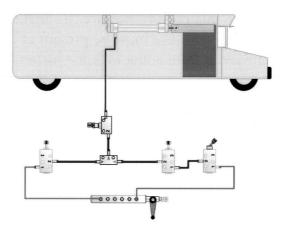

**Figure 8.42** *School bus*

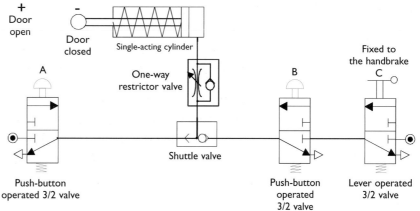

**Figure 8.43** *AND/OR logic circuit for bus door*

+
Door open

−
Door closed

Single-acting cylinder

One-way restrictor valve

Fixed to the handbrake

A

B

C

Shuttle valve

Push-button operated 3/2 valve

Push-button operated 3/2 valve

Lever operated 3/2 valve

### How it works

When the bus has come to a stop the driver pulls on the handbrake, which actuates valve C. The driver can now press valve B to open the door. Valves C and B must be actuated to open the door from inside the bus.

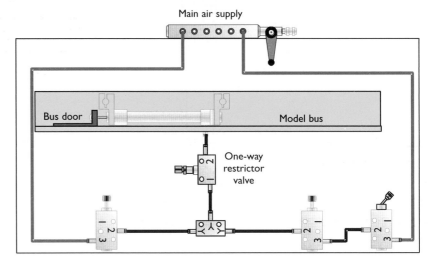

**Figure 8.44** *View of the model bus with AND/OR logic and cylinder speed control*

## Double-acting cylinders

Figures 8.45 and 8.47 show a double-acting cylinder. The symbol for a double-acting cylinder is shown in Figure 8.46. This type of cylinder requires air pressure at port A to make it go positive. If the air pressure is removed the cylinder will remain in a positive position. To make the cylinder go negative again air pressure must be present at port B. The air is prevented from going over the piston by the seal.

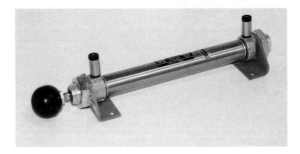

**Figure 8.45** *Double-acting cylinderr*

**Figure 8.46** *Symbol for a double-acting cylinder*

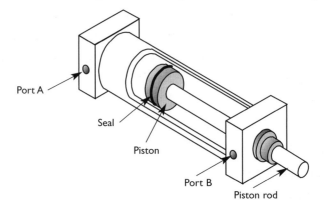

**Figure 8.47** *Cut-away view of a double-acting cylinder*

Two 3/2 valves could be used to control the double-acting cylinders (Figure 8.48). When valve A is pressed the cylinder will go positive. This valve must be released before valve B is pressed. Pressing valve B will cause the cylinder to go negative. Air present in the cylinder can exhaust through valve A.

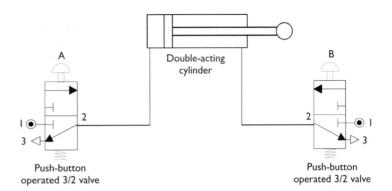

**Figure 8.48** *Circuit diagram for a double-acting cylinder*

# The pneumatic 5/2 valve

It is not normal to control a double-acting cylinder using two 3/2 valves as shown in Figure 8.48. This is usually done with a 5/2 valve. The 5/2 valve would replace the two 3/2 valves. A lever operated 5/2 valve is shown in Figure 8.49.

**Figure 8.49** *A lever operated 5/2 valve*

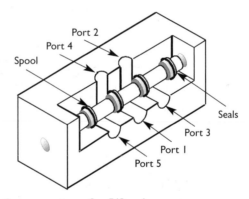

**Figure 8.50** *Cut-away view of a 5/2 valve*

### Drawing 5/2 valves

As with other pneumatic components it is not necessary to draw the actual valve when designing a circuit. You would draw the symbol (Figure 8.54). A 5/2 valve means five ports and two states. The states are air in port 1 and out port 2, or in port 1 and out port 4.

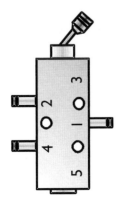

**Figure 8.51** *Drawing of a lever operated 5/2 valve*

### 5/2 valve with ports 1 and 4 open

The symbol for this state is shown in Figure 8.52.

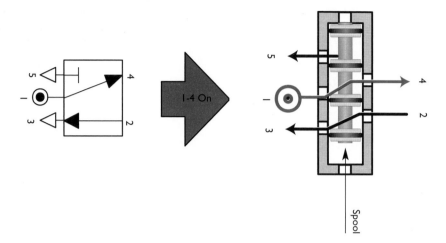

**Figure 8.52** *Ports 1–4 open*

### 5/2 valve with ports 1 and 2 open

The symbol for this state is shown in Figure 8.53.

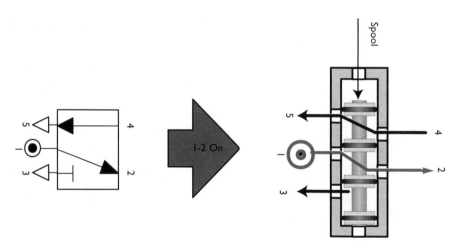

**Figure 8.53** *Ports 1–2 open*

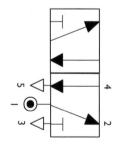

**Figure 8.54** *Symbol for a 5/2 valve*

### Symbol for a 5/2 valve

The graphical symbol for a 5/2 valve must include both sets of port combinations (Figure 8.54). This symbol does not show the means by which the spool inside the valve is made to move.

The symbols for mechanical and electrical switching are the same for both 3/2 valves and 5/2 valves (see Figure 8.13).

## Double-acting cylinder controlled by a lever/spring return 5/2 valve

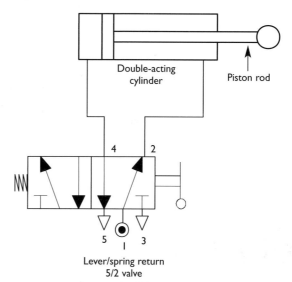

Double-acting cylinder

Piston rod

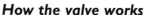

Lever/spring return
5/2 valve

**Figure 8.55** *Circuit diagram for a lever/spring return 5/2 valve*

### *How the valve works*

### Cylinder going negative

When the spool is in the position shown in Figure 8.56 then the main air will come in port 1 and out port 2. When this happens the compressed air forces the piston back into the negative position. The exhaust passes out through ports 4 and 5.

### Cylinder going positive

When the spool is in the down position then the main air will come in port 1 and out port 4 (Figure 8.57). When this happens the compressed air forces the piston out into the positive position. The exhaust passes out through ports 2 and 3.

### Controlling two double-acting cylinders from one 5/2 valve

This circuit will require two 'T' pieces to connect both cylinders in parallel. A 'T' piece is shown in Figure 8.58. When two air lines are joined in this way the diagram should show a small black dot to indicate the connection. Crossover lines are drawn one on top of the other without the dot. A circuit diagram in which two double-acting cylinders are controlled by a 5/2 valve is shown in Figure 8.59.

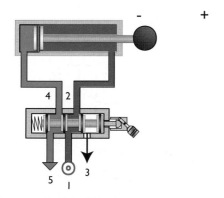

**Figure 8.56** *Cylinder going negative*

**Figure 8.57** *Cylinder going positive*

**Figure 8.58** *'T' piece*

243

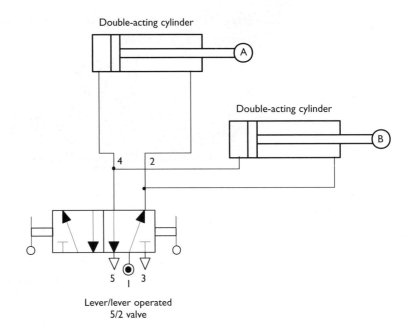

**Figure 8.59** *Controlling two cylinders*

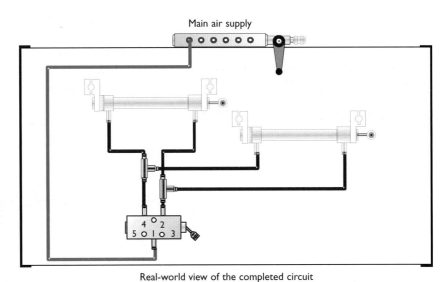

**Figure 8.60** *Modelling the circuit*

Real-world view of the completed circuit

### Pilot/pilot air operated 5/2 valves

So far we have used a lever operated 5/2 valve to control the double-acting cylinder. The next circuit uses a pilot/pilot air operated 5/2 valve to control the double-acting cylinder. This is the commonest method for controlling a double-acting cylinder. A pilot/pilot air operated 5/2 valve is shown in Figure 8.61. The spool inside the 5/2 valve is moved by air pressure rather than by mechanical means. This air pressure is called signal air and is represented by a dotted line on the diagram.

Figure 8.62 shows a pilot/pilot air operated 5/2 valve changed by means of two push-button operated 3/2 valves.

**Figure 8.61** *A pilot/pilot air operated 5/2 valve*

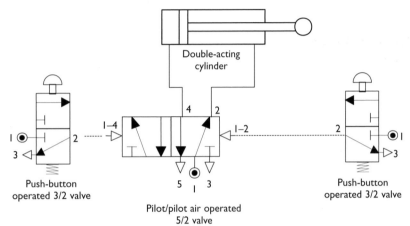

**Figure 8.62** *Controlling a double-acting cylinder*

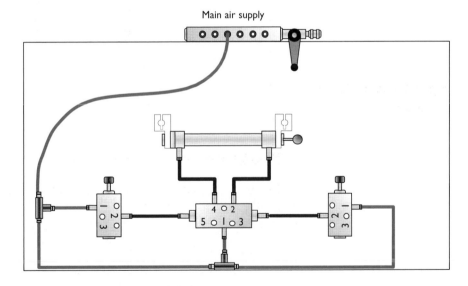

**Figure 8.63** *Modelling the circuit*

## Automatic return

You can use the air signal from a 3/2 valve to automatically change the state of the pilot/pilot air operated 5/2 valve.

In the example shown in Figure 8.64 the push-button operated 3/2 valve starts the cycle. This makes the double-acting cylinder go positive. A plunger operated 3/2 valve is pressed by the

245

piston rod at the end of the positive stroke. When this happens, air passes through the 3/2 valve down to the end of the 5/2 valve, causing the spool inside to change state. The valve changes from a 1–4 to a 1–2 combination.

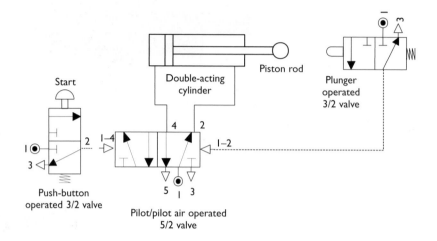

**Figure 8.64** *Circuit diagram for automatic return circuit*

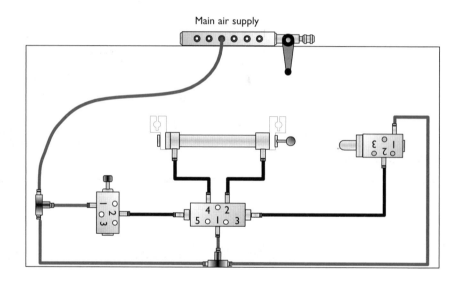

**Figure 8.65** *Modelling the automatic return circuit*

# Time delay circuit

There will be times when it is necessary to have a small time delay in your circuit. The circuit in Figure 8.66 has a time delay between the time when the piston rod hits the plunger operated 3/2 valve and the cylinder going negative.

The time delay is achieved by using a reservoir and one-way restrictor valve. A reservoir is simply an empty container. The one-way restrictor valve controls the rate of fill. By decreasing the amount of air passing through the restrictor valve you can increase the time it takes to fill the reservoir. Only when the reservoir is full will the air be able to flow down the second half of the pipe with enough force to change the pilot/pilot air operated 5/2 valve.

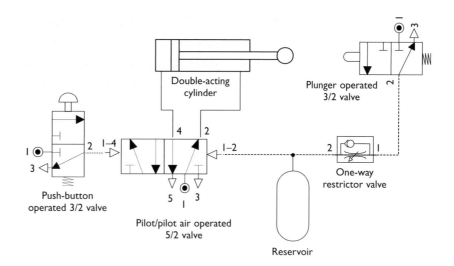

**Figure 8.66** *Time delay circuit*

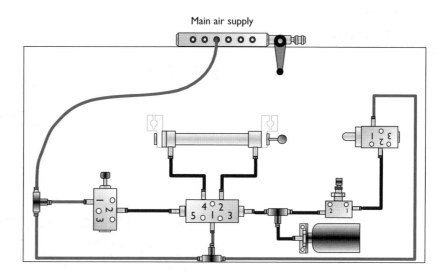

**Figure 8.67** *Modelling a time delay circuit*

---

**Conveyor system**

### Design situation

A manufacturer of portable and wide-screen television sets would like to sort these by size into two different containers. The boxes come down the same conveyor and are currently hand-sorted down their respective conveyors into the containers.

You are asked to design an automatic system to sort the boxes.

### Solution

The solution was to have roller trip 3/2 valve A set at the edge of conveyor 1. This is shown in Figure 8.70. Only the large boxes would activate this valve. When the valve was pressed, a time delay would happen in the circuit before the double-acting cylinder went positive, giving enough time for any small boxes

**Figure 8.68** *A reservoir*

**247**

to continue down to conveyor 2 before the gate was changed over. The changeover would send the large box down conveyor 3. This is shown in Figure 8.71. Once the large box reached roller trip valve B on conveyor 3, the circuit would cause the double-acting cylinder to go negative again, returning the gate to its original position.

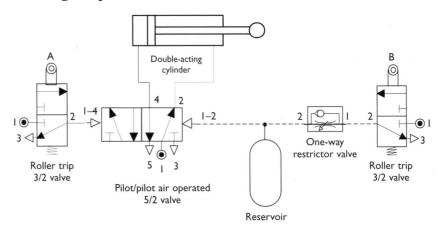

**Figure 8.69** *Circuit diagram for the conveyor system*

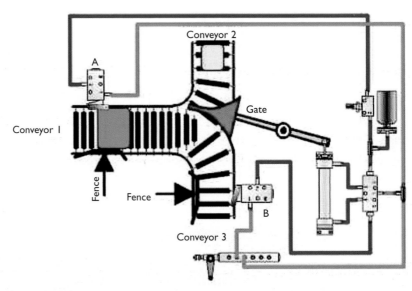

**Figure 8.70** *The large box activating roller trip 3/2 valve A*

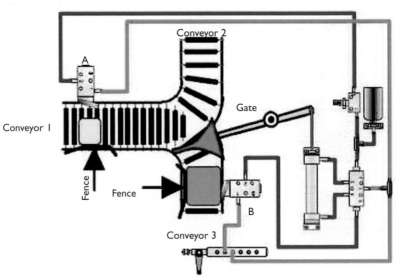

**Figure 8.71** *The large box activating roller trip 3/2 valve B*

# Diaphragm operated 3/2 valves

**Figure 8.72** *Diaphragm operated 3/2 valve*

Diaphragm operated 3/2 valves are similar to mechanical valves such as the push-button operated valve. With the push-button valve you have to press the spool inside the valve down with your hand. The diaphragm operated 3/2 valve has a small soft plastic membrane inside a chamber. Figure 8.72 shows a diaphragm operated 3/2 valve. Its symbol is shown in Figure 8.73.

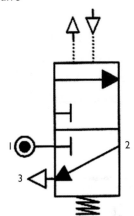

**Figure 8.73** *Symbol for a diaphragm operated 3/2 valve*

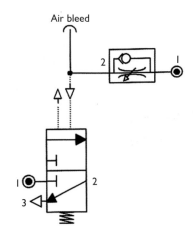

**Figure 8.74** *Air bleed*

When the diaphragm is inflated it pushes down the spool in the same way as the push-button did. To make the diaphragm inflate you have to use a one-way restrictor and a T piece.

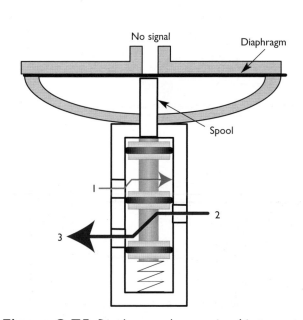

**Figure 8.75** *Diaphragm when no signal is present*

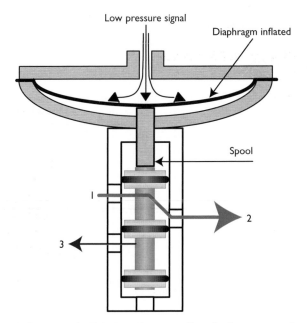

**Figure 8.76** *Diaphragm inflated when a signal is present*

249

The restrictor allows just enough air to go down to the diaphragm and at the same time allows some to escape out into the atmosphere. The pipe used for the escaping air is called an **air bleed** (Figure 8.74). To make the valve actuate (come on) you must block this air bleed. This will send all the air down to the diaphragm, inflating it.

### Diaphragm start/automatic return

Cover the air bleed pipe and the air is forced down to turn on the diaphragm 3/2 valve. An air signal flows along to the pilot/pilot air operated 5/2 and creates a 1–4 airflow through it. Air flowing out of port 4 causes the double-acting cylinder to go positive (Figure 8.77). At the end of the positive stroke the piston rod hits the plunger operated 3/2 valve. Air passes through this valve and flows along to create a 1–2 air flow through the 5/2 valve. Air flowing out of port 2 causes the double-acting cylinder to go negative.

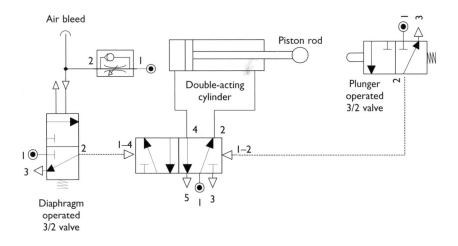

**Figure 8.77** *Circuit diagram of a diaphragm 3/2 valve used to make the piston go positive*

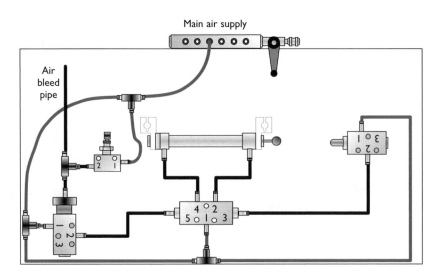

**Figure 8.78** *Modelling the circuit*

### Single-acting cylinder controlled by a diaphragm operated 3/2 valve

In this circuit (Figure 8.79) the diaphragm operated 3/2 valve is used in conjunction with a one-way restrictor valve and an air bleed, to control a single-acting cylinder.

The main advantage of this type of circuit is that the 3/2 valve will actuate with physical contact: all you need to do is block the escaping air.

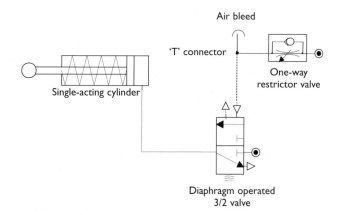

**Figure 8.79** *Circuit diagram using a diaphragm operated 3/2 valve*

| Example | **Conveyor belt system** |

The system in Figure 8.80 is designed to push the boxes from conveyor belt 1 on to conveyor belt 2 using two single-acting cylinders. The cylinders will go positive when the box blocks the air bleed at the end of belt 1.

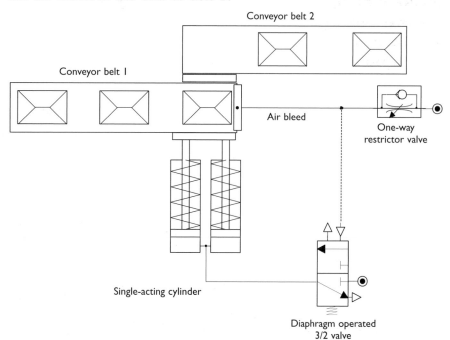

**Figure 8.80** *Conveyor system*

# Reciprocating motion

Reciprocating motion happens when the piston goes positive and negative automatically.

It is possible to create reciprocating motion using two roller trip 3/2 valves, a double-acting cylinder and a pilot/pilot air operated 5/2 valve. This is shown in Figure 8.81. The 3/2 valves alternately provide the air signals that change the state of the 5/2 valve from 1–2 to 1–4 port combinations repeatedly, until the air is switched off. Main air passing through the 5/2 valve causes the double-acting cylinder to go positive and negative.

Care is needed when testing this circuit as it immediately becomes active as soon as the main air supply is turned on.

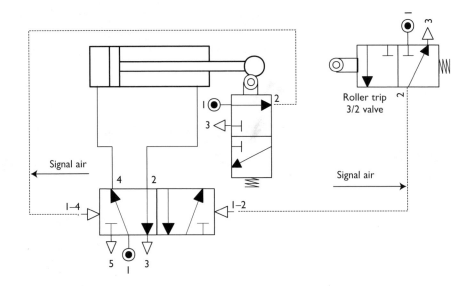

**Figure 8.81** *Circuit diagram for reciprocating motion*

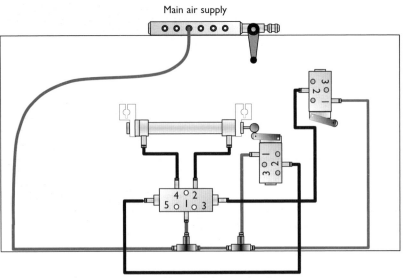

**Figure 8.82** *Modelling reciprocating motion*

Real world view of the completed circuit

### Design situation

A small biscuit manufacturer wishes to use a hopper system to load a range of their snack bars into a wrapping machine. Design and build a model hopper that will continuously push snack bars into the wrapping machine.

### Solution

The solution incorporated reciprocating motion. The push rod had a cam that operated the 3/2 roller trip valves.

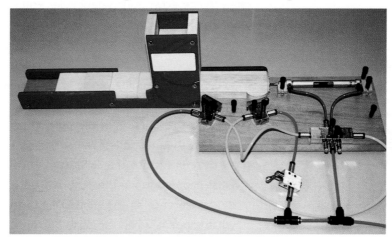

**Figure 8.83** *The final solution*

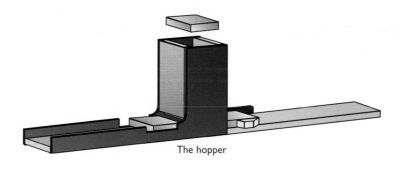

The hopper

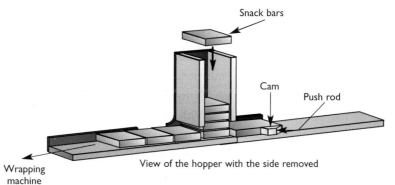

Snack bars

Cam

Push rod

**Figure 8.84** *View of the hopper*

Wrapping machine

View of the hopper with the side removed

### Modification

During testing it was found that the hopper would become jammed. To enable this to be cleared safely a lever operated 3/2 valve was added to the main air supply going to the roller trip 3/2 valve closest to the cylinder. When the lever operated 3/2 valve was closed, signal air was not able to flow back to the pilot/pilot air operated 5/2 valve with the result that the cylinder remained in the negative position.

## Questions on pneumatics

1 Copy the following sentence and add in the missing word.
Pneumatics is a system that operates with compressed _____.

2 Write down one use for pneumatics.

3 When working with pneumatic equipment it is important to work safely. Write down four safety rules you should follow when working with pneumatics.

4 Figure 8.85 shows the symbol for a push-button/spring return 3/2 valve.

   a What is the meaning of the term 'push-button/spring return 3/2 valve'?

   b What is the function of the push-button on the 3/2 valve?

   c What is the function of the spring on the 3/2 valve?

   d With reference to the air passing through the valve, write down what happens when the push-button is pressed.

   e With reference to the air passing through the valve, write down what happens when the push-button is released.

   f The push-button is only one of a number of mechanical tops that can be used on 3/2 valves. Draw and write down the names of three others.

5 Figure 8.86 shows a circuit incorporating a push-button/spring return 3/2 valve and a single-acting cylinder (SAC).

   a Copy the drawing and add the positive and negative symbols to your drawing.

   b What is the meaning of the term 'the cylinder goes positive'?

   c What happens when the push-button on the 3/2 valve is pressed then released after 5 seconds?

   d Suggest one possible use for the circuit shown in Figure 8.86.

6 Figure 8.87 shows a pneumatic logic circuit that is used to control a bus door.

   a Write down the names of the components A, B, C, D and E.

   b With reference to valves C and D, write down the function of component B.

   c Write down the function of valve A and explain how it works.

   d Write down the name of the logic function created by valves A and B.

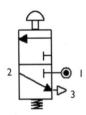

**Figure 8.85**

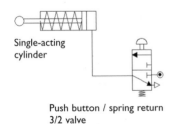

Single-acting cylinder

Push button / spring return 3/2 valve

**Figure 8.86**

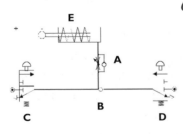

**Figure 8.87**

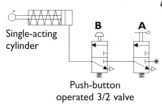

Single-acting
cylinder

**B**    **A**

Push-button
operated 3/2 valve

**Figure 8.88**

**7** Figure 8.88 shows a pneumatic logic circuit used to control a safety
gate on a metal cutting milling machine.

   **a** Write down the name of the logic function created by valves A
      and B.

   **b** Write down the full name of valve A.

   **c** Write down how the circuit works.

**8** Figure 8.89 shows a double-acting cylinder controlled by two push-
button/spring return 3/2 valves.

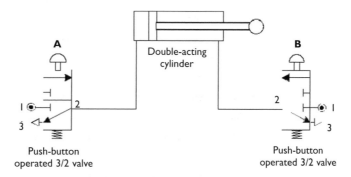

**Figure 8.89**

Push-button
operated 3/2 valve

Push-button
operated 3/2 valve

   **a** Write down how the double-acting cylinder in this circuit can be
      made to go positive, wait two seconds, then go negative.

   **b** Valves A and B could be replaced with one 5/2 valve. Draw the
      circuit using one 5/2 valve to replace valves A and B.

**9** Figure 8.90 shows a double-acting cylinder operated by a pilot/pilot air
5/2 valve which in turn is controlled by two push-button/spring return
3/2 valves.

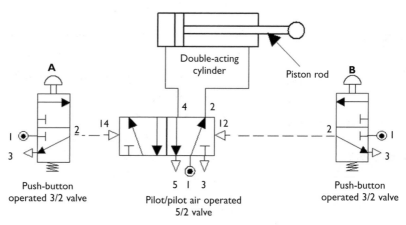

Push-button
operated 3/2 valve

Pilot/pilot air operated
5/2 valve

Push-button
operated 3/2 valve

**Figure 8.90**

   **a** Write down how you could make the double-acting cylinder in this
      circuit go positive and wait two seconds before going negative.

   **b** With reference to the signal air (dotted lines) and the air passing
      through the pilot/pilot air operated 5/2 valve, write down what
      happens in the circuit when valve A is pressed.

   **c** When the circuit was tested it was found that the piston rod on
      the double-acting cylinder was going positive and negative too fast.
      Copy the circuit and add in the components you could use to
      control the speed of the piston rod on both the positive and
      negative strokes.

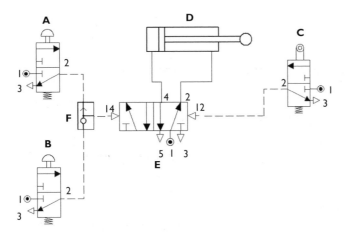

**Figure 8.91**

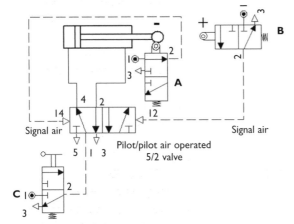

**Figure 8.92**

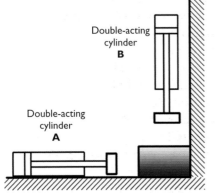

**Figure 8.93** *Pneumatic clamp*

10 Figure 8.91 shows a double-acting cylinder operated by a pilot/pilot air 5/2 valve.

  a Write down the names of components A, B, C, D, E and F.

  b Write down one advantage of the start valves A and B in the circuit.

  c What is the function of valve F?

  d Either valve A or B can be pressed to make the cylinder out-stroke (go positive). Write down how the cylinder is made to in-stroke (go negative again).

  e Redraw the circuit to include a valve that would control the speed of the piston on the out-stroke (going positive).

11 Figure 8.92 shows a pneumatic circuit diagram.

  a Write down the names of valves A, B and C.

  b What happens in the circuit when valve C is turned on?

  c What type of motion is created by this circuit?

  d Suggest one possible use for this circuit.

  e Redraw the circuit so that valve C will stop the circuit when the piston rod is in the negative position only.

12 Figure 8.93 shows part of a pneumatic clamp used to hold a block of metal in place for drilling. Draw a pneumatic circuit so that:

  a Both cylinder A and B must move at the same time.

  b The circuit should be operated by a single lever operated valve.

  c It has been decided to modify the circuit so that cylinder B has a time delay before it clamps the metal block. Add this time delay to your circuit.

  d Explain how the time delay can be adjusted.

13 Figure 8.94 shows cylinders A and B arranged in sequential control. The sequence of operation is:

Step 1: Start button is pressed and released.
Step 2: Cylinder A goes positive.
Step 3: Cylinder B goes positive.
Step 4: Cylinder A goes negative.
Step 5: Cylinder B goes negative.

Draw the complete circuit shown in Figure 8.94 by adding the pipe work to give the required sequence.

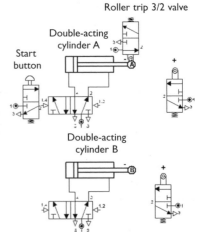

**Figure 8.94** *Sequential control*

# Index

Complete Technology and Design